T0382976

Relational Feedback

People are increasingly disenchanted with performance improvement techniques that fail to deliver. This book offers a new and refreshing way of engaging in authentic feedback that is willingly given and well-received. It demonstrates that focusing on the quality of relationship improves the activity of feedback.

The Relational Leadership WAY© that is the core of this book was created from a thematic analysis of a doctoral research study. The framework encourages effective relationships and works through perfecting a 'way of being' that is generative and productive in interactions with others; especially in feedback conversations, whether we are the giver or the receiver. The 10 themes integral to the framework are organised into 3 parts that relate to pivotal points in a conversation and that when given focused attention will improve relationships:

1. *What* needs preparing to establish relationships that stimulate constructive conversations
2. *Active* engagement in co-creating generative conversations through adopting relational behaviours
3. *You* both noticing and *reacting* to what emerges and impacts on sustaining the quality of the relationship.

This book will appeal to those seeking an innovative approach to performance management and who welcome a reprieve from the relentless pursuit of a universal feedback tool. It is essential reading for:

- Business managers and leaders expected to motivate teams to become high performing work units
- Organisational and independent coaches, mentors and practice supervisors developing trust by building effective relationships that encourage disclosure through engaging and authentic feedback
- Managers, leaders, HR and OD specialists to use as a business text for performance management programmes
- Training organisations to use as a core text for delegates.

Lise Lewis is the founder of Bluesky International and an EMCC Global Special Ambassador. She is also an EIA Master Coach, ESIA Coach Supervisor, provider of global coach and coach supervisor training virtually and in organisations, as well as a researcher and author contributing to *Coaching Supervision: Advancing Practice, Changing Landscapes* and 'CIPD Coaching Toolkit'.

'Wounds from knives and sharp objects heal with time. Wounds from words do not. So use feedback, in the context of Relational Leadership, with great care and precision. The innovative approach of Lise Lewis, using The Relational Leadership WAY©, through the "use of self," is a welcome guide to achieve the above.'

– See Luan Foo, Founder ICF Singapore Chapter and Asia Pacific Alliance of Coaches (APAC) Former Director, Global ICF Board

'As Bernard Shaw said: the single biggest problem in communication is the illusion that it has taken place. I welcome the arrival of this relational book about feedback that helps us to be more courageous and to reflect as we speak.'

– Professor Erik de Haan, Director of Ashridge Centre for Coaching, and Professor of Organisational Development, Ashridge Executive Education at Hult International Business School

'This book is long overdue. It is an evidence based approach to providing feedback with full appreciation of the impact and influence of the relationship within which the feedback is given. It steps back from the temptation to simply provide a one-size-fits-all tool and instead explores the factors which impact and how they can be harnessed to perfect "a way of being" that generates the conditions for effective feedback and its utility. Written in an accessible style speaking directly to practice, it will be an invaluable resource for managers, leaders and their coaches.'

– Annette Fillery-Travis BSc, MA, PhD, CChem, FRSC, Pennaeth Athrofa Cymru ar gyfer Dysgu Seiliedig ar Waith, Head of the Wales Institute for Work-based Learning

'Drawing on research and professional experience, Lise Lewis provides a compelling case for improving relationships and feedback through a rich, step-by-step model. If feedback is so easy, why do we avoid it? If relationships are so easy, why do we fail at them? Relational Feedback offers essential information and frameworks to guide and support leaders at all levels as well as those who provide professional coaching and mentoring. In this "must read" book, we will all benefit as we build and maintain relationships that support growth, development and productivity. Read it; use it!'

– John L. Bennett, PhD, PCC, BCC, Professor of Business and Behavioral Science, Queens University of Charlotte (USA)

'Lise embraces the power and magic of feedback!

'She reveals unique insights, stories, strategies and the unique WAY relational framework that leaders can practically apply to combine coaching and feedback. This powerful framework provides a way of motivating performance, probing deeper thinking, pushing boundaries, engaging transformational and breakthrough conversations in feedback.

'Injecting the feedback process with artificial intelligence AI is likely to foster more human interaction especially with the millennial generation who grew up with social media.

'Based on significant research this book demystifies moving from "knowing to doing".'

– Lydia Goh, President of the Institute of Management Consultants Singapore, Past President of Asia Pacific Alliance of Coaches (APAC)

'Lise Lewis' new book on Leadership Relational Feedback comes at a most opportune time in our need, globally, for leaders who can not only produce results and feed the bottom line, but also build positive relationships in their organisations. If you are a leader, manager, coach, consultant, supervisor or executive, then this book introduces a transformational approach to managing performance through the skill and competence of relationship building and dialogue. Leader-managers today are not skilled in building productive relationships that enhance and extend relationships as well as building self-esteem and self-confidence. The relational tool for feedback that Lise Lewis has created represents an authentic way to introduce powerful and constructive feedback within the organisation.

'Her feedback tool is evidence-based and she shows how it has been used to achieve high quality feedback to develop and grow people. Performance can only be improved if feedback is meaningful and addresses the purpose not just of the organisation but the individual employee. Lewis also talks about the darker side of feedback, and the difficult challenge of helping people understand where their behaviour needs to change. Most leader-managers give mixed messages when delivering feedback, which diminishes the impact of how individuals can reinvigorate their own performance management.

'Her focus is on the 'quality of the relationship' and the 'act of feedback' to inspire a "growth mindset" and willingness to engage in transformational learning. Lewis explains her well-researched WAY Relational Framework® which encourages joint responsibility between both parties. This framework offers a tool for personal development and feedback that is both engaging and transformative.'

– Dr Sunny Stout-Rostron, Director, People Quotient Pty Ltd.; Founding President, COMENSA; Faculty, University of Stellenbosch School of Business, Cape Town

Relational Feedback

Why Feedback Fails and How to Make It Meaningful

LISE LEWIS

Routledge
Taylor & Francis Group

LONDON AND NEW YORK

First published 2020
by Routledge
2 Park Square, Milton Park, Abingdon, Oxon OX14 4RN

and by Routledge
52 Vanderbilt Avenue, New York, NY 10017

Routledge is an imprint of the Taylor & Francis Group, an informa business

British Library Cataloguing-in-Publication Data

A catalogue record for this book is available from the British Library

Library of Congress Cataloging-in-Publication Data

A catalog record has been requested for this book

ISBN: 978-1-138-06391-4 (hbk)
ISBN: 978-1-315-16072-6 (ebk)

Typeset in Dante and Avenir
by Swales & Willis, Exeter, Devon, UK

Contents

Acknowledgements   *xi*
Foreword   *xiii*
Author overview   *xv*

Introduction   **1**

1 What perceptions exist about feedback?   **17**

Definitions of feedback   19

Willingness to engage in feedback – the psychological
perspective   22

The effectiveness of feedback – for both the giver and receiver   34

2 Why feedback and whose responsibility is it?   **40**

The business case for feedback   43

The leader/manager's perspective   44

The people professional's perspective   49

The team's perspective   50

The coaching/mentoring practitioner's perspective   52

The individual employee's perspective   55

3 Current practices in feedback exchange   **60**

Business performance improvement tools: appraisal systems,
competence frameworks and self-assessment   62

Proprietary tools: psychometrics   72

Popular feedback techniques   76

**4 The importance of relationship and how it influences
engagement in feedback**   **80**

The importance of 'being relational'   82

Types of relationship and how these impact on our
view of feedback   88

The dynamics impacting on relationships   91

Power in relationships   93

The cultural perspective   96

The common features of productive relationships   98

Creating productive relationships   102

**5 Part 1 of The Relational Leadership WAY©: *What* needs
preparing to establish relationships that stimulate
constructive conversations**   **105**

Theme 1 of The Relational Leadership WAY©: Self-Management
with the sub-themes of Confidence and Compassion   108

Theme 2 of The Relational Leadership WAY©: Readiness for
Feedback with the sub-theme of Impactfulness   132

**6 Part 2 of The Relational Leadership WAY©: *Active* engagement
in co-creating generative conversations through adopting
relational behaviours**   **142**

Theme 3 of The Relational Leadership WAY©: Objectivity   146

Theme 4 of The Relational Leadership WAY©: Mindfulness   156

Theme 5 of The Relational Leadership WAY©: Presence
with the sub-themes of Flow and Breaking Flow   159

Theme 6 of The Relational Leadership WAY©: Timing
of Feedback   169

**7 Part 3 of The Relational Leadership WAY©: *You* both noticing
and *reacting* to what emerges and impacts on sustaining the
quality of the relationship   177**

Theme 7 of The Relational Leadership WAY©: Physicality   179

Theme 8 of The Relational Leadership WAY©: Emotional State   184

Theme 9 of The Relational Leadership WAY©: Intuition   193

Theme 10 of The Relational Leadership WAY©: Metaphysical   198

**8 How artificial intelligence (AI) may impact on the future of
feedback   202**

Bibliography   211
Index   222

Acknowledgements

Putting the final touches to this book gives me the opportunity to reflect on the great people who have touched my life and supported me on this writing journey.

I am grateful beyond words to the coaches who so generously gave their time to provide data and unstinting support and friendship throughout the doctoral research study, the foundation for this book. Together we delved to the very depths of our practices to work with ambiguity, wrestle with meaning-making and maintain a sense of humour. My hope is that the learning justified the effort made by a special network of colleagues. A huge thank you goes to Alison Kane, Ann Sherrington, Dawn Bentley, Professor Erik de Haan, Helen Harrison, Dr Lesley Roberts, Dr Lucy Ryan, Nancy Kline, Rich Horton and Dr Vikki Powell.

How can anyone complete a work of this nature without support and love from family and friends? My husband David has willingly taken on the role of author champion, chief comforter and even listened with apparent interest to the complexities of feedback. Adam, Claire and Katie, my son, daughter-in-law and daughter, have understood without complaint when time spent with them has been shorter than they deserve. When it comes to supportive friends and colleagues who believed I could make this book happen – I am truly blessed and hope you all forgive me for hearing probably one too many times in response to your question, 'How's the book coming along?' – 'Well – it's coming along!' Special thanks to those colleagues providing testimonials and to Lucy Ryan: writing buddy extraordinaire who provided 'silent' moral support on those days we 'took ourselves off' to be creative and diligent writers under the watchful eye and refreshment breaks choreographed by Elizabeth Ryan and Bracken.

A special mention is deserved by Dr Vikki Powell who willingly volunteered to be my critical reader and who proved she is already expert in offering developmental and validating feedback! Vikki's enduring encouragement helped me through the 'dark despair of making progress' and her expertise, incisive observations and recommendations were invaluable in informing the content of this book. Words cannot express my sincere thanks for her care and generous support.

Foreword

'Can I give you some feedback?' – six words guaranteed to stimulate the fight-flight reflex in human beings. The very word 'feedback' is associated with interference (as in audio feedback) and runaway systems that may end in disaster. The research on performance appraisals, which typically involve feedback of impressions and interpretations between two people of different levels of power and hierarchical status, shows that both appraisers and appraisees find the process uncomfortable and unsatisfying – even when the feedback is positive. There is surprisingly little evidence that feedback of this type leads to improvement in performance.

The overhyped 360-degree feedback, designed in Russia by the Communist trade unions to keep line managers in check, can be even more damaging to morale and performance. The problems with this procedure are many – not least that people have an instinctive negative reaction to anonymous feedback. (An analogy is poison pen letters!) 'Rater bias' typically makes the data highly unreliable and it appears that sociopaths (who don't want to hear bad news) often receive higher scores than empowering managers (who do).

Now, there is a fad for creating 'feedback cultures', where brutal honesty is the norm. Of course, this is a nonsense. What marriage could survive for long in such an environment?

Yet well-managed feedback has great value in all aspects of life and commerce. Customer feedback is essential in designing and adjusting products. Executive coaches frequently offer feedback on what they are experiencing in the room, or as a result of observing clients in key situations, such as leading meetings. Sports coaches help athletes refine performance by sharing their observations about often tiny but significant facets of posture.

The key – explored in great depth in this book – is to create the conditions where feedback is sought and welcomed rather than delivered and resented. When 360 is useful is when it is driven by the appraisee, focused on a small number of issues that they have accepted as important for them to address (rather than on a generic bunch of issues that may or may not be relevant) and given by people whose opinion they respect (they don't necessarily have to *like* these appraisers, simply to value their opinion).

The psychological contract between appraiser and appraisee is an essential element here. Knowing that the other person has your best interests at heart, having confidence that they will meld honesty with compassion – these are fundamental, along with the simple rule that the appraisee has to own the process.

I welcome this book as a much-needed antidote to the unintelligent use of feedback.

David Clutterbuck

Author overview

Dr Lise Lewis

What is this appeal that feedback has for me? I have reflected on why it became such an important topic for me to explore more systematically than an occasional fleeting curiosity. I soon realised it was because I was as dissatisfied as many others about how it works or – to be more precise – how it doesn't work! Past experiences, starting with childhood, reveal memories of an imbalance in positive: negative ratio. As I progressed in my career, seldom was I disabused of this idea by evidence of any advancement towards changing perceptions. Feedback often feels a necessary evil – one that has to be endured instead of having dedicated time to talk about our performance and aspirations with a caring and trusted colleague.

This text draws on a career in human resources and now as a coach and is illustrated with enriching case studies from clients, colleagues and literature review. As Past Global President I also reference the work of the European Mentoring and Coaching Council. The purpose of the EMCC is to encourage professionalism by developing standards for practitioners and practitioner training.

Doctoral research on 'Creating the Conditions for Receptivity of Feedback' gives underpinning integrity to an evidence base. This validates the 'relationship' as key to productive feedback conversations. The book provides a comprehensive explanation of The Relational Leadership WAY© created from the research data. This framework gives you solutions to a 'way of being' that produces the quality of relationship conducive to feedback.

The Introduction gives context for what to expect in this book:

- Why is feedback so important?
- The relationship dilemma
- What this new research into feedback revealed
- Why we resent feedback

- What drives the perception of feedback in business relationships?
- Line manager and direct report
- Coach/mentor and client
- Positioning the feedback discussion
- When's the 'right time' for feedback?
- How to connect with 'someone we don't like'
- How connected am I anyway?
- How do we compensate for systemic influences on the relationship?
- So why this book on feedback?
- How this book works, including an overview of the chapters, and supplementary resources supporting The Relational Leadership WAY©.

I'm delighted to share this work with you and my wish is that together we can elevate the power of feedback!

Introduction

Have we moved on from the days of the 'blame culture' in which learning from unintended errors or heroic risk taking is sacrificed to gratify depleted egos? Sadly not! The only change that seems to have emerged is a later model: 'name, blame and shame.'

No small wonder that the practice of 'feedback' conspicuously struggles to gain the prized recognition it deserves as a fundamental learning tool. Workplace relationships become fractured by mismanaged development interventions.

A staggering 87% of employees worldwide are not engaged! Many companies are experiencing a crisis of engagement and aren't aware of it. Companies with highly engaged workforces outperform their peers by 147% in earnings per share (Gallup, 2016). Can you afford to ignore these findings?

This text is written to stimulate and invite a review of current working relationship practices. Demographics, the digital age we've now entered and the increasingly integrated workforce of humans and artificial intelligence place even greater demands on creating and sustaining effective workplace relationships. The traditionally labelled 'soft skills' which deserve a title more reflective of their crucial role are becoming even more vital now that routine tasks are increasingly the domain of bots and chatbots! The new roles emerging from this radical upheaval will place greater dependency on interpersonal skills and emotional intelligence as the skills profile of the future. Our children may not even be aware of the careers open to them, which are likely not yet created!

This text reviews current feedback practices, what makes many outdated and why feedback has such a disabling reputation. You will have fresh thinking and a new route to feedback through the concept of relational leadership.

The Relational Leadership WAY©, enabling a 'way of being' and recommended as the cornerstone of relational leadership, gives managers, leaders, coaches and mentors the capability to fulfil the anticipated skills profile of tomorrow. It is basically the 'how' of achieving 'what' are productive relationships in business. The framework created from a doctoral research study (Lewis, 2014b) emphasises the value of the relationship.

How we relate creates the conduit for fulfilling the expectations of the workforce in business today and into the future. The key to effectiveness in relationship management places personal attributes above technical skills. Simply applying a 'box of tools' to achieve the quality of feedback essential for satisfying the hungry mouth of progress is quickly becoming insufficient.

Why is feedback so important?

The pressure to improve performance, linked with a desire to cope with the complexity and ambiguity of the working environment, is a challenge in today's competitive market. The inherent obstacles of doing more with less are likely to increase with the anticipated changes in demographics of five generations being employed in the workplace (Salzman, 2017). Technological developments in this digital age will add to this uncertainty.

Top performing companies are top performing companies because they consistently search for ways to make their best even better. These companies are serious about 'continuous improvement' from across the entire organisation, are good at accepting feedback and deliberately ask for feedback (DeFranzo, 2015). Managers are increasingly acting as coaches for direct reports as part of a renewed approach to performance management (Ellinger et al, 2014 cited in Ladyshewsky, R., and Taplin, R., 2018). The change in management and leadership style is obvious.

Human performance improved and informed by meaningful and purposeful feedback remains high on the agenda for business success. The inherent difficulties of engaging with feedback are well known and overcoming these is critical where feedback is essential. A move away from traditional models and theories that offer a template for leadership practices increasingly focuses on the person and the demonstration of personal attributes: 'followers are not satisfied with leaders that are not authentic (and) authentic leaders (need to) develop higher levels of self-awareness' (Nichols & Erakovich, 2013).

The relationship dilemma

How often do we think about our impact on others? How often do we evaluate the quality of our relationships in a business environment to keep them healthy and effective? Most of us know that relationships don't miraculously materialise without effort, yet we often neglect to reflect on how well they're functioning in the 'busyness' of our daily working routines. The fact is that feedback is always present! We see it in our daily observations of each other and it's in every communication we have. Of course, we don't always notice the signs and we don't always act or wish to act on chance or intentional feedback opportunities.

Consequently, how many of us avoid offering feedback both as a giver and receiver because of feelings of uncertainty and insecurity about the quality and robustness of our relationships? If we do nothing improvement is unlikely. If we do initiate feedback we may need help in both delivery and receipt to encourage active participation rather than avoidance.

> Do not bruise the lotuses, or taint the water with stirred mud
> (Bua Mai Hai Chum, Nam Mai Hai Khun)

The above proverb, based upon Thai philosophy, reminds us that we need to be continuously alert to the effect on others of what we say and how we say it. For me this proverb encapsulates the potential for damage to self-esteem that happens by giving 'feedback' without careful attention to its impact. Words affect our hearts more than we know. Although the popularisation of resilience makes this a normative word, we do not all have the same ability to proverbially 'bounce back'. Maintaining wellbeing through nurturing the lotuses and keeping the water clear comes through respect and valuing each other in our decisions about what and how we exchange feedback. As we move further into the digital age of increasingly impersonal communication, protecting a safe and secure working environment can only become more critical.

What this new research into feedback revealed

'Use of self' and a 'way of being' are a more powerful influence than process tools alone.

I found during my time in HR that feedback featured most frequently in recruitment, selection and career progression. Successful candidates received validation for demonstrating the desired attributes for appointment and those unsuccessful were offered supportive developmental feedback. People wishing to further their career could discuss potential openings for promotion. A typical conversation explored the 'expected' and 'desirable' competency profile for each role and invited completion and offered feedback on psychometric reporting. The outcome was to co-create a development plan in readiness for future job applications. This type of feedback felt rewarding, was perceived as being helpful and wasn't personally demanding. Feedback of this type was the upside of HR if I'm to place a value judgement on the activity.

More challenging times came with the 'capability' conversation. People experiencing long term sickness were automatically offered health advice and a phased 'return to work' as their health improved. Usually this resulted in people resuming their substantive role and continuing employment as before. In some circumstances this approach was unsuccessful when an unresolved health condition necessitated a change of role. An engineer was no longer able to find the concentration levels demanded for design or a social worker had to be 'removed' from a stress-inducing caseload. The complexity of the feedback conversation largely depended on the psychological state of the individual. This could range from the extremes of understanding the need and even welcoming a change of role to total denial that work activities had to be different for the benefit of their wellbeing. There were no tools to easily apply in this type of feedback. Expertise in human functioning was essential and the quality of relationship vital. Finding the best pathway to managing the emotional fallout of what was sometimes loss of identity for the individual could be elusive and draining for both.

The darker side of feedback came from downsizing due to budget cuts. The outcome was usually redundancies, often for long serving employees who were not ready to leave the job that gave meaning to their lives and sustained a chosen lifestyle. These feedback conversations were again sensitive. My energy became depleted when digging deep to 'sit compassionately with another' who was struggling to find meaning and searching for ways to adapt to changes that loss of employment brings.

Clearly feedback is not only the domain of HR; it is also a key function of line management. Observing the diversity of delivery, or in many instances non-delivery, of feedback gave me the impetus to undertake a research study. The aim was to challenge existing practices and intentionally create a new image for feedback.

This text draws on examples from research – my own and others' professional and life experiences. The focus is on 'use of self' and a 'way of being' to generate a more powerful influence than process tools alone when creating the right environment for feedback.

As the content of this book has a business perspective let's begin with how feedback features in this context. Feedback in organisations is usually part of a formal performance management system and viewed as pivotal to improving the capability of individuals at work. The ideal scenario that many businesses aspire to is that feedback is part of day-to-day conversations. This gives the advantage of making observations 'in the moment' when examples for discussion are readily available.

The default position for encouraging feedback is its inclusion in the interview as part of the performance management discussion. The intention is that feedback celebrates successful work activities, identifies strengths and specifies performance improvement. This approach is pragmatic and can be perceived as simple to implement. In reality, my own and others' feedback stories paint a different picture: one of disenchantment and disengagement.

A common scenario is chasing targets often set by managers and regularly without the individual's full involvement. How can performance objectives be assessed as realistic and achievable without an evaluation? The process – feedback – for reviewing progress in achieving these targets may not be clear or subject of a throwaway comment: 'we'll catch up on this later.' All too often 'later' doesn't materialise and naturally leads to disenchantment. The busy manager perceives lack of commitment and the direct report feels unsupported.

A combination of working in HR and as an executive coach led me to recognise that performance management systems claiming to have robust processes for improving the way people work were disregarded and largely abandoned. I believe the roots of this dilemma grew from over reliance on documentation guiding the performance discussion and a failure to recognise the 'human factor.' Let's remember that who we are and how we're regarded as human beings determines how we behave at work.

Managers often surreptitiously avoided sharing what they interpreted as 'bad news' or criticism. I noticed that the preferred option was to exaggerate 'good news,' deluding themselves that positive reinforcement alone equals improved performance.

This phenomenon is mirrored in my work as an executive coach when I hear of conversations about mismanaged – or absence of – meaningful feedback. Stories of reluctance and 'fear' to engage because of the perceived consequences also feature in shared tales of despondency. Clients speaking in the secure environment of coaching make disclosures bordering on 'harassment and bullying' at one end of the continuum and at the other end 'withdrawal through abdication' from feedback conversations.

Figure 0.1 The continuum of feedback behaviours; this polarisation of feedback behaviour is not an assumption typical of *every* performance discussion and recognises the existence of good practice

The chilling realisation is that both extremes in the model can be oscillating behaviours when lack of self-awareness and inhibition cloud our judgement.

Why we resent feedback

The apparent frailties of handling feedback reinforce images from earlier in life. You can probably also recall memories of those feedback moments that dented self-image and some that had lasting effects. Personal recollections evoke memories of unexplained 'one way' feedback from within the family that were later paralleled in the education system. These episodes of mixed messages, punctuated with blocks on requests for understanding by those 'in authority' and 'who *obviously* knew better,' left me confused and self-doubting about my own interpretation of events. Consequently, from a young age the seeds of fascination for understanding human behaviour were germinating into a desire to learn how to gain reciprocity in relationships. I became resigned to accepting that feedback was given and received with a splash of serendipity. The result was that my journey to adulthood unconsciously encouraged me to be a keen observer, participant and critical reflector on how we use feedback to influence each other.

Milner (1987) talks of 'knowing who, what, one is. What one is, [w]hat any self is. Do we know the answer to that?' Another question asks whether 'it's possible to pass from knowing the phenomena of the real self to being the real self' (Milner 1987). I don't have the answers to these intriguing questions. What is evident and reinforced by the research is that the better the quality of our relationships, and the more the willingness to share feedback, the greater the level of self-awareness.

We inevitably interpret feedback through our own lens, and when key messages oppose our worldview we simply can't make sense of them and are likely to disregard the content. 'Getting it in perspective and scaling it to its correct size is often the first task,' notes Bluckert (2006) when describing the activity of feedback. A clear challenge for both the giver and the receiver of feedback.

What drives the perception of feedback in business relationships?

Two scenarios you may be familiar with and that drive the behaviour that diminishes the feedback conversation in business relationships involve:

1.   Line manager and direct report

One of my tasks when working in human resources was to reinvigorate the performance management paperwork. Seeking fresh thinking I attended an 'Upward Feedback' workshop. The programme content describing workplace scenarios included scripted guidance showing how a direct report can offer feedback to their line manager. Fine in a classroom setting, but how likely is this to happen in reality? Who wants to potentially alienate a line manager who influences career progression and pay?

Appraisal time can make and break working relationships depending on how the human aspect and emotional impact are respected. Direct reports can be guarded when salary increments are dependent on positive regard from a line manager. Only a brave person will ignore the potential hazards of being seduced into making observations that are less than complimentary about their manager's leadership style.

Genuine two-way 'constructive' feedback is clearly advantageous; however, the willingness to participate varies considerably depending on the culture prevalent within the business.

2.   Coach/mentor and client

Clients may see a coach/mentor as the 'expert' in the relationship and project attributes that may or may not be in the practitioner's skills set. They may prefer taking a secondary role by deferring to the coach's perceived wisdom providing escape from taking responsibility and owning their own best solution. At the same time, the coach may enjoy the superior position bestowed upon them by willingly stepping into the role of sage and creating dependency in the client.

This is not the intention of coaches who follow a code of ethics for professional practice. Neither is it the intention of this book, which promotes a learning partnership creating effective conversations.

So – as practitioners how do we role model a learning partnership?

Positioning the feedback discussion

- *When's the 'right time' for feedback?*

Giving thought to the timing of feedback demonstrates a willingness to relinquish power in the relationship and to encourage respect and equality. The process for gauging the timing is, of course, debatable:

- What influences the decision to offer feedback in the moment?
- What's more acceptable: asking permission to give feedback or offering spontaneous feedback?
- How effective is conjecturing what's happening during periods of silence – are these psychological moments, an invitation to speak, a reflective moment or something else?
- What is the actual meaning of intuitive feelings that encourage whether or not to offer feedback? There are reasons for these felt sensations, but what are they?

How to connect with 'someone we don't like'

Having a positive feedback conversation assumes both parties are prepared to willingly engage and want the best for each other. Naturally, this isn't always necessarily the situation. An individual may feel disassociated from a line manager's style. A line manager may feel a direct report doesn't 'do as they're told'; a cringing indictment of management style! These differences may stem from personality, values, development needs or other disengaging events.

In these circumstances how do individuals let go of their personal agenda?

How connected am I anyway?

- How we affect others depends greatly on our level of self-awareness and willingness to understand how we impact on others
- How aware are we of what our physiology discloses or infers about how 'present' and engaged we are in our interactions with others?

How do we compensate for systemic influences on the relationship?

The short answer to this question is that we may not be able to! However, we can be aware. Looking beyond the immediate relationship we can visualise what may be happening in the 'field surrounding and between' us. The meaning of 'field' has several interpretations ranging from metaphysical influences immediately impacting on the relationship to the wider system of the environmental context in which people are working. Systemic forces impact on relationships and may distort or aid communication. Although the complexity of this phenomena and its bearing on our interactions may remain somewhat elusive we need to be aware that there may be more influencing our relationships than what is immediately evident. There will be more on this in later chapters.

So why this book on feedback?

The purpose of this book is to demonstrate that the quality of relationships improves the activity of feedback. At the very least, respect for each other is the baseline ingredient for encouraging reciprocity.

The 'relationship' as a 'resource' appears marginalised and is deservedly regaining recognition. We accept relationships through a tacit understanding that can sometimes ignore the benefits gained from an explanation about their creation. Until something goes wrong – then our attention is, of course, drawn to relationships that need 'fixing.'

The content of this book is informed by doctoral research findings on feedback and supported by extracts from literature and case studies from business and coach/mentor practice.

The context for the field research within the doctoral study focused on feedback in coaching. The relationship between the coach and client was perceived as potentially holding significant data worthy of investigation. Relational aspects of the conversation and any external phenomena perceived to impact on the quality of communication between individuals were recorded, analysed and interpreted.

The analysis of the data assessed whether significant observable phenomena will spontaneously recognise the quality of a relationship, and when combined with tacit knowledge can inform a 'summoned way of being' through 'use of self.' The aim is to create conditions that are more enthusiastically engaging for feedback than may be apparent. Inducing this state is representative of eliciting or encouraging a 'growth mindset' with its focus on development as identified by Dweck (2006).

The outcome of the study is offered as having universal replication for strengthening interpersonal relationships generally. However, the primary intention is to improve the activity of feedback within a business context and in coaching/mentoring and coach supervision practices where learning and improvement are key indicators of organisational and people development.

The use of proprietary tools and techniques is common practice for establishing a platform for discussion including feedback. When designing the research study, these customary 'processes' were perceived as underestimating the emotional impact of feedback and the relational context. The emphasis for the study was, therefore, on producing an alternative. An overview of occupational testing will, however, be included in one of the chapters as recognition that it is a popular intermediary in the feedback discussion.

The study also assumed that the purpose of feedback is that it results in transformative learning so that the desired changes for improved performance at work are achieved. This usually occurs through 'critically reflecting on the feedback received (assumptions of others: objective reframing) or on one's own assumptions (subjective reframing)' Mezirow (2000). The research analysis of the feedback dialogue was examined to identify indicators reinforcing the quality of the relationship and how this informed the activity of feedback. Assessing the relationship between feedback and adult learning theory was not included as a feature of the study.

The outcome of thematic analysis of the research study data collected from coach practice produced The Relational Leadership WAY© core to this book.

The Relational Leadership WAY© encourages effective relationships and works through perfecting a 'way of being' that is generative and productive in all interactions with others and specifically in feedback conversations, whether we are the giver or the receiver. The 10 themes integral to The Relational Leadership WAY© are organised into 3 parts that relate to pivotal points in a conversation and that, when given focused attention, will improve relationships:

1. *What* you need to *prepare* to encourage relationships that stimulate constructive conversations
2. *Active* engagement in co-creating generative conversations through adopting relational behaviours
3. *You* both noticing and *reacting* to what emerges and impacts on sustaining the quality of the relationship

The underpinning themes of the 3 parts

1. *What* you need to *prepare* to encourage relationships that stimulate constructive conversations:
   The first part of The Relational Leadership WAY© introduces the themes for *prepare:*
   1. **Self-management:** emotional state, level of confidence and compassion for each other

2. **Readiness for feedback:** assessing receptivity and possible reaction to feedback

2. *Active* engagement in co-creating generative conversations through adopting relational behaviours:

The second part of The Relational Leadership WAY© presents the themes that encourage everyone to actively participate and signposts what relational behaviours are:

3. **Objectivity:** being non-judgemental and aware of personal biases

4. **Mindfulness:** maintaining total focus on all aspects within the relationship and in the conversation

5. **Presence:** generating flow in the conversation through holistic and grounded participation

3. *You* both noticing and *reacting* to what emerges and impacts on sustaining the quality of the relationship

The third part of The Relational Leadership WAY© completes the themes that alert both to what needs attention to sustain a productive relationship:

6. **Timing of feedback:** predicting the best time for sharing feedback

7. **Physicality:** noticing levels of energy, somatic and kinaesthetic signals and physiology

8. **Emotional state:** observable fluctuations in emotional stability

9. **Intuition:** level of accessible 'brainpower' through conscious learned experience and unconscious and subconscious channels

10. **Metaphysical:** paying attention to the sensation of what feels to be impacting on the relationship from the wider system.

The flexibility of The Relational Leadership WAY© gives the potential for the themes to be developed and adopted to meet individual personal development programmes. Learning can focus on a specific theme, a combination of themes, an element, or for the more adventurous the whole framework!

The Relational Leadership WAY© is featured as a leading-edge approach. The anticipation is one of co-creating together a 'way of being' through 'use of self' in a way that facilitates the sharing of feedback. The purpose is to achieve the desired transformational change in capability gained through raised self-awareness. Taking this joint responsibility encourages 'gentle exposure to things feared and avoided and practising thinking differently, in an atmosphere of support' (Gilbert, 2009b).

The framework is, therefore, recommended as an alternative or as complementary when used together with customary feedback processes.

The Relational Leadership WAY© also recognises that feedback cannot always be planned and is likely to emerge spontaneously in conversations. In the context of coaching

> the aim is to help coaches deal with the fact that the unique, dynamic adaptive nature of coaching relationships means that coaching is a radically unpredictable, almost iterative process in which the next step is informed, in large part by the conditions immediately preceding it
>
> (Lane & Corrie, 2006)

I believe this observation similarly applies in all relationships. To be respectful to others and to truly demonstrate the empathy that feedback demands invites us to emulate Charon's (2006) observations that practitioners are required 'to learn the science of their craft to meet the needs for replicability and universality in attending to its advancement and the art of their craft to meet the needs for singularity and creativity in attending to individual clients.'

Dirkx and Mezirow (2006) refer to a 'progression from knowing what works, to how it works, to why it works, to when it works.' Knowing 'what to do and when' is the gift offered by the application of The Relational Leadership WAY©.

Preparing the narrative for feedback is clearly important; however, there is a 'growing emphasis on the emotional, physical and spiritual development, to be able to sustain (self) in the moment and across time (in the conversation) and amid increasing complexity and diversity' (Drake, 2011). Managers, leaders, coaches, mentors and everyone with responsibility for helping people to improve at work are represented in this umbrella statement.

How this book works

This book will appeal to you if you're seeking an innovative approach to transformational change in performance management and welcome a reprieve from the relentless pursuit of a feedback tool guaranteed to succeed. You will have noticed that people are increasingly disenchanted with performance improvement techniques that fail to deliver. You are invited to share a new and refreshing way of engaging in authentic feedback that is willingly given and well received.

The aim is to offer a different route to feedback and to counteract the 'bad press' often accompanying this activity. This book acts as a catalyst for personal development and as a recommendation to those wishing to improve feedback skills:

- Business managers and leaders expected to motivate teams to become highly performing work units. To achieve this involves transparent and honest feedback that builds not damages relationships
- Organisational and independent coaches, mentors and practice supervisors who wish to develop trust by building effective relationships that encourage disclosure through feedback that is engaging and authentic
- Managers/leaders/HR/OD specialists to use as a business text for performance management programmes
- Coach/mentor/practice supervisor training organisations as core text for delegates

We want to maintain our natural way of being and with the support of the 'way of being' recommended in The Relational Leadership WAY© – without being formulaic in its application you will create the productive relationships that will enhance your working and extended relationships.

This book is written for you to 'dip into' where your interest takes you. At the same time, the chapters have a logical sequence with each building on the one before to provide a pathway helping you to improve how you give and receive feedback. Hopefully the messages will also prove effective in your personal exchanges with friends and family.

The chapters

To help you with your choice of reading here's a brief taster of each chapter:

Chapter 1: What perceptions exist about feedback? visits current thinking on feedback and why it's important. You will find a range of definitions illustrating what industry voices believe to be the purpose of feedback and how the psychological perspective impacts on people's willingness to engage in this type of information exchange.

Chapter 2: Why feedback and whose responsibility is it? brings to the stage the stakeholders and their role in feedback seen through various lenses.

In **Chapter 3: Current practices in feedback exchange**, these practices are explored, reviewed and evaluated before introducing the alternative perspective in **Chapter 4: The importance of relationship and how it**

WHAT you need to prepare
to encourage relationships
that stimulate constructive conversations

THEMES

1. Self Management

2. Readiness for Feedback

Figure 0.2 Part 1 of The Relational Leadership WAY©

influences engagement in feedback, which prioritises the relationship as the primary vehicle for feedback. Chapter 4 closes with the introduction to The Relational Leadership WAY© graphically illustrating the framework of 10 Themes organised in 3 parts (see Figure 4.1).

Chapter 5: Part 1 of The Relational Leadership WAY©: *What* **needs preparing to establish relationships that stimulate constructive conversations** covers what you think about, reflect on and source before the feedback discussion. You will be given a definition of the two supporting themes 'self-management' and 'readiness for feedback' and how to apply these in the feedback discussion (see Figure 0.2).

Chapter 6: Part 2 of The Relational Leadership WAY©: *Active* **engagement in co-creating generative conversations through adopting**

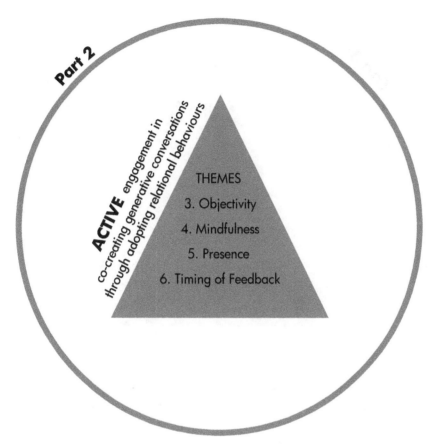

Figure 0.3 Part 2 of The Relational Leadership WAY©

relational behaviours explains the themes to introduce into the relationship to gain *active* engagement: 'objectivity' – 'mindfulness' – 'presence' – 'timing of feedback'. These themes create a foundation for the type of relationship that activates willingness to participate in feedback (see Figure 0.3).

Chapter 7: Part 3 of The Relational Leadership WAY©: *You* **both** *noticing* **and** *reacting* **to what emerges and impacts on sustaining the quality of the relationship** explains and guides on working with the themes of: 'physicality' – metaphysical' – 'emotional state' and 'intuition' that emerge and that we become cognisant of in the conversation. Noticing and working with these phenomena are vital in maintaining and sustaining positive relationships (see Figure 0.4).

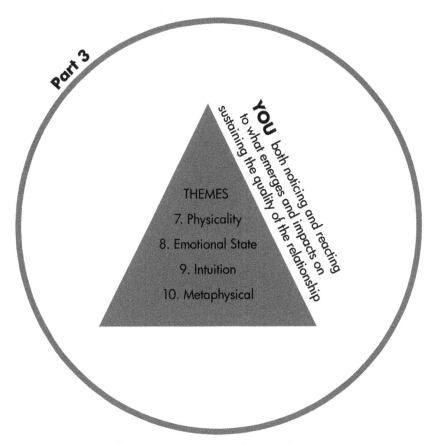

Figure 0.4 Part 3 of The Relational Leadership WAY©

Chapter 8: How Artificial Intelligence (AI) may impact on the future of feedback offers a glimpse into what feedback may look like in the age of the integrated workforce of humans and robotics. This chapter is also a segue to further research for future development of The Relational Leadership WAY©.

Supplementary resources supporting The Relational Leadership WAY©:

- Webinars are available for registration to aid learning for each theme, for engaging in discussion groups and practice forums. The webinars are available at www.liselewis.com

What perceptions exist about feedback?

1

'How to give feedback is one of the hottest topics in business today.'
(Buckingham & Goodall, 2019)

If feedback is this high on the business agenda, why is it so susceptible to tokenism and sometimes completely avoided? My observations when listening to and participating in feedback conversations was to notice that the behaviours underlying this reaction were often driven by negative feelings – anxiety about what to say and how to say it so that the feedback was sympathetically received, and fear at the haunting prospect of what might be said. This is a strange dichotomy when feedback is both the saviour and persecutor of people development.

Talking with receivers of feedback exposes diverse scenarios ranging from benevolent mentors offering a guiding hand to a gripping fear synonymous with heavy footsteps following you in the dead of night! The individual's perception of feedback is influenced by their worldview, coupled with the significance of the giver and their perceived and actual competence in delivering feedback. Without acknowledging these factors the efficacy of feedback will be questioned.

Cavanagh (2006) states that 'we need to have an understanding about how to nurture effective levels of openness'; suggesting 'openness' as an antidote to avoiding what he describes as 'derailment.' I take this reference – relating to managers – as advice to nurture a culture of transparency. In this environment employees are persuaded to voice suggestions through joint feedback on different and improved ways of working. Ideally, everyone is encouraged to take responsibility for their own personal development. Such an improvement culture avoids people being unaware of how to meet expectations and managers inadvertently being held responsible for undermanaging. This accepting of responsibility chimes with the article 'Dealing Positively with Criticism' (Warner, 2013) in recognising that 'despite our natural suspicions, as adults, we also appreciate that criticism can be valuable, particularly if it is well intended or constructive and not maliciously intended or destructive.' I prefer the terms 'supportive' or 'developmental' feedback to 'criticism'; however, the message is clear that given the right conditions people are willing to be open to others' opinions.

Setting aside the ideal world we need to acknowledge that some people just don't like feedback; in fact in my experience most don't! People fear that their performance will be perceived as poor or that they will be criticised for making mistakes and automatically assume the feedback message will be negative (Zenger, 2016). Managers and leaders may fear that their direct reports will react adversely to even the mildest of criticism – possibly with anger and tears. This explains the unwillingness to welcome or give feedback and contributes to perpetuating a cycle of avoidance or diluting the improvement message.

The timetabled scheduling for planning performance management meetings can, therefore, arrive and clash with the urge to procrastinate in arranging these conversations because of the negative associations about content. Even when performance conversations do happen the result is that feedback is reduced to a sterile and disingenuous activity confined only to cosmetic positive comments.

Case study

This fear exhibited by managers and leaders was illustrated by a client who introduced their topic for coaching with the statement: 'We just don't do performance management here; no one wants to tackle it.' Further exploration elicited a scenario of frustration with 'working around' one specific manager, resulting in reorganising operational teams to avoid potential confrontation with direct reports at 'breaking point.'

The prevailing culture was one where managers generally colluded or were in denial about the toxic potential of this attitude. We can conjecture on the reasoning: hoping the situation will 'go away'; not taking responsibility; believing it's the role of human resources; mobility of roles meaning that managers were in transit to various locations much of the time and more. In this case study the reason was that 'everyone is afraid of this person, particularly the immediate line manager.'

You can probably identify different solutions to gain resolution; however, for this client the options were limited. The 'likelihood of anyone being prepared to listen or discuss the situation was doubtful' and 'my only choice may be to leave; a decision I'm starting to accept.'

This may be the best solution for this individual although not necessarily for the business who may be losing a competent employee. Neither does the individual leaving resolve conditions for those remaining. The 'disrupter' also continues to damage business operations. The problem will perpetuate until someone has the courage to give feedback and manage the consequences.

In this chapter, I share case study examples from performance management discussions and coach/mentoring conversations to illustrate a range of perceptions about feedback. You will also learn more about the psychology of feedback and how this influences our ability to engage as individuals, teams and leaders, with particular emphasis on reaching the realisation that it's time to move on from outdated assumptions about feedback. We have to recognise that the catalyst for reciprocal learning and transformational insights informing the continuous improvement essential for the future of work is fostering authentic relationships.

Let's start this voyage of reframing by giving feedback definition before moving towards how feedback can be viewed differently by using the relationship as launch pad.

Definitions of feedback

An internet search will find you a range of descriptions for feedback confirming that there is not one universally agreed. A simple explanation is that feedback is a 'reaction to behaviours and actions.' This may be implicitly recognised without comment or explicitly observed and expressed through shared experiences of feelings, thoughts and perceptions.

Heron, (2009) offers a menu of feedback 'types.' I see these as informing an entry to or regulation within the feedback conversation.

- **Verbal:** content, meaning of what is said, choice of words, construction of statement, tone, volume, pitch, speed, pauses, silences

- **Non-verbal:** eye contact/use of eyes, facial expression, touch, posture, gestures (arms, legs, head, neck), relative position (near – far – beside – in front of – behind – opposite), breathing
- **Awareness:** distinguishes between behaviour that is 'aware of' and that is apparently 'unaware of'
- **Source** (prioritised in order of importance): self, client, others, practitioner
- **Corrective:** obvious error or omission
- **Subjective:** general impression, unsupported by evidence
- **Objective:** with supporting reasons.

CIPD (2017) tells us that 'essentially, performance appraisal is a means for managers and their employees to review and discuss the latter's performance, to identify areas for growth and improvement and inform suitable development plans.' I don't get a sense of reciprocity or signs of a learning partnership from this definition.

An example from coaching literature is Starr (2012) who defines feedback as 'normally information or opinion given to a person, who is related to that information or opinion.' This is a simple description of relaying data attributable to the receiver although the source generating the feedback remains undefined and intangible, giving a feeling of detachment similar to the CIPD definition.

I like the definition offered by Scoular (2011) as this explicitly refers to 'relationship'; a key feature in this book: 'the coaching relationship offers a unique opportunity for a client to receive from their coach that rare thing, direct and honest feedback, (relatively) free from the influence of hierarchy, politics, history and expectations.'

In my experience from HR and as a coach, when this transfer of 'information or opinion' is lacking, the individual inevitably makes their own assessment about their performance. People understandably assume their contribution at work is at least acceptable and at most valuable. This reinforces the intention of most of us to 'do a good job,' and why wouldn't we believe we do in the absence of data disabusing us of this perception?

This impression of 'acceptability' generally results from a culmination of life experiences informed by the sociological perspective. Oetting (1999 pp. 947–982) illustrates this when stating:

> Developmentally, the only primary socialization source for the preschool ... child is the family. In early grade school years, the primary socialization sources are the family and school. Peer clusters emerge ... later, with ... greatest effect occurring during adolescence.

The psychological debate adds another dimension when contesting 'nature vs. nurture' by emphasising innate ability over learned capability and vice versa. Consequently, various factors shape our knowledge of self as well as the individual's propensity for self-reflection and scrutiny. An example of this impacting on performance can be comparisons of self with the opinion of influential others. My experience suggests that some people can be highly introspective and externally focused in gaining a sense of self. Others seem to have little interest in self-reflection or knowing what others think of them, to the extent of exhibiting the adage 'I am what I am.' Most of us will probably judge ourselves as being at different points along this continuum.

When providing HR expertise to organisations, I noticed recurring misconceptions about what represented potential sources of data for forming opinions of others and informing feedback:

- people's perceptions of each other shaped from anecdotal exchanges of perceived or anticipated behaviours
- observations peppered with bias and stereotypical judgements
- psychometric test reports claiming to be an objective diagnostic measure based on test publishers' statistical data and assumed as a definitive profile.

These examples inherently carry varying degrees of subjectivity and complexity when founded on diverse interpretations of perceptions and evaluative observations.

Defining feedback, therefore, is a challenge in itself. As creating a new definition was not an outcome of the research, a simple definition was chosen for identifying the context of the study and the definition assumed in this book:

> Feedback is an activity to raise self-awareness and improve the contribution of individuals in a business environment.

The purpose of the 'activity' is to have a conversation that alerts the receiver to how their behaviour is perceived by the giver. This conversation is intended to draw attention to opportunities for change by identifying a shortfall in performance expected by the business and creating development needs for the receiver. 'Performance' in this definition focuses on personal attributes and behaviours rather than the task completion or technical expectations in the receiver's role. The reason this route was chosen was that, in my experience, a shortfall in technical/task-based skills is usually easily remedied. Feedback on task-based competence can be endorsed with evidence of capability aligned to business standards. A solution is addressed by a range of training interventions matching the individual's learning style.

The more challenging performance issues arise when behaviours create disruption in interpersonal relationships. These disruptions are based on perceptions which are, of course, reality to the individuals experiencing the disconnect. The research informing this book will disrupt in the opposite direction and demonstrate the positive power of relationship that nurtures rather than diminishes mutual growth and produces a thriving working environment.

Willingness to engage in feedback – the psychological perspective

'Successful organisations actively embrace feedback accepting that recognition of both weaknesses and strengths are vital contributors to continuously improving. Feedback, when effective, benefits both the giver and the receiver' (DeFranzo, 2015).

Logically we know that feedback is best managed 'in the moment.' The challenge is how we do this reflexively and substantiate our perceptions in a non-judgemental way. This challenge is all the more complicated when you factor in two particularly confounding variables:

1. Our worldview may believe the feedback to be confrontational, when in fact the receiver may welcome it!
2. The other's resistance to hearing unsolicited negative information, however well-intentioned the feedback

How do we know what the reaction will be when we 'hold up the mirror'? How can we 'change the feedback message' when unwelcomed behaviours are repeatedly displayed?

Let's take a look at what happens in organisations faced with these challenges. In leading HR functions, I was frequently tasked with evaluating how effectively performance appraisal systems were recognised and utilised as an essential management tool. This review highlighted that people felt most 'comfortable' when using the appraisal documentation as a guide for establishing task-based goals. In effect, the 'what' of task achievement appeared to be adequately covered. In contrast, the 'how' conversation was often limited to discussing resources needed for task completion with little or no emphasis on individual performance indicators informed by developmental feedback. Without this informative conversation, what hope is there for encouraging improvement and learning? The apparent superficial attempts to talk about performance resulted in the appraisal process falling into disrepute as a 'waste of time' with both parties abandoning the process.

Managers became frustrated that their expectations of direct reports were not fulfilled – although without a direct dialogue they seemed to expect this to happen by osmosis! Those who resorted to asking HR for help were usually looking for remedies to improve breakdowns in relationships that were fuelling dysfunctional teams.

Typically, most managers avoided giving feedback on inadequate performance, preferring to prevaricate, disregard areas for improvement or expect HR to wave the proverbial 'magic wand.' Disappointingly, case study facilitation time built into performance management trainings didn't receive the anticipated applause to share performance challenges and explore solutions. This discontent is demonstrated in the statement 'Employers are also finally acknowledging that both supervisors and subordinates despise the appraisal process': an attitude endorsed by companies such as Adobe, Microsoft, Deloitte, PwC, and GAP who have abandoned appraisals in favour of regular feedback conversations (Cappelli & Tavis, 2016). Whether the 'regular feedback conversation' – which is not a new concept – is promoted as completely replacing the appraisal will be proven or otherwise when recorded evidence emerges. Those demonstrating a dogged determination to make the appraisal work may believe it's not the process that's deficient and may be seeking *how* to gain the desired results. There will be more later on what relational leadership achieves in this direction.

This evaluation of performance appraisal also emphasised overstated feedback as the norm, with managers significantly embellishing direct reports' performance – the anticipation being that positive reinforcement encourages spectacular improvement. Reluctance to give accurate feedback often stemmed from concern about being accused of bullying or harassment with the veiled threat of a grievance complaint or claim for constructive dismissal. Basically, managers craved a script to protect them against reprisal and that also guaranteed a way of resolving improved performance. This was customary behaviour prevailing in this case study of a highly unionised culture. Managers' working practices were often weighted in favour of the employee when regulated by national terms and conditions and supplemented by EU legislation.

This environment led to the unintended result of colluding with unacceptable performance and provided an 'escape route' for avoiding line management responsibilities. Procrastination based on perceived constraint developed a situation that finally became untenable. Workplace targets were not met and/or other team members felt aggrieved at the lack of remedial action being taken by line managers. From an HR perspective, resorting to a disciplinary procedure to address poor performance was viewed negatively and to be avoided whenever possible. Quality feedback was, therefore, considered both imperative and, at the same time, elusive.

Paradoxically, the recipient appeared to experience a similar anxiety on hearing the 'feedback' word. So, what is it about the word 'feedback' that instils a sense of vulnerability and exposure and generates the emotion of fear in both the giver and the receiver? The obvious answer for the receiver is the prospect of hearing something perceived as potentially negative about oneself; therefore, feedback is not an activity to welcome or actively seek. However, we learn if we get feedback and its absence clearly diminishes our ability to develop competence.

I'm confident that both these scenarios from the organisation and individual perspectives are prevalent in other business sectors.

Reflections on coaching practice and reviewing capability indicators for coaching and mentoring (EMCC, 2015) suggest that we are more receptive to raising our self-awareness on performance when we are free from the fear of being judged. We also value hearing another's view if we trust the source. Nurturing this attitude reduces the fear and anxiety assumed at the prospect of feedback that has the potential for damaging rather than enhancing relationships. The key is finding the route to authentic feedback from a place of safety.

An alternative to setting 'performance goals' and one which is suggested as seeing feedback in a positive light is to have a 'learning goal' focus. VandeWalle et al., 2000, cited in Clutterbuck and Megginson (2013), suggests that those with a 'learning goal' orientation 'are more likely to seek and benefit from feedback in the pursuit of their goals than those with a performance goal orientation.' I completely agree that 'development' discussions are more productive than 'performance' discussions. This important change of vocabulary changes the emphasis from what can be perceived as a judging conversation to one of support. However, Clutterbuck and Megginson (2013) remind us that a strong learning orientation doesn't eradicate the perception of feedback:

> on the basis of receptivity (willingness to hear message incongruent with established beliefs or assumptions), the perceived credibility of the feedback source, individual differences (e.g. openness to experience, curiosity) and emotional skills (e.g. the ability to navigate and manage the motions generated by the feedback).

Another possible interpretation for disregarding the 'human factor' as significant in the performance discussion may be a lack of adequate support for the activity of feedback delivery. McDowall et al. (2009) evidence this in their journal article on best practice in feedback. They state that 'individuals have subjective reactions to feedback' and 'it is also imperative that those who give feedback are appropriately trained and self-aware.' We are invited to recognise that feedback for the receiver is influenced by their worldview coupled with the competence of the giver in its delivery. The suggestion is that without establishing the impact of these factors the efficacy of feedback is questionable.

Barber (2008) reminds us that fear is multidimensional with somatic, experiential and cognitive features as well as a subjective energy that, though felt, cannot be directly observed. Fear nestles in our expectations; in the space before a 'happening'; in a limbo zone where the worst is expected but has not yet come. Fear escalates in this 'in between' time with 'not knowing' what to expect.

So, what is this antidote to 'fear' that apparently feeds the rejection of feedback? Let's first take a look at the 'good guy' fear, what others say about fear and what we can learn from neuroplasticity.

The fear factor

The culture at Netflix was 'described in the *Wall Street Journal* as "encouraging harsh feeback" through "intense and awkward" real-time 360 degrees' (Buckingham and Goodall (2019). The strength of vocabulary says it all!

The emotion of fear alerts us to the possibility that we may be harmed and may need to protect ourselves. Fear helps us to survive and is a helpful reminder of the environment we occupy. If we hear or see something unfamiliar, we seek reassurance that we're not in danger. Being this alert means we can take evasive action:

- We **don't** pull out of a side turning if we see an oncoming car as we know if we do we're likely to crash, causing injuries.
- We **don't** enter malarial zones without taking precautions to protect our health if bitten by mosquitoes.
- We **do** avoid feedback if we think we're going to be 'exposed' in some way that damages our self-esteem.

Psychologically, fear affects our concentration and attention by priming our 'state of readiness' for threat, blocking our thoughts and leaving us confused. When our self-image is threatened, and our intellectual and emotional defences are weakened, this is when fear steps up.

25

We have an element of fear in our everyday routines that keeps us alert to potential hazards; real or imaginary. In the feedback scenario we may fear being controlled and judged by others and conjure up fantasies of rejection of us as individuals or our efforts, augmented with feelings of being 'disciplined.' Jeffers (1991) believes 'fear will never go away as long as you continue to grow as fear is a natural consequence of facing change.' We have to 'face the fear' to borrow from the title of her book. We all have levels of fear calibrated by our individual experiences.

This innate safety alarm stems from the time when we had to protect ourselves from the dangers of roaming predatory animals and marauding tribal conflict. Although most of us no longer have these fears to face in our everyday lives, this survival instinct prevails to keep us safe – just as it did then. We know the 'flight or fight' syndrome that has become hard-wired as part of our evolution (see Figure 1.1). Do we run away from the perceived danger, or do we confront the perpetrator (see Figure 1.2)? Basically, fear is our friend in these situations and is taking care of us.

A simple explanation of the 'flight or fight' syndrome

The organising principle of the brain is to minimise danger and maximise reward. When we're engaged at work, we're in the reward state of mind and focused on solutions. When we're disengaged through feeling threatened, possibly because of job insecurity or a dysfunctional relationship with our line manager – or even the prospect of unwelcome feedback – we become problem-focused.

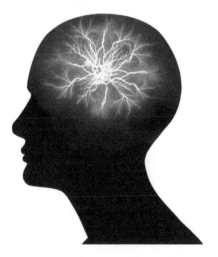

Figure 1.1 Elements of brain function

Thalamus	reacts to stimulus from our eyes, ears, mouth and skin
Sensory cortex	interprets this data
Hippocampus	retrieves previously stored memories
Amygdala	analyses emotions and determines possible threat
Hypothalamus	activates the 'flight or flight' response

Figure 1.2 The brain's response to change (Rock, 2008)

Threat produces adrenaline to prepare the body for 'flight or fight.' We now find mention of four 'Fs' as:

* Flight
* Fight
* Freeze
* Flock (come together to gain reinforcement for response to stimulus)

Threat ('away') is faster acting, stronger, longer lasting, more likely to put levels of adrenaline up and dopamine down, while reward ('towards') is slower, milder, and shorter-lived.

Neuroscience explaining the source of the emotion 'fear'

Most of us can easily relate to 'feeling under threat' at the prospect of feedback. The resultant emotion is likely to be one of fear most commonly associated with the likelihood of being criticised and perhaps feeling personally 'under attack'. Whatever our definition of fear reveals individually for us, the outcome is that we 'sense' the likelihood of change.

Whatever our propensity for change, none of us actually welcome it without some degree of trepidation about unknown consequences. One reason is that we form 'habits' through repetition. Over time and with practice we know how to complete the routine tasks of our work and can unconsciously press our autopilot button to deliver these. Neuroscience tells us this autopilot button activates our 'hard-wired' neural pathways in the brain.

27

When change is expected of us through feedback this autopilot reflexive action is disrupted – and we don't like it! The thought of change causes us discomfort and we resist it.

Further reading on neuroscience explaining the source of the emotion fear and how 'change is pain' is available at http://www.strategy-business.com, in an article titled 'The Neuroscience of Leadership' by David Rock and Jeffrey Schwartz (2006).

Our brain is basically a connection machine and up close no two brains are alike. The brain 'hardwires' everything it can and builds neural pathways. If we've had either negative or positive experiences of feedback in the past our brains will hardwire these memories and drive an 'automatic perception' informing how we respond to similar situations in the future. These hardwired automatic learned responses drive our behaviour. The good news is that our brain can create new wiring!

Through neuroplasticity (enabling new connections) we know that the first time a signal crosses the pathway to hardwiring is the hardest, just like crossing a ravine, and then the next journey gets easier, so learning is easier. Making this same crossing repeatedly embeds the learning until the 'crossing' becomes effortless.

Figure 1.3 Tiger's Nest: 'Crossing the ravine; the end in sight!'

How do we 'unlearn' and change a behaviour?

We may be reluctant to change if 'protection of self' is the main function of fear. There are likely to be several reasons for this, depending on the context for change, emotional impact and many more. My experience is that people reject change because they're rarely involved in the process. We really dislike a vacuum in our understanding and we know that without sufficient information we will 'join the dots'! We may not necessarily dislike change – we just don't like not knowing how the change is likely to impact us (Stern & Cooper, 2017).

We can change a behaviour if we understand the enabling principles that create new ways of thinking! Neuroplasticity is the ability of the brain to change; each time something new is introduced the brain changes. This enables us to rewire whatever response we have to feedback if we have sufficient reinforcing experiences.

As we become more competent, much of what we do at work is hardwired and handled by the basal ganglia; those 'unconscious competences' we don't have to think about! Functioning on automatic pilot, we become less aware of habits we've developed when communicating with others, running meetings and completing activities in our daily routines.

Lasting transformation needs new circuits in the brain. In a trusting relationship we can help others to rewire automatic responses to build new neural pathways by introducing small steps of new learnings. We need to recognise that a 'leap across a ravine' to do something new takes courage, and this is where we can support each other.

This process is slow and needs intense effort and attention to carve new pathways. Persistence and patience are key for transformative processing to work:

- We can leave the 'unconscious' to work on our behalf
- Encourage others to switch off the conscious linear thinking process
- This connects our unconscious so that ideas emerge from the subconscious when we go back to the 'task': we start to build positive/ negative reinforcing memories.

Our brain is a bedrock of activity; neurons are continuously firing and sending messages to and from our brains. 'Mirror neurons' operating at great speed and not necessarily at a conscious level help us in the feedback situation by noticing what's happening in others.

These neurons influence what we do next. When our conscious attention is elsewhere, we unconsciously mull over other thoughts. If we're consciously perceiving feedback as a learning opportunity, our hardwired experiences will be unconsciously interrupting our conscious thoughts. Most decisions are not based on conscious reasoning! (Brann, 2017).

Using brain plasticity to change mindsets

Dweck (2012) discovered that there are two main mindsets in both children and adults: a *fixed mindset* and a *growth mindset*.

People with a fixed mindset believe that talents and intelligence are essentially set. These people are reluctant to try new ways of doing things and don't significantly change as adults when retaining this fixed mindset. 'They are more interested in *appearing* smart and avoiding failure than in actually getting smarter' (Dweck, 2012).

Those with a growth mindset understand that they can continue developing their capability and competence and increase their mental capacities throughout life.

How to increase brain plasticity

- Practice any exercise: dancing, walking, making music
- Try a new activity: learning a different language, art classes
- Nurture wellbeing: quality sleep, healthy diet, meditation

Developing brain plasticity encourages new habits!

Duhigg (2012) introduces his concept of 'keystone habits' that can cause a chain reaction in our life or in an organisation. An example of a keystone habit is exercise. When we start habitually exercising – even as infrequently as once a week – we often start changing other, unrelated patterns in our lives.

Duhigg agrees that change might not be fast and it isn't always easy. At the same time, he reassures us that with practice and effort almost any habit can be reshaped. He talks about a simple researched neurological loop at the core of every habit, which consists of three parts:

- A cue
- A routine
- A reward

To recognise our habits we have to identify the components of our 'loops'. Once we've diagnosed the habit loop of a particular behaviour, we can look for ways to supplant old vices with new routines. Duhigg offers us a framework, which I've supplemented below with *italicised* examples:

* Identify a cue: What stops us changing a habit?
  Getting feedback is 'bad news'!
* Identify a routine: The behaviour we want to change
  Thinking feedback is a negative experience
* Experiment with rewards: Try different rewards for attempting to make the change
  If I get feedback I can learn more about what I do well
  If I get feedback I will know how to build on this
  If I get feedback I will be able to progress in my career
* Isolate the cue: what is the payoff for changing our habit?
  I don't get feelings of anxiety at the prospect of feedback
  Feedback is a positive development activity
  Receiving and acting on feedback will get me the rewards I want
* Have a plan: Continuously review a plan of action to change the habit
  Identify someone I trust and feel relaxed with to give me feedback
  Arrange a meeting and explain why I want feedback and how I value their opinion
  Review the feedback and take action that will achieve the rewards
  Search online for motivational tools that I can use to adopt methods that build good habits and break the ones I don't want.

Does negative brain plasticity exist?

Let's remember that not all changes in the brain are for the better! The phrase 'use it or lose it' applies to the brain as well as to muscles. When we don't use certain neural connections they eventually wither and die. Areas of the brain can actually get smaller from disuse.

Also, not all neural connections are positive. Undesirable habits, destructive addictions and objectionable self-talk can become firmly entrenched and hard to change due to the effects of *negative brain plasticity*.

I'm sure we've all experienced negative self-talk from our 'inner critic' at times that's had the effect of undermining our confidence to the point of convincing us we may as well not make the effort as we're sure to fail. Negative self-talk is a superfood for fuelling negative brain plasticity.

Here's a personal story that's made a lasting difference to how I developed a positive neural pathway, assisted by brain plasticity, through reinforcing a defining moment that changed my way of thinking.

I well remember the incident that was nearly my undoing in gaining a leadership coaching contract. This was early in my self-employed career when I was transitioning from a regular monthly salary to finding work to replace the missing pay cheque! I was on my way to make the requested selection presentation and during the 2-hour train journey the nasty confidence-sapping gremlin was taking a stronger hold the nearer I got to my destination. By the time I was 10 minutes away from the venue, I believed the voice that told me my presentation was inadequate, and worse still so was I. What made me think that I had the skills, knowledge and experience to step into a coaching role with an organisation recruiting coaches for large corporations? My energy and enthusiasm for making the presentation drained along with my confidence that I could do a good job in convincing the panel that I was worth engaging. My steps slowed, my shoulders dropped and my emotion changed from the excitement I felt on leaving home to dejection with a rising sense of failure.

I was seriously thinking about turning around and taking the next train home when I noticed a life-size statue of a man standing grandly on a substantial plinth with the name FRANKLIN engraved at eye level. I didn't realise until reading the plaque below that the statue was of Rear-Admiral Sir John Franklin, an English Royal Navy Officer who was also an Arctic explorer in the 1800s. He died on his last expedition, attempting to chart and navigate a section of the Northwest Passage in the Canadian Arctic.

So what had this to do with the negative self-talk my inner critic was energetically sharing, you may be asking! Well, this was my epiphany – my 'moment of sudden and great realisation'. Franklin was my surname before marriage and John was my elder brother's name. Noticing this statue was obviously a coincidence, I told myself. However, as I stood there with all my doubts about capability, I replied to my

Figure 1.4 Sir John Franklin, 1786–1847

self-talk with a different statement. 'Well, I can go home and feel defeated or I can make up my mind to go to this interview and enjoy myself whatever emerges.' I still find the use of the word 'enjoy' enigmatic. Why didn't I choose something on the lines of 'I'm going in there and making the best presentation they've seen today and they'll be amazed at the skilful way I've promoted my offering and expertise – and they'll recruit me on the spot'?

Let me share with you what happened next. I decided I was going to 'enjoy' the experience whatever happened. The impact of this decision was astonishing. As I made the decision my energy returned, my shoulders lifted and extraordinarily my mind cleared. My step noticeably quickened as I walked towards the venue. I reminded myself that I had prepared well and my presentation was focused, informative and visually appealing.

The outcome: I was confident in greeting the panel, put on my best welcoming smile and happily shared the ritual banter that accompanies these situations. Was I fazed when the projector failed to connect with my laptop? No! Any tension in the room came from the panel who were kind and apologetic about the technology malfunction. One of the panel remarked that, 'I've never seen anyone so calm at interview, especially with an IT issue.' Success! The outcome was a hiring and I worked with this organisation for several years.

Although all this happened a while back, the encouragement I gained from discovering that statue of Sir John continues to inspire me. Whenever these moments of self-doubt come to mind, the anchor of Sir John rushes into my pre-frontal cortex to remind me 'I've prepared well, I know how to do this and I can give it my best effort.'

In the article 'Fear is Nothing to Be Feared' (Schpancer, 2017), we're told the long-term solution is learning to manage the fear and manage yourself in the fearful territory. It takes time and it's uncomfortable. As with any behaviour we want to change we have to 'build the muscle.' The more we practice, the nearer we get to the goal we want to achieve.

Schpancer (2017) reminds us that the fear is not 'us' and it does not represent reality in full; it's only part of the experience. He asks us to remember that while we feel fear we can also tap into our values, courage, logic, past experience and general worldview to get a fuller representation of what is actually happening.

Taking this view helps us to appreciate that fear is nothing to be feared. Fear keeps us safe; however, having this realistic view of fear will lose its power to control our lives when we don't find it helpful.

Reinforcing this view is Gilbert (2010b) who uses the term 'anxiety' to describe this 'basic defensive emotion which is focused on threats.' I like that the description about anxiety possibly distorting our thinking alerts us to this sense of potential warped reality. When we feel that our emotions are being focused on creating a state of 'readiness', I believe this is our trigger for some self-talk saying, 'Hey, let's wait a minute and see what's really going on here.' This action gives us choice that we can use to determine what other possibilities exist for us in the feedback conversation, both as giver and receiver.

The effectiveness of feedback – for both the giver and receiver

We all know that feedback makes sense; it's how effectively it's managed that makes the difference to the way people react and respond, both negatively and positively.

Let's start our discussion of the purpose of feedback with a case study from an internal coach working in human resources:

> My client's topic was to talk about the advisability of non-disclosure of previous ill health to her line manager and HR before starting in her current employment, believing this to be detrimental to career progression. Her condition had been serious and operable. During our conversation, she realised that the fear of this health condition recurring was stopping her from fulfilling all aspects of her role.
>
> I was reminded of the Johari window model, which prompted me to give feedback that because of keeping this information within her 'private hidden self,' her manager had assumed she was either incapable or didn't want to do the work. My client wasn't aware of this and felt strongly that this wasn't the case (her blind spot). I was able to help her see through my feedback that by making this health position known to others (open public self), she could work with her manager to find ways to do the role fully without making her ill.
>
> I learned how powerful feedback can be. I felt it appropriate to give this feedback to my client as she was unaware about how her manager perceived her. The use of the Johari window really helped to highlight the situation to my client and helped me to structure my feedback.
>
> I felt really excited during this session. It was really useful to get some experience of giving feedback and was interesting using the Johari window to help me work out what my client's blind spot was and to help her realise the impact this was having on her and her manager's perception of her.

In this case study the coach identifies the purpose of this feedback as in service initially of the client and then of the client's manager. We may also assume this will ultimately benefit the business. The coach also acknowledges the personal and client satisfaction experienced in this feedback example and the usefulness of a technique as a feedback aid – more on tools and techniques in Chapter 4.

This example reminds us that the intended purpose of feedback is positive and to help the recipient. There's also a gain for the giver from a sense of helping and unblocking a barrier to performance. Who doesn't want this!

Of course, the most effective feedback is *self-feedback*. Most of us recognise our strengths and weaknesses and know when we've done a good job or will benefit from a learning experience. Our self-esteem stays more intact when we judge ourselves rather than being judged by others. This is where we know that feedback is to raise our self-awareness and for us to take responsibility for our personal development and improved performance. Being responsible for ourselves means we identify a personal development plan with the added benefit that we choose development options that best meet our personal learning preferences (see Figure 1.5).

However, in the not-so-ideal world we rely on shared responsibility for taking ownership of supporting each other to raise the bar in performance.

CIPD (2017) believes it's a line management responsibility and states that the purpose of feedback is to 'inform employees on their performance and progress and on what's required to perform well in the future. This can focus on behaviour or how things are done.'

Feedback is recognised as a critical element in performance management for focusing on learning and improvement and so that individuals can

Figure 1.5 Taking personal responsibility for improved performance

monitor their progress towards goals and stay motivated. The importance of regular feedback is highlighted with a recognition that many organisations are moving towards more continuous feedback. This is a move away from relying on annual or six-monthly reviews that are now well-evidenced as not happening!

Just as regular feedback conversations are not a new concept, neither is this recognition about the viability of appraisals – any Google search will bring a myriad of examples where appraisals are recognised as defunct. It's more than time to change and move on from a good intention.

At the same time, we have to recognise that the content of performance discussions is undeniably enduring:

– Sustainability of performance and assessment of achievements
– What's helping and hindering performance and what needs to continue and what needs to change
– What practical support and learning and development is needed and can be given to help reach, maintain and exceed the expected performance
– How the person's current role and longer-term prospects can be developed and realised
– Agreeing actions and a delivery plan to achieve the outcomes of the performance.

CIPD (2017) recognises that sharing 'effective feedback and taking it on board is much easier when there is a trusting relationship.' I fully agree and a primary function of this book is to give guidance on developing the personal attributes for creating trusting relationships through a 'way of being.'

A trusting relationship will achieve another purpose of feedback, which is to encourage open exchanges in which both share an honest dialogue covering mutual expectations and concerns.

Heron (2009) talks of the purpose of feedback as being a 'valid intervention – in service of the personal development of the client.' She describes a 'degenerate intervention' as not fulfilling a 'valid intervention' because the practitioner lacks personal development, or training, or experience, or awareness. A 'perverted intervention' is deliberately malicious and intended to harm the person. These are forceful descriptors of interventions, with the latter a disturbing indictment of a damaging purpose of feedback for the individual.

O'Brien (2019) quotes a contra humane approach from Buddhist practice that alerts us to 'Right Speech' that counteracts 'modern communication technology (that) has given us a culture that seems saturated with "wrong" speech that engenders disharmony (and) acrimony.' This article equates violent words, thoughts and actions as 'arising together and in support of each other.' We can't imagine using violence in feedback, yet the power of the spoken word delivered without sensitivity can have a similar impact. 'Right Speech means using communication as a way to further our understanding of ourselves and others and as a way to develop insight.' This type of speech is truthful, honest and based entirely on compassion as 'always giving somebody support or help or a chance to grow.' Language is used to reduce anger and ease tensions; 'if your speech is not useful and beneficial, it is better to keep silent.' This is a compelling illustration of how 'a way of being' draws people together and increases the probability of productive feedback by sowing the seeds of healthy communication.

Berger (2004), based on observations from education, suggests that the 'work of a transformative teacher is first to help students find the edge of their understanding, second to be company at that edge, and finally to help students construct a new, transformed place.' Ultimately, she argues, this process will help students find the courage they need to transform. She believes that the purpose of feedback is to 'create new forms of thinking, new discoveries – reflection that takes us to the edge of our meaning.' This reflective space has the most power to be transformative; 'to move outside the form of current understanding and into a new place.'

This 'edge of knowing' or liminal space is the initial stage of transitioning to a new place, which Berger (2004) describes as a 'psychological, neurological, or metaphysical subjective state, conscious or unconscious, of being on the 'threshold' of or between two different existential planes.' This means that we experience an oscillating state of 'knowing' and 'not knowing.' As we move on from a place of knowing to a new place we're likely to experience a sense of loss followed by a realisation of new beginnings.

If our purpose of offering feedback is to encourage this transformation, we're expecting a new behaviour, way of working, or another outcome. The intention is developmental. Expectations are that we will recognise our need to change and will take responsibility for this. This may take us into new uncomfortable territory; however, transformational change demands we challenge the status quo. Given our reluctance to change, we can anticipate resistance to the feedback discussion. The key is to name and modify this anticipation and create a curiosity that keeps the receiver of feedback on that 'edge of understanding' and holds the space for the time it takes to transition to the new condition.

Success arrives when feedback raises self-awareness to a level at which we understand what we need to change, how we think differently about behaviours and feelings we previously accepted and how we see situations in new ways. These may be 'ah-ha' moments which take us immediately to a new way of thinking, feeling and being. However, there may also be uncertainty and insecurity as we grapple with developing a new perspective.

The state of 'stumbling, stammering, rambling and circling back' that Berger observes in her own experience of the 'edge of knowing' reminds me of those 'I don't know' responses we get when we ask a question that challenges a current way of being. This statement is often followed by anything but 'not knowing' as a flow of new understanding emerges, or at least a sense of new opportunities and curiosity as the possibility of change gives feelings of excitement and anticipation.

I believe this highlights that although the purpose of feedback is intellectually simple to understand the activity itself is complex. We are all somewhere on the continuum of transformational change (see Figure 1.6).

We may think we want to change, but the realisation of what this change attracts can keep us in the current state, however undesirable that may be.

We've all heard stories or may even have experienced being in a toxic relationship that we want to leave. We know it makes sense to leave, but the prospect of actually leaving is more frightening than the prospect of staying in a familiar situation.

A word of caution, therefore, for us to understand more about and to have concern for the human psyche and emotional fitness of each other and to treat feedback with the respect that is often overlooked or underestimated.

If our purpose for feedback is to seek and encourage transformational change, our role in this journey is to:

- listen intently and ask incisive questions that seek out this state between 'knowing' and 'not knowing'
- slow the pace of conversation and hold a safe and supportive space that gives time for reflection and curiosity about new perspectives
- affirm willingness for change
- encourage adoption of the desired change

Figure 1.6 Continuum of transformational change

Offering solutions or rushing people into agreeing actions for change are not the most effective way of encouraging change. We can all remember being 'told what to do' and how ineffective this is. Given the time and the space we will find our own solutions.

A scenario that is regularly brought by coaches to me as a coach supervisor goes something like this:

'We had a great conversation; talked about alternatives to reach the desired goal and agreed actions for between coaching sessions that would achieve the goal. Next time we met, nothing had been done.'

There may be many reasons for this – change of goal, workload issues, personal events unexpectedly emerging and so on. However, what can be the cause is that the client hasn't taken complete ownership of the 'agreed' actions.

Coaching clients can sometimes agree to actions to 'please their coach'; direct reports may want to appear positive in the eyes of their manager or may just agree to end an unpleasant performance discussion and hope the issue goes away!

If we see the purpose of feedback exchange as one of helping others to accept responsibility for personal change, the more likely we are to adopt a habit of continuous self-reflection. We will eventually believe that the idea of transformative change is fulfilling and generative in our personal growth.

This results in reduced dependency on others to be responsible for telling us what to do, how we should do it and when we should do it. The ability to blame a line manager, a colleague, a coach or a mentor for our actions is removed.

In the next chapter we will see the activity of feedback from different perspectives; notice where you fit into this scenario, especially where you hold multiple roles.

Why feedback and whose responsibility is it?

2

Feedback isn't optional – it's critical to survive and flourish! People, teams and organisations only develop and harness the agility to move forward through recognising the need for change and anticipating what this is, when it needs to happen and how it will be implemented. Change happens through people, of course, and many of us need help in recognising the dynamics of making this happen. We can take short sharp action with or without the understanding that people casualties are inevitable. However, sustainable change and maintaining the psychological contract happens most effectively when people are respected for the intelligent beings we are and involved in the change process. Ideally, good and bad news sit equally at the table of truth and transparency, placing feedback high on the everyday schedule of work practices.

In my experience, the most successful businesses are those where people genuinely care about others and actively value the contributions of everyone. The leadership in these organisations model relational values and champion the behaviours they want to encourage and expect to see in others. Culture isn't an independent entity; culture is created and perpetuated by people. Feedback that enables thrives best in a nurturing culture. Feedback also depends on inhaling the energising oxygen generated by a systemic framework of facilitation capable of smothering any restricting constraints on its ability to breathe life into people development.

Peer into the organisational kaleidoscope and you will find not one but multiple stakeholder perspectives, each with their own reality, both as giver and receiver of feedback. What are the motivations driving engagement and what is the responsibility of each stakeholder who will have differing views and vested interests about feedback (although all are likely to promote its merits)?

Who are these stakeholders? Undeniably, everyone in an organisation has responsibility for feedback:

- leadership/management
- human resource professionals
- teams
- coaching/mentoring practitioners
- individual employees.

The aim of reviewing how these stakeholders fulfil their role in feedback is to give you insights into the typical organisational scene as a benchmark for auditing the prevailing culture for feedback within your own business. You may also want to reflect on your own stance as a giver and receiver of feedback. By reviewing the examples of current practice and case studies you can assess:

- what is reinforced for you as powerful attributes accelerating the impact of feedback
- what needs to change and be enhanced for you to excel at feedback
- how you will make these changes supported by The Relational Leadership WAY© featured in Chapters 5, 6 and 7.

To start on this journey of 'why feedback' and 'whose responsibility it is' let's ask ourselves, where would we be without feedback? Some may wish to avoid the whole subject by claiming we can exist in blissful ignorance of what others think of us, what impact we have and what difference we do or can make in the world.

The reality is that we absorb a continuous flow of data, whether it's our own self talk, a meaningful glance from a loved one or an appreciative smile for a job well done – and that's on a good day! The challenge, if we wish to accept it as the saying goes, is to recognise the possibilities open to us by bringing this information flow into consciousness. We can be much more effective if we act on this information and pay attention to the feedback whether it's self-reflection, unsolicited or from a well-intentioned other.

Naturally, as members of the human race we satisfy our social needs by feeling supported and accepted in our relationships. There is sufficient available research to remind us that it's vital for our wellbeing to have some kind of barometer signalling fluctuations in our interactions with others.

Feedback in its many forms will be present in all our daily activities. Those following the discipline of positive psychology posit that we are motivated to do well by being happy at work. As social beings and with the nature of the workplace it's likely that we will achieve this ideal through harmonious relationships.

Heron (1989) talks of how at work we interact daily with others who need our help, support, advice or expertise. Precisely how we deliver this help determines its success and impacts the relationships we build. The model Heron created offers categories of helping style and we're encouraged to ask for feedback on how others define the style we use; that 'F' word again!

The six different styles that Heron presents are cited as a valuable resource for informing our way of communicating with others. The aim of this book on relational leadership is to move beyond this stage by expanding on 'what to say and ask' as the Heron model suggests into the 'how we behave.' I define this approach as a 'way of being' for nurturing productive relationships that take us to the core of genuine and authentic connection.

This concept of relational depth stems from the evidence-based research that led to this book, presenting The Relational Leadership WAY© as a means of stimulating confidence in giving and receiving feedback by developing capability in building receptive relationships. The role of the framework is to signpost ways of inspiring performance and development discussions that genuinely encourage change and a desire in others to make this happen. Being competent in applying the themes of the framework accelerates a raised sense of self-awareness for both in the relationship. The quality of awareness is proposed as producing more enduring results than reliance on each person's capacity for reflection and/or application of traditional feedback processes and proprietary products.

A primary purpose of the framework is to eradicate those feelings of wanting to avoid giving and/or receiving feedback for whatever reason. Previous experiences may have left us daunted by the prospect, or perhaps simply feeling totally disenchanted by the whole idea of feedback taking any meaningful form. Whatever the reason the bottom line is that we know avoidance isn't the answer. In my experience the quality of connectivity with others appears to be a major factor contributing to this apparent avoidance and was a prime motivator prompting my research into feedback. Empirical and anecdotal evidence supports the idea that developing and improving interpersonal relationships is labelled as a 'soft' skill. The complexity of human relationships often tells us a different story with the 'hard' work of 'soft' skills being potentially traumatic for those involved in achieving transformational change that necessitates challenging feedback.

More recent research recognises a deficit in spotting the signals that assess the temperature of relationships: 'outcome research has generally been silent on what happens within a coaching relationship, such as the many gestures, speech acts, and attempts at sense making that make up the whole of the intervention' (de Haan & Nie, 2012). How often do we ignore these signals in favour of capturing the meaning of the spoken word? We know that tone of voice features strongly in how we interpret communication from others. However, the actual language used apparently becomes insignificant when compared with how we behave towards each other. I agree that interpreting this behaviour goes beyond the well recorded body language signals, such as crossed arms meaning resistance to engage. This interpretation may be true and worth checking out. What The Relational Leadership WAY© emphasises is when and how to react to these signals. More on this in Chapters 5, 6 and 7.

Accepting that feedback makes sense, the role of this framework is to cultivate the conditions within the relationship that facilitates delivery and acceptance of what needs to be said, heard, reflected on and acted on.

Next, we look at the context in which the stakeholders' relationships operate.

The business case for feedback

Whatever type and size of organisation we're employed in, most of us know that we now increasingly operate on a global platform. Technological change is moving at such a pace that algorithms are replacing humans in many roles – more on this in Chapter 8.

What is evident is that businesses must remain competitive to survive and be sufficiently agile to embrace new roles emerging from artificial intelligence. Knowledge management and the 'ability to produce innovative products and create high value service' (Lane et al., 2006) will provide the differentiation to succeed. Human skills of adapting and working with complexity will be in greater demand. Meeting these expectations necessitates an enabling culture that places emphasis on nurturing relationships that encourage transparency in conversations, with feedback playing a defining role in orchestrating a developmental framework for improvement.

What does this generative culture look like? CIPD (2017) suggests that the ideal conditions for effective conversations include:

- A culture of trust and openness
- People managers who are appropriately skilled, for example in asking good questions and active listening

- Employees who are receptive, prepared to align with business objectives, learn and take responsibility for their performance

The purpose of feedback may take many forms and the participants contributing to this research study gave their perspectives on why and how feedback is important to them:

- Using feedback as a remedial coaching tool
- Being a critical friend and having positive intent when providing feedback
- A situational perspective involving sales personnel where a ratio of positive:negative feedback was used as a motivation tool
- An acknowledgement that experience and education systems mould the way we receive feedback, resulting in this often having a negative effect
- When impacting on self-esteem the perception can be that direct or honest feedback is negative
- A perceived reaction of fear of what one will hear is not likely to be experienced when clients unfold feedback for themselves through reflection

Extrapolation of these examples is likely to identify even more reasons for feedback. At the same time, creating the conditions to fulfil the expectations raised in these business case scenarios is unlikely to happen without some re-engineering of the discussion itself.

This is especially true when, as identified by the research participants, 'a general acceptance existed that clients and, in some instances coaches, could be reluctant to engage in these discussions.' It's clear that the business case for continuously improving performance to survive in a competitive and sometimes hostile marketplace is vital. Not surprisingly, expectations are that managers/leaders within the organisation will motivate direct reports to take responsibility for making this happen or, ideally, individuals will take personal ownership for self-development. Whether this is achieved is largely dependent upon the organisational culture valuing and promoting every employee taking responsibility for self-development.

The approaches that organisations take for nurturing and facilitating a culture of improved performance vary and are reviewed in the next chapter.

The leader/manager's perspective

As we know, the role of the leader/manager is manifold, covering a range of operational and leadership responsibilities. The designated person to give feedback in the workplace is generally the line manager, who has been known to nominate human resources to take over this responsibility 'if the going gets tough!' The sad truth is that managers continue to be recruited and promoted based on professional knowledge and technical expertise. Rarely are those with line management skills asked about their leadership style or supported with development opportunities to upskill their approach to people management. This is dangerous territory for businesses that neglect nurturing human capital to be the best they can be and perform at optimum capacity. Potential disaster for those direct reports who are dependent upon line managers for career progression.

The ideal scenario is one facilitated by and necessitating endorsement from top leaders who are best placed to advocate the regular practice of feedback. Here's a sterling example donated by Flight Lieutenant Andrew Armstrong of Command and Recruit Training Squadron, Royal New Zealand Air Force, which I believe excellently endorses the importance of relationship through the application of the DEB/DESC Feedback Framework.

Flight Lieutenant Brad Marra graduated from the Royal New Zealand Air Force's Initial Officer Training Course on 26 June 2019. He was awarded the top prize for all-round performance. This accolade is only ever bestowed upon the individual who in the eyes of their peers shows the greatest potential for

Figure 2.1 Flight Lieutenant Brad Marra, Royal New Zealand Air Force

leadership. At the conclusion of the 15-week programme, Marra comments that 'a great deal of my progress is attributed to the feedback I received.'

Early in the course, Marra was taught the valuable skill of giving feedback. One technique he learnt was the DEB/DESC feedback framework. He explains: 'while the tool was easy to use it was also our collective commitment to openness, honesty, and timeliness that has enabled important feedback conversations.'

While giving feedback has been essential to growth, Marra believes the ability to take feedback has been just as significant. He claims that 'even the very best skills giving feedback have the potential to be lost, unless the receiver actually has the capacity to take on the feedback.'

If the art of 'receiving' feedback is so vital to one's progress, what has Marra learned are the necessary qualities for getting the most from feedback? He offers three key messages to help people better prepare themselves to receive feedback:

- Learn to value a growth mindset. Early in the course, Marra and his team embraced growth mindset as a group value. 'We set expectations for ourselves including group values. Using a growth mindset approach helped with our feedback conversations' Marra explains
- Credibility – Marra comments; 'while multi-source feedback has helped me, the most valued feedback came from credible providers. I was able to seek feedback from anyone of my choosing.' Tools like the Feedback Wheel can help all learners identify their most trusted and useful feedback networks
- Focus on the trends. Sometimes one small piece of harsh feedback can dominate thought processes. Marra believes that focusing on feedback trends has served him better than concentrating on the isolated pieces of poor feedback. He mentions that 'when I look back on the feedback I was given – I put more effort into noticing the trends in my feedback rather than the one-off remarks. This helped me focus on the real issues.'

DEB/DESC feedback framework

Useful for communicating negative or constructive feedback

D Describe the situation or event
E Provide a clear **example**
S Suggest ways for improvement
C Comment on the **consequences** of that change

Useful for communicating positive feedback

D Describe the situation or event
E Provide a clear **example**
B Describe the **benefit** of that change

Feedback wheel

Create a multi-source feedback network.

Unfortunately, all too often those with the ability to drive change at the top of the organisation appear reluctant to personally participate as givers and receivers of feedback. They too may have possibly moved up the promotional ladder without adequate sponsorship for developing leadership capability and competence. This, combined with the realisation of lacking people management skills, often attracts a sense of 'impostor syndrome.' The underlying fragile self-worth generated by assumed deficiencies as a leader is likely to fuel a resistance to feedback when perceived as exposing imagined weaknesses. Those in more junior positions may be reluctant to provide feedback from a sense of perceived reprisal. 'Good feedback is powerful and rarely given, particularly to those most senior in organisations' (Scoular, 2011). 'People have a tendency to "shoot the messenger" deeming innocent bearers of bad news unlikeable' – John et al., 2019 make the case that 'if you want a pay rise say what the boss wants to hear not how they can improve as your line manager!' Other possibilities include those organisations operating an outdated environment and who don't

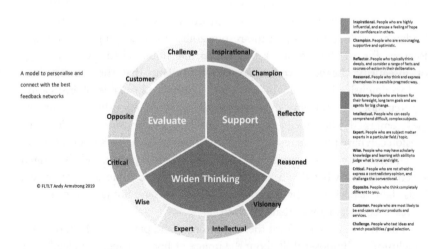

Figure 2.2 Feedback Wheel (created by Andrew Armstrong, 2019)

endorse feedback, or 'start-ups' growing organically and necessarily placing emphasis on the operational and technical aspects of business development. There are likely to be many businesses working on the hypothesis that the key to business success is focusing effort on strategic choice, direction and business planning and underestimating the vital human factor.

Feedback is often a casualty of this organisational deficit. Although there is much to support the belief (both anecdotally and in the literature) that managers are negligent in offering feedback to direct reports, the same is true about telling people they're doing a good job (Stern & Cooper, 2017). This behaviour reinforces the 'lack of recognition' being an instigator of disengagement.

The reality is that organisations don't have enough socially skilled managers to recognise the warning signs of disengagement. They're too busy working 'in' the business at the cost of working 'on' the business.

If they do notice, it's likely they have insufficient competence and/or time to step up to their role as motivators. Implicit in the lack of organisational support for people management is lack of relevant training in how to give feedback. The fleeting comments often delivered with awkward and urgent delivery in an otherwise hectic day fail to impact as intended. Not the fault of the line manager; it's the reality of a lack of investment in focused management and leadership development.

Continuing to reward specialist knowledge over relational expertise undermines the vital role that people play in organisational performance. What became evident from my research study was the lack of emphasis on leadership style impacting on the responsibility for managing relationships. Reasons for avoiding feedback pointed to the 'potential to invoke feelings of insecurity.' Leaders were reported as noticing that these insecurities 'led to defensive behaviour that can be harmful and capable of instigating repercussions for the line manager/direct report relationship.' A different view emerged when focusing on the coaching relationship in which 'this tension can have positive results when the coach is viewed as a critical friend.'

The majority view from the research data was that people feel challenged when receiving what they perceive as being difficult or negative feedback. This claim is backed up by the comment that 'skills are not taught for giving critical feedback in a way that's receptive.'

What do we all learn from these comments and perceptions? An obvious conclusion is a mindset shift about the image of line managers and leaders as 'punishers' or 'abdicators' of feedback to one of 'developing partners' creating learning relationships. This means a shift away from sterile performance management systems and futile superficial target setting that have little or no alignment with strategic business objectives. I suggest that we can no longer suppress feedback in the unconscious hope that people will know what's expected of them at work and assume they will understand development and improvement expectations by osmosis! We need to wake up to the reality that leadership and management also need support in personal development, including feedback, for them to fulfil their role in stimulating and energising a workforce that excels. We owe it to all those we employ, to colleagues and to ourselves to be alert and agile about predicting the future of work.

Feedback is the role of line management and leadership in all organisations.

The people professional's perspective

Human resources, now known as people professionals (CIPD, 2018), have traditionally been the guardians of performance management systems, owning responsibility for documentation, training and sometimes monitoring the completion of appraisal timetables.

Excluding those enlightened businesses which recognise people professionals as strategic partners in organisational development, the norm is for this function to be budgeted as an overhead that diverts finance away from frontline services. That is, until people issues become problematic and managers seek rescue! Regrettably, this is often after a long period of ignoring or hinting at deficits in performance until the working situation becomes untenable. As staffing budgets reduce and expectations for productivity increase, tensions escalate and those labelled as 'passengers' are no longer tolerated by the team. I've experienced and still hear of professionals desperate for a solution to help managers resolve situations when long-term employees fail and sometimes refuse to adapt, especially where technology features. These situations are, of course, complex and result from firmly entrenched working practices; other scenarios involving different sectors of the workforce can be similarly identified.

When answering the question, 'Why feedback and whose responsibility is it?' I think that people professionals can play a key role in adding to the value they crave to demonstrate as their worth to strategic leadership. A CIPD survey (2018) paints a picture of experiencing the 'conflict between their professional beliefs and what their organisation expects of them (ethical values) demonstrating the challenging role professionals often must play in organisation decision-making.'

Fertile territory exists between people professionals and strategic leadership to role model the power of relationship and shared ethics by placing people at the centre of corporate values. If you're a professional reading this, how effectively is feedback elevated beyond performance management systems and recognised as the commonplace activity it is in all conversations in your organisation?

Feedback is not a discrete entity; it exists in some form in every interpersonal exchange we have.

Professionals are well-placed to provide the evidence base for feedback. However, collecting the metrics and making the case for feedback as an essential business tool will not necessarily make it happen. Evaluating the cultural climate is a stronger indicator of whether transparent and transformational feedback can thrive.

A few questions for reflection:

- What is known about the stories people share about the workplace culture?
- How often are corporate values showing up in workplace vocabulary and behaviours?
- How might the political scene be described in the organisation?
- How does this enable or impede?
- What is the temperature of the professionals and top leadership relationship as a catalyst for change?

The team's perspective

Feedback in a team setting is rich in complexity. We've reviewed the leader's perspective and discovered some of the constraints on their ability and willingness to be part of the equation impacting on effectiveness. A trend is evolving for teams to come together on a project-led basis and where team members are selected for technical skills. These teams fulfil a specific function, and when this is achieved individual members move on to the next project. Occasionally a leader emerges to fulfil a function such as sourcing resources. Although organisational reporting suggests that team working, with or without a leader, is on the increase, many organisations still operate with the traditional manager and direct report composition. I'm wondering what managers and direct reports did before, if not working as a team?

The 'leaderless' team surely negates the role of the leader as provider of feedback, so where does the feedback come from in this scenario? We gain some insight from these examples of team definitions:

'The ability to co-operate with others, directed at accomplishing the project objectives. It involves an honest and open attitude connected with respect for all human values' (Muzio et al., 2007). Doesn't this 'ability to cooperate with others' signpost a feedback opportunity and offer the suggestion of how to implement this through an 'honest and open attitude?' Personal accountability seems evident here and in an ideal world we'd all be able to understand what we need to do and how to do it and give ourselves feedback. The reality is our inability to notice 'blind spots' in our performance that can only usually be revealed by working with another in a trusted relationship.

'A small number of people with complementary skills, who are committed to a common purpose, performance goals and approach, for which they hold themselves mutually accountable' (Katzenbach, J. quoted in Clutterbuck, 2007). Does this being 'mutually accountable' place a responsibility on the team to give and receive feedback? Yes, it does, and let's remember that the team is made up of individuals who will define accountability through different prisms. For this definition to work for feedback, there has to be common acceptability of a way of sharing meaningful feedback for the team to be 'accountable for delivering the common purpose and goals.'

According to Hackman (2002), team effectiveness is measured by products or services that exceed customer expectations, growing team capabilities over time, and satisfying team member needs.

All of these definitions rely on team members' full understanding and recognising what's needed, both individually and collectively, to fulfil their purpose. The missing link is *how* we help each other to gain this 'full understanding!' Feedback is an obvious prerequisite in the 'how' of this process, and again, 'how' we share feedback impacts on the team's effectiveness to fulfil its purpose.

I find Gallwey's equation (2001) easy to understand and impressive in interpretation when applied to team performance:

(Team) Performance = Potential – Interference

Interference is defined as individuals overcoming an 'individual' mindset and moving to adopting a 'team' mindset, emulating today's corporate environment of promoting the team – not the individual – as holding the key to business success. This is a reinforcement that collective efforts create synergistic results, as long as everyone has the team goal at the centre of their individual contribution.

A final thought in this section on feedback within a team dynamic. Now that we're working in a digital age, we're becoming even less reliant on the human factor. This is evident with the proliferation of machine learning and artificial intelligence (AI) increasingly replacing routine tasks. Downloadable apps for improving team effectiveness use algorithms to manage our diaries, meetings, project timelines and communications. I can see the logic of supporting a communication framework for virtual working, but what happened to speaking to the person sitting right next to you! For me, this encourages increased remote working within the team, and then what happens to feedback? Perhaps this will also become the role of AI? We hear horror stories of the pain caused, especially to our young people, by critical comments recorded behind the facade of a social media platform – not face to face – but that doesn't do anything to protect the recipient when the feedback arrives in Messenger or WhatsApp.

The coaching/mentoring practitioner's perspective

Participants in the research study reflected on their approach to feedback and scrutinised current practices around them. This emphasis on self-examination isn't always comfortable. The new learning inevitably impacted on practice and gave the practitioners more awareness of their personal responsibility for feedback. The impact produced mixed reviews:

'I've become much more aware of the fact of when I'm giving feedback – I've just become much more conscious of that and I think that actually has been a good experience and I think it's actually benefited my coaching... this research has certainly impacted on my coaching.'

(Leadership Coach)

'I think I've certainly become more conscious of feedback. I think it's good to be conscious but in the moment I'm not convinced that's been a good thing so I found the research quite disruptive in a way... Trying to keep that third eye whilst you're present in the moment with someone, I found very hard, I don't have that way of thinking clearly! However, being conscious of when I go into feedback has been useful.'

(Business Coach)

Inviting study participants to observe and record phenomena emerging in their practice proved a barrier initially. Most were practised at using a 'process' or 'technique' for feedback, and we revisited the definition of the activity of feedback several times in the context of this study. We also attempted to replace the word 'feedback' with another that had fewer negative connotations. Even the occasionally preferred concept of 'feed forward' left a sense of 'incompleteness' in gaining an understanding of holistic development. Our conclusion was to acknowledge that substituting a word in regular use both in business and in coaching was a major challenge. Instead, our thoughts focused on how to improve the activity and tap the resource of 'use of self' as a more valid replacement for processes. We felt that recognising the potential to be gained from the relationship would also contribute to the evaporation of the fear of the feedback by concentrating on the experience rather than the word itself.

This research aroused a curiosity in study participants about extending their practice to what we viewed as the richer domain of relationship. Some thoughts from study participants:

Pre-study observation

- 'It's all based around appreciative enquiry so it tends to be [a] very positive sort of feedback around their strengths.'

This observation from coach practice illustrated the reliance on models as a feedback tool. The use of appreciative enquiry encourages self-determined change by recalling actions that have worked in accomplishing past events and that are perceived as being transferrable to benefitting a current event. Focusing on strengths in this way has its merits for building confidence in overcoming issues based on past successes. The question emerging is, how can feedback increase its scope for raising a deeper level of self-awareness beyond the boundaries of the specificity of models?

Post-study observation

- '… and I've been [trying] a process intervention as opposed to a content intervention. That's really where your research has taken me to, trying a new approach and conceptually really feeling comfortable with it and in terms of results, feeling comfortable with it.'

Working collectively as participants in this research study, we found ourselves venturing into new territory of explicitly rather than implicitly holding a mirror to ourselves. We were vigorously challenged to review our model of working with clients by adapting our practices to accommodate new learning. Sometimes willingly, and sometimes with a degree of discomfort, we moved away from the familiar modes of exchanges with clients. Nuggets of enlightenment emerged throughout the journey that gave a sense of accomplishment and a new way of viewing the responsibility of feedback through the lens of self.

What was taken for granted in client work was the 'relationship.' We knew the relevance and importance of building rapport; however, even as experienced practitioners, we were unprepared for the deeper level of connection gained by observing and examining previously unexplored features manifesting within the relationship.

The value to be gained from this level of interaction in business conversations is gathering momentum. 'Looking forward, coaching is likely to play a major role in leadership development activities' (Jarvis et al., 2006). A CIPD (2019) update on the use of coaching confirms that 'coaching and mentoring can be effective approaches to developing employees. Both have grown in popularity, with many employers using them to enhance the skills, knowledge and performance of their people around specific skills and goals.' The quality of feedback will inevitably play a major role in gaining credibility for and recognition of coaching as an intervention for change; one does not happen without the other. As we know, change is integral to our working lives and no longer one event to manage; change is continuous as we operate in complex and uncertain times, set to become more so with the developments in AI.

'As people do not change something until they first become aware of it, one of the key aspects is to facilitate heightened awareness in clients of the lenses through which they see the world and themselves' (Bluckert, 2006, p. 82). The coach becomes 'the mirror' for the client to reflect on shared observations that enhance their performance at work.

The coach as the 'mirror' in client work

The topic of a recent supervision session with a practising coach was how to work with a client who is 'arrogant.' The coach defined his interpretation of arrogance as 'someone who knows best' and 'doesn't want to listen to anyone else's point of view.' Further insights revealed that this client's demeanour was clashing discordantly with the coach's values. The coach's reaction was to be directive in their feedback about how others viewed this behaviour. The result was entrenchment by the client, who rejected what was perceived as anecdotal comments with claims of acceptability of his style by others.

So, what happened here? Well, one thing was evident – the coach had made assumptions about the relationship. Being peers in the organisation, he had the expectation that he could be forthright in his feedback and that this would be accepted by the client. The opposite reaction left the coach wondering what to do about the situation.

We first talked about managing his state when his values were disrupted and how to adopt a sense of curiosity and use of exploratory questions to discover the client's motives for driving his agenda. Discussing the quality of the relationship from the client's perspective as well as his own helped the coach to question his assumptions about anticipated 'permissions' on how feedback can be given and how it may be received. The coach's resolve was to focus more attention on the quality of the relationship at the next meeting and apply a lens of compassion to further discussion about how the client was presenting to others.

Mezirow (2000) helps us understand the role of the coach as a feedback 'mirror' and partner in adult learning:

- The aim is to coach others to be reflective and reflexive as a precursor to understanding oneself and one's situation
- The skill of coaching is to know when to intervene, what to follow up, what to ask, when to suggest an activity, whether to share a hunch
- When strong feelings are expressed, a learning situation can be transformed from what may appear to be a 'difficult' situation by sharing an empathetic statement that communicates an equal relationship

The individual employee's perspective

Whether we're a line manager or a leader or admit to the more realistic label of combining both roles – we are all individuals. We seem naturally to bestow expectations on ourselves and others for what we assume the roles of a line manager, a leader and team members to be. These inevitably colour our views and inform our motives, reactions and accountability for feedback.

This example from coaching practice of a client's experience illustrates circumstances that can lead us into an entanglement of mixed emotion and logic when unresolved issues continue to impact and affect working relationships.

The goals of the client:

- Confidence building/assertiveness – wanting to say 'no' more
- 'Stand up' to colleagues and to 'speak up in the moment'

The coach used the 'scaling' tool and asked the client to rank their current level of ability in these two goals on a scale of 1–10. The client thought she was at a 1 or 2.

The client gave an example of a recent incident and explained how she had been 'dropped in the deep end and had to manage it.' She was upset about a comment from a colleague, whose responsibility it 'should' have been. The client spoke to her line manager who gave advice about how to give feedback to the colleague. The client didn't feel comfortable or confident enough to give this feedback.

She felt stressed that she hadn't taken action, dwelt on it and reran it in her head. She was also nervous about giving the feedback her manager had told her to say.

When asked why she struggles to give feedback her reasons were:

- To avoid confrontation in a work environment
- Wants to smooth things over
- Doesn't want to make people cross – wants to keep her head down, do her job and go home
- She was concerned that if she confronted someone they would turn it back on her and make it her fault
- The individual concerned is an extrovert and very intelligent
- The client feels it's easier to give feedback or challenge by email but often the reality just becomes suggestions
- When face-to-face, the client's first response is to say 'sorry'
- The client found it easier to give feedback to more junior colleagues as she had more confidence in what she was saying

When the coach explored further with the client her reasons for the above she responded:

- I'm not like this at home – 'I wear the trousers'
- I feel a need to respect my elders; this is the way I was brought up

- I didn't go to university
- I lost confidence through a previous work experience where they are trained to argue/win
- I didn't get on with my previous manager and didn't challenge their bullying

As we see, the client recognises personal development needs, but their line manager has offered guidance which the client feels unable to carry through. We can trace the erosion of the client's confidence in this case study culminating with the inability to address an anticipated conflict situation with a peer. The expectation now is that a coaching experience will deliver the desired result identified in the goals.

What a different scenario may have presented if the original bullying incident had been managed at the time it happened, avoiding erosion of the client's confidence. A second opportunity presented when the current line manager could have checked out how the client felt about delivering the offered advice for feedback. This client is left feeling deficient both as a receiver and giver of feedback.

We can all conjecture where responsibility lies in this case study, and rigorous subjective observation suggests that if we want to apportion responsibility for learning from experience it is the individual who is responsible for their own feedback. This isn't to suggest self-talk alone is sufficient, but something deeper and more complex that needs the ability to be aware of holding both affirmation about self and the ability to self-critique the situation. This behavioural example of reflexivity demonstrates 'reflecting in the moment' rather than after the event.

There are many theories and practices informing adult learning. Reflective practice is mentioned here as offering a primary source for apportioning the responsibility of feedback. The answer, of course, it that the responsibility rests with us all! We can gather our own feedback and choose to be a positive recipient and giver of feedback.

I regularly train in-house coaches and delegates are asked to request feedback from their coachees on practice, including benefits and practitioner style. The purpose is to encourage reflection to be a regular feature of their continuing professional development. Some find it difficult to persuade coachees to provide written feedback, but perseverance usually reaps rewards. We're very conscious, of course, of coachee bias in wanting to 'please' their coach who may be the only person to have listened to them without interruption in a long while! The end result is that by asking we have some chance of feedback; by not asking we have no chance. This practice can easily be transferred to the workplace. The more we ask, the more likely we are to receive and – as this book suggests – the better the quality of the relationship the more authentic the feedback is likely to be and the more easily it will be accepted.

Another case study from coach practice illustrates a shortfall in relationship reciprocity. Feedback can be openly welcomed by the coachee in the 'way of working together' conversation ('contracting' is the definition used by coaches) which is the basis of building a trusting relationship – except the reality when feedback emerges tells a different story!

'How would you like us to manage feedback?' says the coach.

'Oh, tell me like it is,' says the client, 'tell me straight.'

The goal of the coaching session is to improve the client's leadership style. The client was keen to complete a psychometric questionnaire relating to leadership competences. Outputs from the questionnaire were discussed and observations reviewed on personal style.

Taking the discussion to the next stage of encouraging disclosure about impact of behaviour on others (contracted to discuss), the client became defensive and reluctant to participate.

What created this tension at this time and what was the driver for staying in that place were the thoughts of the coach.

Trying to take the discussion to another level resulted in client withdrawal.

We can possibly speculate that feedback is welcomed as long as it's favourable!

Also observed on other occasions is that while people are usually welcoming of coaching when the topic of feedback is raised, I observe body language showing reticence although the spoken word is articulating full agreement to receiving feedback.

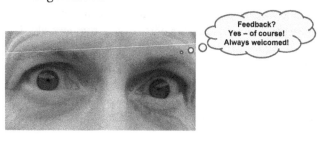

An illustration of the dilemma and tension for us as individuals involved in giving and receiving feedback comes from the work of Baxter and Montgomery (1996). They talk about how the 'need for connection can be opposed by ... associations such as autonomy, independence, privacy, and self-assertion. Feedback, therefore, may be viewed ... as something which is attractive in terms of connectivity with others and ... intrusive into one's perception of self.' We want to hear what others think about us or share our view of reality about another; however, this may only be on our terms!

This desire for connection stems from the psychological need for a sense of belonging that is essential to our identity and becoming our true selves (McGoldrick et al., 1996). Can feedback, therefore, be viewed as informing 'a sense of belonging' – through engaging with the process and being noticed by the other – that enables us to become our 'true' selves by accepting or rejecting the feedback?

Relational leadership creates the conditions for receptivity in relationships, and at the same time a leader must know when to step out of the connectivity and into a 'separateness' that achieves objectivity in the feedback exchange; a theme within The Relational Leadership WAY©.

'There are only two ways to influence human behaviour: you can manipulate it or you can inspire it.' Simon Sinek

No choice – inspire it is!

Current practices in feedback exchange

3

Perceptions about our effectiveness in giving and receiving feedback may well be analogous with our belief about our driving skills: we're great at it!

Ask a leader how to approach performance improvement feedback and you may well be regaled with success stories of 'saying it like it is' and 'it's best to be direct and say exactly what's expected of people.' Such replies echo the redundancy of paperwork claiming, 'I have frequent conversations with individuals about their performance.'

However, this example from research suggests scope for improving the quantity and quality of feedback. In a study by Thach (2002), participants maintain they want 'more constructive feedback' (26.2%) and that coaches should 'be more in depth' and 'define an action or development plan.'

Empirical evidence available from working in organisations suggests that leaders are reluctant to admit they don't have regular informal conversations with direct reports about work performance. The formal performance management discussions were spasmodic and, in my experience, even less evident was the completion of the recording paperwork designed for corporate schemes – much to the frustration of human resource specialists as champions of encouraging the business benefits of continuous improvement. The reason for this apparent antipathy wasn't obvious; leaders seemed overwhelmed, to the point of burnout for some. Others seemed to appreciate that these conversations were essential and part of their role, but the conversations just didn't happen. What seems an obvious route for busy leaders to benefit from performance discussions that lead to people development facilitating delegation may not reach consciousness in a disrupted state of mind. That some didn't follow through with these conversations for no obvious reason possibly reveals that even conscientious leaders have scope for development.

The question that continues to emerge is: what's the missing piece of the jigsaw that encourages these discussions to happen, and – can we dare hope – to be 'welcomed.' A colleague shared how a client's use of 'solutions focused' questions encouraging people to visualise what an ideal picture of working to one's best ability can look like created a segue to the 'how can this be achieved' scenario. Improvements were evident, although not perfect.

Green (2014) proposes that 'everyone wants feedback – even millennials and even experienced, expert workers.' Accepting this as indicative, the question remains: where is the elusive piece of the puzzle? A more recent perspective on millennials suggests an expectation for development opportunities demonstrating the differing views emerging from quoting this demographic age group as a benchmark.

Applying tools and techniques is recognised practice in feedback. Typical examples are positive:negative ratios, the feedback sandwich, feed forward and similar algorithms. Diagnostic reports produced from psychometric tool analysis offer what can be claimed as a richer source of data from psychologically informed self-rating questionnaires to feedback discussions.

Dweck's (2007) work has a different focus for technique with the psychologically based 'growth' and 'fixed' mindsets. We're encouraged to 'praise effort,' which has a motivational effect, rather than 'praise smartness,' which can produce the opposite outcome. Later research in P'Pool (2012) both supports and expands on Dweck's Theory of Motivation. Support is reinforced for the 'right' type of praise and also the idea that teachers can have a direct role in helping students change their view of intelligence as a fixed trait (entity view) to a malleable trait (incremental view) and able to change through personal efforts. I make no apology for suggesting that the teacher role is interchangeable with the relationship as being key to making the difference.

One of the primary drivers for the research on feedback was to find an alternative to these more familiar processes which have clearly lost popularity – with the exception of Dweck's work – despite their claims of effectiveness. What these techniques tend to assume is the emotional readiness for acceptance of the reporting which, as we can expect, isn't always present. I like the idea that 'the real leverage is creating pull' from Stone & Heen (2014) whose statement justifiably recognises that best results arrive from being responsible for our own learning.

The impact of feedback is often underestimated in the administration of these tools, techniques and processes, or may not be considered at all where a preoccupation exists that face validity and ubiquitous usage equals accuracy. However, they do have status as a springboard for working in tandem with The Relational Leadership WAY© showcased in later chapters. This chapter, therefore, makes a referenced review of popular feedback tools, techniques and frameworks. These emerge from business and coach/mentoring practice including the latest developments in, for example, social media organisations that have totally abandoned the use of performance appraisals.

Business performance improvement tools: appraisal systems, competence frameworks and self-assessment

Appraisal systems

Both standard feedback frameworks and appraisal schemes in common practice appear inadequate to improve performance where a relationship is already deteriorating. Let's face it, appraisals are outdated and we need to do something about it – urgently!

However, although there is evidence of some departure, discussed later in the chapter, appraisal systems continue to be accepted as fundamental for improving performance. They are usually held annually and preferably with regular reviews. A key feature of their purpose is to provide feedback that both validates work well done and enables an improved way of working where necessary. The more critical the role to the business, the greater the frequency of feedback is advisable. The judgemental review of the appraisal is the most commonly used although other evaluation methods are also sourced.

The traditional approach, using the generic label of performance appraisal, usually operates similarly in most organisations. Other labels may be applied to the activity, for example: performance review, staff development interview or employee review.

What each has in common is that the process is usually supported by documentation that offers guidance on completion for both the appraiser and appraisee. The purpose of the process is to regularly review an employee's performance at work and offer suggestions for improvement.

Standards for performance at work are usually predetermined through role profiles, competency frameworks and criteria that contribute to organisational objectives. These objectives may itemise team as well as business objectives. These indicators underpin the agreement of work performance goals identified to improve individual, team and business performance. As well as reviewing current performance, the aim of the performance appraisal is to predict future career potential guided by a personal development plan.

The interview part of the appraisal process is easily recognisable as the ideal opportunity to provide feedback. Direct reports can be invited to instigate this conversation with encouragement to ask, 'What are your expectations of me?' and 'How am I doing to meet these expectations?' The essence of feedback is to help employees understand how to align with organisational performance expectations. Any perceptions of uncertainty can be eradicated and replaced with affirming clarity. Distractions that detract from work performance can be reassuringly resolved.

One solution for achieving the effective delivery of feedback is to support through training the primary giver of feedback – the line manager – to inspire productive energy and to work within cultural, legal and operational boundaries. The ideal outcome from the feedback discussion is for employees to feel positive, have a clear idea of what's expected of them and a personal plan that has a developmental and future focus. The aim is that employees feel welcomed to participate in the conversation and to take joint responsibility for building trust and improving communication flow

Sounds easy, doesn't it? Despite this logical assumption that appraisals will produce the desired effect, the lack of positive reporting about their effectiveness clearly indicates opportunity for alternative strategies.

Research by Du Plessis & van Niekerk (2017) found that managers often have negative attitudes towards performance appraisal because of its problematic nature. These negative attitudes lead to reduced employee support, inaccurate performance appraisal ratings and, consequently, negative employee perceptions of the performance appraisal process. The main findings of the research also identified that 'performance appraisal is fundamentally an uncomfortable and emotional process' for managers, which results in their adopting defensive attitudes. With these uncertainties, managers do not always display the ability or readiness to conduct performance appraisals. Some of these uncertainties and relevant to this section of the book were quoted as:

- a fear of performance appraisals as they experience it to be a challenge (Torrington, Hall, Taylor & Atkinson, 2009)
- dreading the possibility of damaging relationships with employees (Pulakos & O'Leary, 2011)
- the presence of emotional uneasiness, conflict and failure to provide constructive feedback (Marreli, 2011).

Typically, appraisal recording documentation, competency frameworks and guidance notes for managing the appraisal discussion are meticulously crafted with the positive intention of improving people's competence. A key element in applying the processes is that 'direct reports' engage in performance discussions with managers. The aim is to generate an information exchange including feedback that alerts the individual and ideally the manager to expectations for both these roles. Role expectations may be determined, for example, by business strategy and objectives, role/competency profiles, diagnostic tools, peers, team members and working practices, corporate values and the accompanying expectations for behaviour.

One of the tactical reasons for the failure of achieving the anticipated outcome from appraisals is the incompatibility that emerges in translating business strategy to the point of delivery: the employee. The paperwork trail may be totally aligned; however, the interpretation of business plans, departmental objectives and individual profiles and goals often depicts another picture with dilution of the plans intended. Managers with busy schedules will divert activities to fulfil their remit and individuals will deliver what they prefer to do and 'overlook' job elements that don't hold the same level of interest. 'My job profile bears no relationship to what I actually do,' is a common claim made by employees.

[Appraisal] should always be an opportunity ... to receive honest, fair and objective feedback from your employer. Not all managers are capable of doing this, and sometimes let personal differences, snap judgments, or unsubstantiated comments ... affect their perceptions of you cautions Plimmer (2013).

We also have the dilemma of what appears as double standards. Appraisees criticise line managers for asking them to start the process by 'writing their own appraisal,' presumably misinterpreting the good intentions of inclusivity and viewing this as the line manager's responsibility. Then there are those who criticise appraisal for only being one way. Or are both suggesting an antipathy towards appraisal and (just human instinct) looking to critique whatever the approach?

Managers naturally present different approaches when acknowledging or addressing the potential impact of feedback on direct reports. Some managers believe that forceful feedback, sometimes with personalised statements such as 'you're incompetent,' is justified as acting with integrity and based on their reality when describing expectations about performance. Alternatively, some avoid performance issues, seeing these as too challenging to address. Feedback in these situations can become regrettably confined to positive events, even when performance falls below the desired level. I've noticed instances when the growing realisation of this practice by both parties results in the process being viewed as inauthentic, although neither the giver nor the receiver apparently take responsibility for instigating changes for a more desirable outcome. Avoidance blame is frequently apportioned to the inadequacies of the performance management processes and the perceived bureaucracy of the documentation.

A model that continues to stand the test of time, that positively informs the practice of feedback for given situations and can easily be adapted for the appraisal discussion, is the Hersey and Blanchard (1977) Situational Theory of Leadership. This model reiterates what appears to be the reality that there is no single leadership style that is best. To be effective leaders are encouraged to adapt their style to the situation. The existing model has been developed to produce the SLII model (Blanchard, 2013) with the accompanying slogan that this new addition is *not* 'something you *do to* people, it's something you do *with* people' – a principle echoed by the application of The Relational Leadership WAY©.

This revised version of the existing Situational Leadership model states that 'effective leaders must base their behaviour on the developmental level of group members for specific tasks.' The developmental level is determined by each individual's level of competence and commitment:

Table 3.1 Situational leadership model

Level of competence and commitment	Corresponding leadership style
Enthusiastic beginner (D1): High commitment, low competence	• Directing (S1): High on directing behaviours, low on supporting behaviours • Giving specific direction and instruction
Disillusioned learner (D2): Some competence, but setbacks have led to low commitment	• Coaching (S2): High on both directing and supporting behaviours
Capable but cautious performer (D3): Competence is growing, but the level of commitment varies	• Supporting (S3): Low on directing behaviour and high on supporting behaviours • Encouraging subordinates, listening and offering recognition and feedback
Self-reliant achiever (D4): High competence and commitment	• Delegating (S4): Low on both directing and supporting behaviours.

Being able to pinpoint each employee's level of maturity allows the leader to choose the best leadership approach to help employees accomplish their goals. Implicit within this belief is that style of feedback will also be informed using the same methodology.

Schulz and Schultz (2010) found that those opposed to appraisals generally 'don't receive positive ratings from anyone involved' and are therefore 'less than enthusiastic about participating in them.' They found that most workers don't appreciate 'constructive criticism or any criticism' and tend to be 'hostile knowing they could be given bad news on their performance.'

Gordon (2003) reinforces that 'valid feedback is based on observation, is timely and concrete.' Rancourt (1995) believes that 'real time coaching boosts performance and to work well needs a willing manager.' Clearly, not addressing issues supported by evidence as they arise does little to build relationships conducive to successful performance discussions. We are not impressed at the time of appraisal interview to be told we didn't handle a situation very well six months ago! As a direct report receiving late feedback, we're also unlikely to remember the incident, so will feel demotivated. As a line manager offering the feedback, we may have forgotten the detail that helps our direct report understand what was unacceptable at that time.

Despite appraisal apparently failing as a primary source of feedback, the activity continues to be recognised in a business context as instrumental for improving individual performance. What people do at work is acknowledged as ultimately impacting on the commercial success and, therefore, the viability of the organisation.

As is widely accepted, the anticipated principle of feedback is to raise self-awareness leading to transformational change, to celebrate good performance and to identify areas of learning for individuals and teams. The growing popularity of coaching may be an endorsement that people development warrants the input of a dedicated specialist beyond the remit of line management. This in no way suggests or recommends that coaching is a replacement for the line management role. However, the weight of evidence, both researched and anecdotal, identifies that where a shortfall exists, especially for feedback, coaching may be a welcome complementary addition to fill the gaps in the feedback chasm. Typical individual improvement topics for coaching conversations are interpersonal effectiveness, leadership capability for new appointments and continuing professional development generally. Drake (2011) talks of mastery in coaching a raising 'awareness of what is going on (in themselves, their clients, their conversations and their environment); their sense of what to pay Attention to; their ability to effectively Adapt; and their Accountability for their work and its consequences.'

Sadly, the subjective rather than objective nature of the feedback discussion undermines the intention of the appraisal system. This is not easy to overcome, as even in discussions supported by 'evidence' of performance the subjective interpretation of the giver of feedback is what the receiver remembers and reacts to. This scenario opens the case for working on the relationship between line manager and direct report that fosters expertise in giving supportive performance feedback rather than what may be perceived as potentially disciplinary. Managers and leaders today need to have interpersonal and emotional intelligence skills beyond the technical skills scoped for operational needs.

To enable the strengthening of this golden thread I increasingly found my HR role to be one of encouraging dual perspectives – inviting managers to move beyond their own worldview, to be people-centred (Rogers, 1986) and to see their employee's perspective, particularly in circumstances that lacked earlier specific feedback about improving performance. In effect, without input from others, the basis of direct reports' own perceptions was gained through feedback from tasks and their own feelings and thoughts about what we do (McDowall, Harris & McGrath, 2009). Consequently, when confronted with information incongruent with self-belief, an individual's response is to defend our position of believing our contribution to be acceptable. 'Colleagues at work may be reluctant to give straight, tough feedback,' says Bluckert (2006).

We all need recognition and management today is about offering a mix of praise for a job well done and a review of performance that helps direct reports to develop and grow in their role. This encourages engagement with the organisation and is likely to improve employee retention.

Too easily, the conversation can be influenced by the manager's biases and prejudices combined with the employee's 'likeability'; we know the outcome of the 'horns and halo' effect. 'You can do no good or everything you do is great!' Previous mistakes are remembered and compounded by predictive expectations with efforts to improve going unrecognised. A responsibility as a coach is to remind clients that changes in behaviour take time and repetition of the new behaviour before people start to notice any difference. The manager who becomes aware that their leadership style has not had the intended effect cannot expect direct reports to immediately respond to a new way of being. Even in the unlikely event the change is quickly observed, people will be guardedly awaiting a re-emergence of the 'old' behaviour that has been the norm.

One example I've observed for overcoming this phenomenon is in a client company with claims of improving objectivity. They support the appraisal discussion by accessing feedback data from other managers directly or indirectly working with the individual. Organisational/external coaches/ mentors are commissioned to work on achieving personal development plans with a remit of providing ongoing feedback. A coaching relationship can be an alternative activity for gaining feedback, although this is not a replacement for line management responsibilities.

Appraisals are claimed to become unnecessary if organisations adopt a total quality management approach. Accepting that there are exceptions to this traditional approach to performance management using formal appraisal, here is an example from Google.

Google concedes that 'performance reviews are a critical part of managing any business.' They assert, however, that reviews can often be 'time consuming and ineffective.' To overcome this perceived barrier, Google has adopted an 'internal grading system known as Objectives and Key Results, or OKRs.' Practical translation of this system enables Google employees to set their own goals with measurable outcomes that lead to the achievement of the goal.

The rest of the process works by:

Measuring performance
Googlers are rated by their managers on a five-point scale, from 'needs improvement' to 'superb.'

Soliciting peer feedback
Googlers and their managers select a group of peer reviewers that also includes employees who are junior to them.

The peer reviewers are asked to list one thing the person they're reviewing should do more of and one thing the employee could do differently to have a greater impact on the company.

Calibrating
Groups of managers meet and review all their employees' tentative ratings together. This process is designed to reduce managers' bias because they have to explain their decisions to each other.

From *Work Rules!: Insights from Inside Google That Will Transform How You Live and Lead.*

What the Google system has in common with most others is a rating system (5-point scale), 270-degree feedback (review by peers and those in more junior roles) and consistency checks (rating review). Google also separates annual reviews and pay discussions – another common practice in organisations.

The CEO of Google, Laszlo Bock, suggests that 'employees *want* to be evaluated because they want to grow and eventually become the best at their job. It's up to the employer to show them how to do that.'

As suggested, the Google approach largely appears to be no more than a relabelling of current practice and despite the claims there seems little evidence that the abandonment of appraisals has changed beliefs about the practice of feedback. However, repackaging has its merits and the setting of 'own' goals in Google must be given recognition as encouraging 'ownership' of performance; a primary incentive in motivation theory.

Reinforcing the Google route is the argument that managers fulfilling their role shouldn't need the platform provided by appraisal documentation, and perhaps abandonment of an ineffectual process is advisable.

Some may believe that linking pay to appraisal holds the key to energising this apparently defunct activity. However, research and articles show that when the appraisal is a deciding factor in employee pay awards, any chance of encouraging learning and growth is lost. The majority view is that employees will hide and cover up problems and only bring positives to appraisal and not to expect an honest discussion about improving performance if the outcome affects income. Relating pay to performance loses the goal of appraisal – to help the employee grow and develop.

Businesses that decide appraisals are the favoured option for performance management with or without linked pay may favour a combination of multiple assessment approaches:

- self-assessment: encouraging responsibility for raising self-awareness
- peer-assessment: encouraging accountability
- line/technical manager assessment: short cycles identifying performance gaps and avoids escalation of performance issues.

Despite the efforts of more enlightened employers attempting to energise the appraisal experience in its many forms, there seems to be little change for the activity of feedback. Managers continue to feel uncomfortable about this aspect of their role that expects judgements about others to be made based on a system that lacks attention to the human aspect. Unintentionally the manager is invited to fill the gap with subjective assessments of individuals' capability and performance.

My suggestion is that we can only achieve this through a joint willingness by both the giver and the receiver to become genuinely involved in feedback. The robustness of the appraisal system is only as effective as the quality of the conversation and the robustness of the relationship. Focus on the relationship first, gain a solid foundation for a working partnership to grow and give life to the purpose and not the process of appraisal.

Competency frameworks

Appraisal systems often integrate assessment tools as an objective contribution to measuring employee performance. Competency frameworks are an example offering evidence-based performance indicators against which employee performance can be measured to inform plans for continuing professional development. Other 'off the shelf products' including NOS (national occupational standards) and those aligned with the EQF (the European Qualification Framework) inform organisations on generic competencies to use in assessment and development centres.

Some organisations prefer to design frameworks specifically to reflect organisational purpose, vision and values. I remember designing this type of framework in a previous role with the explicit purpose of providing managers with standards based on corporate values. These standards included statements describing 'acceptable' and 'unacceptable' behaviours aligned with corporate expectations. The aim of creating the standards was to facilitate and encourage regular engagement with the performance management system by both managers and direct reports. The 'statements' represented indicators designed to facilitate conversation between managers and direct reports when feedback focused on a gap in performance. Indicators were developed using reinforcing language for behaviours recognised as supporting the corporate ethos and developmental language for highlighting behaviour to be discouraged.

Did this conversation encourage the desired engagement? No! Not to the anticipated or desired degree.

Reflecting now on why this initiative didn't achieve the desired outcome, I think that although the project was introduced with the best of intentions as an aid to people development, by creating behavioural indicators alone this was insufficient to overcome the reluctance to give transparent and honest feedback. Again, the focus was on the 'WHAT' process and not on the 'HOW' – that is creating the right conditions in the relationship to create a safe and trusting environment for open and honest feedback.

Societal as well as organisational culture also influence the acceptance and adoption of competency frameworks in a similar way to organisational acceptance. What may be valuable traits in one society are not necessarily equally perceived in others. While some cultures value performance feedback as essential and welcoming for raising self-awareness and encouraging self-management, others find the same approach threatening and intrusive.

Coaching and mentoring professional bodies have produced competency frameworks for accrediting training that demonstrate integrating professional standards into learning programmes and for individual practitioners to distinguish their competence as coaches, mentors and coach supervisors. Organisations taking the route of training managers, leaders and HR specialists to be internal practitioners are seeing the benefit and value of using these frameworks as pathways to developing professional practice.

Whilst these benchmarks claim to offer quality in the provision of coaching, mentoring and supervision, doubt is expressed about the inherent problems of competencies (Bachkirova, 2015). The suggestion is that competency frameworks may not include all aspects that are critical to superior performance. Competencies are likely to identify behaviours that were successful in the past rather than addressing the mindset needed for the future (Bachkirova, 2015). There is also a danger that organisations may observe adherence to competencies as a sign of quality and security that provides to be ill founded (Bachkirova, 2015). What is reassuring, however, is that the 'behaviours found most helpful were listening, understanding and encouragement' (de Haan et al., 2011), prerequisites for generative feedback conversations. My view is that it is better to have researched standards as a foundation for professional practice than no standards at all. Developments in any field will inevitably build on or replace what already exists.

Self-assessment

Self-assessment for evaluating our level of capability in behaviours, skills and knowledge has to be the preferred and ideal practice as a starting point for encouraging meaningful feedback conversations. This opportunity makes good sense for encouraging us to take responsibility for our personal development. We also feel we have a voice in determining and offering our perspective on what we see as personal contribution at work. What we won't detect is our tendency for blind spots in our performance; patterns of behaviour or gaps in skills set that are not obvious to us but often clear to others! 360-degree assessments are favoured as an antidote for plugging this gap. More on using psychometrics appears in the next section, including the advantages and disadvantages of using 360.

Despite potential pitfalls the practice of self-assessment continues to be recommended to encourage early and continuous adoption of reflection on our interactions with others and our contribution at work.

Fulfilling both the psychological and employment contracts is likely to avoid the syndrome of inertia that many organisations wish to eradicate: employees just turning up for work, doing what has to be done and no more. The root causes for this may be manifold and at one level can be how performance is impacted differently – if at all – between those who 'live to work' and those 'who work to live.' The bottom line in this equation usually translates as quality rather than quantity. A diligent employee may be industrious doing the 'wrong' things and without feedback, efforts are unlikely to be diverted to meaningful activities. 'Working to live' may conjure up a vision of presenteeism and producing the least amount of acceptable productivity to get through the day, whereas in reality the opposite may be true. Those who place more emphasis on personal life outside of work can still be highly and meaningfully productive – they just have different value judgements about lifestyle preferences.

The value of self-assessment enables individuals to reflect and formulate their worldview on contribution at work and how this compares with others' perceptions. The first stage of feedback becomes operational, and when shared beyond self-adjusting work practices has potential for:

- Avoiding misperceptions colouring the feedback conversation
- Demonstrating a recognition of when change needs to happen
- Taking joint responsibility for performance at work.

Proprietary tools: psychometrics

Psychometrics appear to have regained popularity after a brief period of decline in usage around the millennium. Bluckert (2006) talks of psychometrics as a diagnostic feedback tool. He quotes Wasylyshyn (2003) as saying that psychometrics 'cannot be underestimated as an efficient way to surface relevant information and insights.'

These tools are widely used in recruitment and selection, talent management and succession planning and embrace individual, leadership and team development. The aim of psychometric design and application is to predict anticipated performance capability. The anticipated view on how psychometrics add value is one of providing a platform for discussion in both recruitment and development conversations. The aim is enabling the individual to elaborate on self-reporting responses rather than the questionnaire reporting being the definitive predictor of performance.

A proliferation of psychometrics exists to measure individual qualities and fall into two categories:

- Ability
- Personality.

Ability tests measure, for example, logical, numerical, verbal, abstract reasoning.

Personality questionnaires are designed for individuals to self-assess on a range of traits. Arguably, the more robust questionnaires are designed by occupational psychologists who are likely to base their products on the 'Big 5 Personality Traits' (Rothmann & Coetzer, 2003):

1. **Openness** (to experience): intellectually curious, open to emotion, appreciative of art willing to try new things and may hold unconventional beliefs
2. **Conscientiousness:** how people prefer to control, regulate and direct their impulses; high scorers prefer being planned rather than spontaneous, pay attention to detail and put work before play
3. **Extraversion:** gain energy from external sources, enjoy interacting with people, often perceived as energetic, enthusiastic, action-oriented individuals, like to talk and assert themselves. The lower the score the more people's tendency towards introversion
4. **Agreeableness:** value getting along with others, generally considerate, kind, generous, trusting and trustworthy, helpful, willing to compromise their interests with others, optimistic view of human nature, positively correlates with the quality of transformational leadership skills
5. **Neuroticism:** measures level of emotional stability, may indicate tolerance for stress, level of pessimism and anxiety towards work, high scoring may affect decision making and ability to think clearly; low scoring indicators: tend to be calm, emotionally stable, free from persistent negative feelings.

The 'Big 5' have high reliability and considerable power in predicting job performance and team effectiveness and researches in the emerging field of personality neuroscience have begun mapping these traits to relevant brain regions.

Those of us keen on this approach may like to take a look at the HEXACO model of personality which adds a 6th trait: honesty-humility.

Here is a sample of the more popular products in general usage which add value for identifying feedback topics to discuss in performance, development, coaching, mentoring and coach supervision conversations:

– **360-degree:** invites and analyses feedback from self-reporting and multiple evaluations including more senior managers/leaders, colleagues and direct reports. The advantage of the 360 is gaining feedback from a range of others across horizontal similar functions and vertical from different function relationships. The limitation is that people may introduce unconscious bias by transferring their own agenda and conscious bias by diluting the truth. It's not unusual for a good manager to get low scores because of their likeability and openness to feedback. A poor manager may get high scores because raters don't wish to annoy them and possibly be identified. How many will also take the opportunity of criticising when qualitative statements are guaranteed anonymity?

Smither et al (2005) claim that the extent to which the recipients of 360-degree feedback follow up on it 'depends on their feedback orientation, their perceived need to change their behavior, whether they react positively to the feedback, believe change is feasible, set appropriate action plans and act on them.'

Hernez-Broome (2002) showed that even a 'minimal coaching programme offers significant benefits' in reinforcing developmental activities. Much also depends on how well embedded and transparent such schemes are within an organisation. If every leader is expected to receive and act on 360-degree feedback then everyone knows this and it is harder to conceal their feedback or avoid it all together. A colleague shared a case study of a multinational financial institution making 'publicly' available the action plans of everyone's 360 feedback.

– **Strengths Deployment Inventory (SDI):** helps to understand how motives drive behaviours, how those motives and behaviours change during different situations and how to develop a better understanding of the motive-driven behaviours of others; encourages stronger relationships, more effective teams and identifies how strengths can support weaknesses
– There is growing research showing that appraisals are more likely to improve performance by emphasising strengths and replicating successful techniques in other areas of one's work. The effectiveness of strengths-based appraisals results from adopting a future-focused coaching style

- **MBTI:** indicates differing psychological perspectives in how people perceive the world around them and make decisions; based on the underlying assumption that we all have specific preferences in the way we interpret our experiences and these preferences underlie our interests, needs, values and motivations. The reliability and validity of this questionnaire for consistency of results and rationale for *what* is being measured is challenged (Grant, 2013). To be reliable, a test has to produce the same results from different occasions over time. To be valid a test will identify how well we are likely to perform in a particular job or with a particular group of people. The test continues to be popular so clearly not everyone agrees with this assertion. A criticism I've noticed people make about MBTI is the categorisation of people into a '4-letter box.' Opinions seek more individuality than attaching a formulaic label to predicting human behaviour. There can be a sense of camaraderie in sharing MBTI preferences as people identify with others 'belonging in the same club' amid claims that the underpinning evidence base lacks rigour
- **OPQ32 + OPQ32r Personality Questionnaires:** The OPQ32 is designed to provide information on aspects of an individual's behavioural style likely to impact on their performance at work. The OPQ32r is the latest and most comprehensive version of the OPQ. It provides detailed information on 32 specific personality characteristics which impact performance on key job competencies and provides a clear framework for interpreting patterns of personality solely within the business context. This tool often holds strong credibility, possibly because of its direct association with a work context and due to the quality of the personality characteristics
- **16pf:** The 16pf® (16 personality factors) is a self-reporting tool designed to reveal potential, confirm suitability and identify development needs. A range of reports are available for a variety of functions
- **FIRO-B:** helps to build effective and successful working relationships by showing individuals how to adapt behaviour, influence, improve communication, manage conflict, develop resilience and build trust. Relevant to the context of this book, FIRO-B uncovers deeper human needs that may influence receptiveness to the feedback generated from this tool.

Use of psychometrics therefore comes with a safety warning to ensure ethical administration that is only delivered by qualified test users.

Even statistically designed psychometrics with the integrated rigour of validity and reliability gained from norm table benchmarking are subject to distortion. This stems from test users' subjective bias when interpreting psychometric reporting. The report data based on an individual's selection of test options may also be susceptible to personal subjective bias. These unpredictable assessments when related to an individual's competence at work are unquestionably flawed and support the claim of Hesketh and Laidlaw (2002) 'where feedback (on performance) has not achieved the desired results.'

Test designers integrate specific questions into psychometrics that are crafted to uncover distortions in people's responses. These are sometimes known as the 'honesty' questions where results reflect whether individuals select answers they believe will 'show them in a favourable light.' The distortion can be great enough to render the test report unusable. Generally, individuals can be encouraged to disclose a more realistic interpretation during group dialogue. A development centre activity may run on the lines of bringing 'like types' together to discuss their 'similarities.' This generates a further continuum of the characteristic in the group and encourages reluctant people to consider their blind spots: 'I think I am very creative, but now I've heard Bee talk about his crazy ideas I realise I may not be as creative as I thought.'

What was helpful in my experience of psychometric training was the strong emphasis on the need to give balanced feedback. We were encouraged to steer individuals towards positive traits as well as potential areas for development. We were also alerted to the likelihood of individuals' tendency to zone in on what they perceive as negative feedback and overlooking the positive – a disappointing outcome when attempts to inject affirming language go unrecognised in feedback conversation. Nevertheless, this happens and is reality. I understand cultural influences may persuade this line of thinking where saving 'face' is paramount.

Popular feedback techniques

My initial review of references on 'processes' for feedback revealed what appeared to be mechanistic approaches with only moderate critique on their effectiveness. Several years ago Gordon, (2003) spoke of the 'growing disillusion with processes' for feedback exchange stating that techniques can 'alienate rather than develop the performance discussion' they were intended to facilitate. People are increasingly aware of what to expect with traditional feedback mechanisms. Even so, years on, these same principles and techniques are applied.

What appears to be missing from coaching text is sufficiency of necessary guidance on how to give and receive feedback. I view this absence of guidance as encouragement for researching relational aspects of coaching as a source for improving feedback rather than producing another process tool or technique.

A few are now included as examples rather than recommendations – you may already be aware of most as we cling to the familiarity of well used resources. You may notice that minimum attention is given to practitioner competence in their application or the influence of the giver of feedback within the relationship:

1. **Feedback formula:**

This technique works on the premise that it's important to say what was perceived as happening and what the effect was. How the feedback formula achieves this:

- Tell the person what they did *(The example)*
- Be as specific as possible in describing the behaviour so that there is no misunderstanding about it
- Tell them the effect of their behaviour/action *(The effect)*
- Again, be as specific as possible
- Agree with them how to make a change *(The change)*

2. **Critical:positive ratio:**

Also known as the Losada ratio and developed by Losada and Fredrickson is a positive psychology concept promoting the concept of 'the 3-to-1 ratio.' The idea for use in feedback is that by giving three positive statements to one negative statement people will flourish.

3. **The feedback 'sandwich':**

Almost universally recognised where 'criticism' (sandwich filling) is given in between positive ('either side' praise slices) statements about performance. One view is that what may be perceived as a critical statement will be softened by the praise wrapping.

Another view of the packaging of positive and negative feedback together is seen as more than just a 'softening up' tactic. The suggestion is one of being fair and appreciative of good work. We are reminded that the praise needs to be genuine and descriptive. It's not enough to say 'I think you're doing a good job,' which can be claimed to sound disingenuous without supporting evidence. We may also give a false sense of actual performance causing an undervaluing of the criticism to follow.

This technique seems to have become discredited with familiarity and people ignore the praise waiting for the critical comments; objective defeated! This gives a sense of insincerity and risks diluting our message. Instead, separate praise and improvement feedback and be honest and transparent with both.

The 'sandwich' approach can alienate rather than develop the intended performance discussion. Charvet (2008) states the 'Feedback Sandwich is Out to Lunch.' She comments that with its 'intention to make criticism both easier to give and receive' the 'formula is easily recognized by anyone who has heard it more than once' and who will expect that praise is soon to be followed by criticism.

4. Essentials of effective feedback:

Parsloe & Leedham (2009) acknowledge that 'feedback is a two-way process.' We're reminded that interpersonal communication is 'not so smooth' and 'not to underestimate the sensitivity and care needed to achieve mutual understanding, acceptance and motivation to respond positively to messages we receive.'

We have reference here to 'self' and later to working in the 'adult' state offered by Transactional Analysis theory and viewing the idea of feedback through the other person's lens. More emphasis is placed on the process that *appears* one-way from coach to client:

1. Be sensitive to the situation and treat them as an adult
2. Imagine yourself on the receiving end
3. Be honest and fair
4. Balance negative and positive messages
5. Include weaknesses and balance with strengths
6. Choose appropriate time and place tone and language
7. Keep criticism simple and constructive by concentrating on behaviours, *not* personal attitudes or beliefs
8. Encourage responsibility for own development
9. Be well organised yourself and hold regular reviews
10. You may be a role model so walk the walk.

5. 'Feed-forward'

Feed-forward is presented as having a more positive impact than feedback which is perceived as being 'heavily biased towards performance shortfalls, problems and unwanted behaviour' (Warner, 2012).

The claim is that by looking forward positively we set ourselves 'free of what's happened before – we allow a fresh start.'

Both people in the relationship are asked to follow a 3-step process:

1. Make each question about future possible improvement a dialogue, not a dictate
2. Focus on the future, not the past, when offering ideas – say 'You could ...'
3. Listen to the coach's ideas without clarification and just respond by saying 'Thank you,' before asking for another idea.

Putting feed-forward into practice encourages the other to identify one or two changes, improvements, actions in a similar way that most coaching conversations progress. The client asks the coach to make a 'forward-looking' suggestion about how to achieve the change. The premise is that this approach puts the client into 'improvement' mode. This request for change suggestions can be repeated several times with the same or different coaches. Offering feedback is recognised as part of the client – coach conversation and the addition of feedforward is set to achieve new possibilities for the future.

Can we see the similarities here with the 'Options' part of the GROW model and the Future Perfect concept of the Solutions Focus theory?

6. Upward feedback

This technique suggests giving feedback to those in more senior roles than us. Gallo (2010) recognises that giving our boss feedback can be a 'tricky process to master' and offers 'Principles to Remember':

Do:
- Be certain your boss is open and receptive to feedback before speaking up
- Share what you are seeing and hearing in the organisation or unit
- Focus on how you can help to improve, not on what you would do if you were the boss.

Don't:
- Assume your boss doesn't want feedback if they don't request it – ask if they would like to hear your insight
- Presume you know or appreciate your boss's full situation
- Give feedback as a way to get back at your boss for giving you negative feedback.

This Harvard Business Review by Gallo (2010) reminds us that the 'relationship comes first to create the ability to give and receive feedback' – a great segue to The Relational Leadership WAY© for feedback. Before introducing this we'll take a look at 'the relational' aspect of feedback in the next chapter.

The importance of relationship and how it influences engagement in feedback

4

Let's admit it: relationships can be tough and business relationships may be even tougher without the familial ingredient! This is despite the obvious point that people working in the same organisation are anticipated to be working for the same purpose!

'People' issues seen as apparently unsolvable in organisations usually focus on interpersonal behaviour and not capability; the latter usually being easily resolved through developmental support.

Difficulties arising in relationships may therefore be a contributing factor to feedback being avoided. Where a relationship is struggling, the prospect of a feedback exchange is likely to create further tensions. Even in a healthy relationship working effectively, feedback may be avoided if the individuals feel unable to trust that the relationship is strong enough to withstand such exchanges.

We know that feeling when relationships aren't working and the euphoric harmony of those when we feel totally 'in tune' with the other person. I remember well the first taste of experiencing a 'magical' oneness in a coaching conversation. The sensation was one of suspended animation when I felt truly at one with the client. In the space of the silence created by that moment the client sourced the solution to the quandary he had been puzzling over for some time. I felt I was 'just there' but holding this space for the client served as a resource enabling reflective time. In our feedback exchange at the end of the conversation the client described how he felt the same moment of 'intimacy.' This was a phone conversation – which along with virtual platforms being increasingly used as communication platforms – is still thought by some to lack the 'human' element of a face-to-face conversation. Perhaps digital conversations actually create an environment conducive to this type of experience because of the reduced stimulus that allows us to enter an almost hypnotic, trance-like state by simply being present with that person. In this space we seem to be able to embody the 'transformation that we develop with the ability to step back and reflect on something that used to be hidden or taken for granted and to make decisions about it' (Kegan, 1998).

What is it that draws us to some people and repels us from others? How does knowing this help us to understand more about our relationships at work and the impact on our willingness to actively and authentically participate in feedback?

Can we manufacture this sense of harmony or does it spontaneously happen or not happen? De Haan (2008) believes that the 'relationship is the best possible ... and only genuinely effective ingredient' for conducting helpful conversations.

In this chapter we explore what happens in relationships and how we can develop deeper connections beyond the social cues which inform our first impressions of each other. We go beyond a person's gender, what they're wearing, their accent and other surface characteristics that inform and substantiate, sometimes incorrectly, our perceptions of others. Several facets of relationship will be explored:

- The importance of 'being relational'
- Types of relationship and how these impact on our view of feedback
- The dynamics impacting on relationship
- Power in relationships
- The cultural perspective
- The common features of productive relationships
- Creating productive relationships.

Acknowledging that generative relationships hold the key to productive feedback conversations provides incentive for achieving such relationships through applying the themes integral to The Relational Leadership WAY©. You want to maintain a natural way of being in relationships and with the support of the 'way of being' recommended in The Relational Leadership WAY© and without being formulaic in its application you will create the productive relationships that will enhance your working and extended relationships.

The importance of 'being relational'

Reviewing other theoretical disciplines provided an entry point for comparing experiential observations defining the importance of relationship. This route gave credibility to and substantiated the findings of the research on which this book is based. Comparing the theory with the research gave power to the claim that the relationship is essential as a vehicle for creating the right conditions for the feedback conversation.

Evidence supporting the importance of relationship is increasingly cited in coaching/mentoring literature (Cox, 2013) and in competency frameworks published by professional bodies. The European Mentoring and Coaching Council (EMCC) framework includes 'Building the Relationship' as a competence with capability indicators explaining the process for professional practice:

- Explains their role in relation to the client
- Describes own coaching/mentoring process and style to client
- Demonstrates empathy and genuine support for the client
- Demonstrates a high level of attentiveness and responsiveness to the client in the moment
- Recognises and works effectively with emotional state(s)
- Attends to and works flexibly with the client's emotions, moods, language, patterns, beliefs and physical expression
- Describes and applies at least one method of building rapport.

The EMCC framework validates The Relational Leadership WAY© that also offers another dimension to building relationships step-by-step, noticing all the 'phenomena' emerging and present in both the immediate discussion and the wider system.

Available literature offers many definitions of relationship observed through the lens of the author and based on personal and sometimes researched theory.

Directly linking 'being relational' to feedback, O'Broin and Palmer (2008) state that 'the relative success in relationship-building is likely to impact on … feedback and evaluation.'

The significance of relationship appears in research from Wasylyshyn (2003) who offers the client's perspective by reporting that the 'relationship with the coach' is the client's third preference for a 'coach tool.' Coaching sessions and 360-degree feedback were rated 1 and 2.

Cavanagh (2006) reiterates this reciprocal exchange between coach and client by stating that 'in the complex interaction of the client and coach a conversation is co-created from which the coaching engagement emerges.' A further reference suggests that coaching is seen as 'not so much a methodology as it is a relationship' (Whitworth et al., 2007). Similarly, 'regardless of the preferred theoretical perspective, the foundation of effective coaching is the successful formation of a collaborative relationship' (Grant, 2006). Collective agreement exists between these references and The Relational Leadership WAY©, fully endorsing the importance of the relationship.

An article in the *Training Journal* (2009) champions the role of the client as well as the coach in the relationship based on a Duckworth & de Haan research project started in 2007 entitled: 'What Clients Say About Our Coaching.' An extract from the key findings is:

- 'The quality of the relationship between coach and client, as rated by the client, is what makes all the difference to the success of executive coaching;
- Building strong relationships is more likely to lead to coaching success than introducing clever interventions.'

What is clear and reinforced by the research study is that whatever success criteria are cited by clients, the sense of the quality of the relationship is what is experienced. This sense has the power to make or break the coaching contract. What we need to be mindful of are certain conditions that we can co-create to increase the likelihood of people being more receptive to feedback:

- Creating an environment that radiates safety and trust triggers hormones in the brain and the state of rapport is ignited, felt, implicit and maintained as long as these conditions are satisfied and sustained
- Feeling secure avoids the tendency for being on 'red alert' for unexpected denigration, interruption, blame or shame.

Being in rapport gives us vitality by prompting the sharing of physical energy. We develop a lively curiosity and want to be purposeful about our contribution in the conversation. We want to create that effervescent feeling of animation when words tumble out almost from another source and sense making is effortless. Of course, the 'other source' is the synergy of relationship.

'Qualitative research offers support for the impact of rapport in executive coaching relationships and is described as essential to achieving coaching outcomes,' state Gyllensten and Palmer (2007). Boyce et al. (2010) suggest that 'Rapport is about reducing the differences between the coach and client and building on similarities.' Effective feedback style is seen as 'rapport and active listening, open questioning and probing, non-judgemental style and challenge appropriately' (Bourne, 2008).

Although acknowledging such views, I hesitate to rely specifically on the word 'rapport.' My observations from coach practice make me think that the descriptor 'rapport' is too generically applied as a catch-all describing the awareness of relationship without explaining how to achieve it. Rapport may possibly be too narrow a definition for the type of relationship that encourages the genuine engagement and convergent thinking needed for manoeuvring the complexities of feedback. The working alliance is central to the quality of outcome, so for effectiveness of feedback, more working alliance than chemistry or rapport alone is essential. To awaken and access the full power of relationship we have to extend our efforts beyond the classic 'this is how you build rapport' – nodding, listening, matching – and immerse ourselves in the client; basically, be totally and unequivocally present! 'Presence' is one of the themes of The Relational Leadership WAY© and defining this and how to achieve it appears in Chapter 6.

Coaching texts talk of being 'collaborative with a good rapport' to 'facilitate coachees' trust' (Passmore & Whybrow, 2008) and as the *skill* of building a relationship (Starr, 2012). I agree that creating fertile relationships is something to work at; I don't see these partnerships as something that spontaneously happen, necessarily. However, we do have an innate skill for 'connecting' that I define as 'intuition'; again, another theme in The Relational Leadership WAY©, and that is featured in Chapter 7.

'Being relational' is more than creating rapport to 'oil' the conversation. A 'relational and reciprocal' relationship is clearly about ease and it can also be about real tension and enlightening depth. Sessions with 'feelings of tension' can have 'brilliant relational depth' in those moments of true connectivity. These 'moments' can make the conversation meaningful and worthwhile without necessarily feeling an 'easy rapport.' Exposing our vulnerabilities and revealing that you may get things wrong or sharing a hunch about how you think the other is reacting or might react to a situation can contribute to stimulating the closeness fuelling authentic conversations.

We know the importance of maintaining objectivity in feedback conversations. An illustration from the research data reinforced 'deliberately not colluding' by feeling able to 'say anything' and making this known to the client. The coach's intention was to be transparent and manage any client's expectations of the conversation becoming a 'friendly chat.' Creating 'harmony' was seen as being potentially dangerous where a power dynamic may exist with the other. This dynamic was explained as the client: 'attempting to maintain the status quo and not creating change.' We can recognise this type of conversation in performance discussions with a direct report in long term employment who is reluctant to develop skills to meet the changing needs of the business. Working with new technology is a typical example.

Back to the case study – the thinking was that using 'disharmony in service of the client gave them an experience they haven't had before and to see themselves in another way; they can then choose whether to change.' This coach thought that feedback may not result in anything at that time when responding to the question: 'how does disharmony impact on receptivity to feedback.' Their view was: 'as coaches we don't see all the results of the discord moments because it percolates and can be a grain that grows.' The opinion was that as experienced coaches we are not there to 'make the client feel better; we want to take a risk and get people to take their own risks and think about themselves differently and experience something different.' A similar view on engagement was made by the comment: 'I am involved with ... coaching work where I don't actually have terrific rapport with the other person.' Focusing on productive relationships does not necessarily mean creating harmonious conditions. Revisiting the new technology illustration of the 'reluctant employee' could mean asking them to think about advising on the routine tasks of their role that can be transferred to robotics, enabling them to be available to new opportunities. The desired outcome for the company cannot be guaranteed, although this conversation can alert the individual to the alternative of being replaced by a 'bot.' We have many examples of this already with Amazon employing over 100,000 robots to manage warehouse inventory.

'As people do not change something until they first become aware of it ... one of the key aspects ... is to facilitate heightened awareness in clients of the lenses through which they see the world and themselves' (Bluckert, 2006). In this way, each in the relationship can 'be the mirror' for the other to reflect on shared observations that enhance self-awareness.

Focusing on the components of relationship really alerted me to the magical powers we possess as human beings. There is much we still don't know about how we function as human beings and what is happening at unconscious and subconscious levels. My quest for data informing how these levels of thinking affect the relationship led me to neuroscience. Science has tended to separate the brain from our biological functioning and we're starting to learn that we're much more joined up than was previously thought. The latest research in neuroscience continuously surprises us with insights into what really happens 'inside of us!' Brain scanning detects areas of the brain that 'light up' to show reaction to emotions and naturally this has implications for relationships as we react to the 'signals' we experience from interacting with others.

Reinforcing the impact of the quality of the relationship was voiced in a concern about a possible damaging effects from a coach, illustrated as the 'coach's own agenda,' and how this can 'hamper delivery of the coaching' (Fillery-Travis & Lane, 2006). Although this comment refers to coaching practice, we can easily see how anyone's own agenda can disrupt. Using leading questions to manipulate an outcome destroys the trust essential for productive relationships.

We can find many more references echoing consensus on the importance of 'what to do' techniques in building relationships. *How* to achieve this seems to be elusive. Capturing this 'how' became the primary pursuit of my research with psychotherapy literature guiding the way to revealing the hidden treasures of inter-relational working.

For those of us with interest in underpinning theory, here is a selection of references that contributed to validating the outcomes of the research and the creation of The Relational Leadership WAY©. I summarise the key references below:

In his prologue to the translation of Martin Buber's work 'I and Thou,' Kaufmann (1970) introduces the practitioner and client as equal in the relationship. He talks of the desire for 'genuine dialogue' through 'a shift away from subject-object duality', with its 'seer and seen' towards 'I-Thou'. This 'I-Thou' relationship involves seeing the other as a whole that exists in relationship to us. Similarly, this occurs where 'each participant is being equally affected by the other' and 'genuinely attuned to each other ... responsive and responding' in 'mutual relationships and mutual intersubjectivity.' There is 'both receptivity and active initiative toward the other' (Jordan, 1991a).

The work of Mearns and Cooper (2005) from therapy practice reveals their concept of 'relational depth' as a 'sheer sense of connection.' In their view the relationship is 'a state of profound contact and engagement between two people, in which each person is fully real to the Other, and able to understand the value the Other's experiences at a high level.' This sense of 'profound contact' was 'not all the time, but at some moments.' Evidently, this 'profound contact' happens from a 'sense' of being 'engaged, enmeshed, intertwined' as if 'when I turned I affected my clients, and, when they turned they affect me' (Mearns & Cooper, 2005). At these times, the 'pace of work is much slower' and the experience is a 'profound sense of genuine human contact' created by meeting the client 'on their terms' (Mearns & Cooper, 2005).

McMillan and McLeod (2006) build on this concept, stating that 'deeply facilitative therapy relationships are characterized by a willingness to "let go" on the part of the client and enter into an enduring relationship with their therapist. A sense of connection ... ambient energy ... shifts of consciousness.'

With relational depth we have an acceptance that the 'client' as well as the 'practitioner' has equal responsibility for enabling the quality of the relationship. This extract of 'meeting them on their terms' and pace is not a technique; it's a result of interest. If the coach can generate continuous interest in where this person will go next in their thinking and feeling, their pace will slow down – indicative of respecting the input of both in the relationship.

Mearns and Cooper (2005) use the term 'relational depth' to refer both to specific *moments* of encounter and also to a particular *quality* of relationship. Their 'moments' of relational depth are similar to 'moments of meeting' (Stern, 2004). Emphasis is given 'not just to a specific moment of encounter, but an *enduring* sense of contact and interconnection between two people' (Mearns & Cooper, 2005).

The explanation of Mearns and Cooper (2005) as 'seeing this as a phenomenon relevant to the whole spectrum of human encounters and not just limited to the therapist–client relationship' is encouraging in seeking portability into relationship working generally.

Rogers (1957; 1959) is legendary for creating this 'client-centred approach' and identified his now famous conditions for change, which exemplify the importance of relationship:

- 'A relationship between client and therapist must exist, and it must be a relationship in which each person's perception of the other is important'
- 'The therapist is deeply involved him or herself – they are not "acting" – and they can draw on their own experiences (self-disclosure) to facilitate the relationship'; a debatable tenet by professional coaching practitioners, although 'use of self' is increasingly gaining wider acceptance
- 'The therapist accepts the client unconditionally, without judgment, disapproval or approval. This facilitates increased self-regard in the client, as they can begin to become aware of experiences in which their view of self-worth was distorted by others'; a nod to mutual respect in the relationship
- 'The therapist experiences an empathic understanding of the client's internal frame of reference. Accurate empathy on the part of the therapist helps the client believe the therapist's unconditional love for them.' Compassion for self and others in the activity of feedback continues in Chapter 5
- 'That the client perceives, to at least a minimal degree, the therapist's unconditional positive regard and empathic understanding.' Again – more on this in Chapter 5.

Siegel (2010) talks of interconnectivity between two people referencing empathy as a person 'trying to sense the inner world of another' and then to 'really understand that world.' The explanation continues that as 'human beings we have a whole system of neurons that are detecting the intention of another person.' The emphasis is that the one receiving the empathy will feel the care as well as the 'sense of connection' leading to trust and a feeling of safety; a 'sense of security.' This thinking develops to include mindfulness as a way of being 'really present in an open way … to what's going on inside of you as it's happening … without … judgement' providing a 'gateway to being open and present to other people' as well as yourself. 'The more you are aware of your own bodily sensations, the more you could be aware of other people's internal emotional states' (Siegel, 2010).

'Being relational' is defined as the ability to create productive relationships. When starting the research informing this book, the 'relationship' was perceived as implicitly impacting on the activity of feedback. As the study evolved and reached conclusion, 'relationship' and 'being relational' became paramount for producing fertile conditions encouraging receptivity to feedback. 'We are in this together' and creating 'a safe space,' says a coach who participated in the research study.

Generative relationships become the springboard to deep dive into engaging, powerful and inspiring conversations both as givers and receivers of feedback.

Types of relationship and how these impact on our view of feedback

We will have several relationships in our lives and each play a part in moulding our worldview and how we subsequently react to feedback. Factors such as early attachment patterns, personality, level of wellbeing, resilience and self-esteem each play a part in how we absorb feedback and the impact that others have on colouring our perception of feedback. We may or may not be aware of how we transfer behaviours onto others when we are reminded of someone in our past who has left a positive or negative impression.

Although this book is designed to help with improving the activity of feedback, let's first remember that sometimes, for a variety of reasons, we experience a revelation that eclipses the less favourable instances. Illustrating this is a powerful case study that Zena Vardaki (2018) has agreed to share as an example of how feedback can be positively welcomed in a potentially threatening scenario:

Feedback ... what a wonderful gift when accepted

'If you are irritated by every rub, how will you be polished?'
Rumi

A few years ago, I attended a seminar about communication. One of the exercises that we had to make was to give bad feedback about one of the about 40 participants that we barely knew. The trainer asked for a volunteer. Guess what? Just one hand was raised. Mine. I generally love challenges and taking risks and since I was not afraid to listen to bad things about myself, I went for it.

Forty chairs were placed in a circle and just one single chair for me in the middle. I was ready! I told myself that I would embrace all the negative feedback. I would filter the comments and discard the things that were not relevant and keep the good stuff. I wore my armour and I sat on that chair ready to ignore or accept whatever I chose.

One of the pieces of negative feedback I received was about the colour of my hair. I did not mind; I did not feel less important because of it, since I loved my brown natural hair. One down.

Another negative feedback was that my skin was too pale. I discarded that as well. Two down.

The next one was that I spoke too fast, and in some cases the other participants could not keep up with my pace. Noted. I took that one with a smile. It was true but I did not realise it before. I decided at that moment that I would work on this and I would become a better speaker and adapt my pace accordingly. That feedback was a gem!

After about an hour the 'torture,' as the trainer said, was over and it was time for me to share my feeling on getting all that negative feedback.

First, I was relieved, since it was not as bad as I thought it would. That was because I decided beforehand that I was going to filter it before accepting it.

Second, I realised with astonishment that giving bad feedback was extremely hard for some of the participants. I remember that one woman refused to join the exercise because she felt very sad about the idea of making me unhappy.

The trainer asked me why I volunteered first. I replied that my urge to grow and become a better person was greater than my need to belong in a team. (So maybe that is the reason some people don't speak their truth, because of the fear of losing their position in the tribe.) I had a difficult childhood that turned me into a warrior. I knew who I was, I loved myself, and if you love someone, you are willing to 'die' in order to reach heaven.

This case study, reminiscent of a childhood experience, reminds us that the impact of feedback starts at an early age, carries on through education and is coloured by family and friends until we reach the workplace with a well-formed opinion of feedback. The workplace can strengthen or dilute these perceptions as we enter the mix of prevailing culture, demographics and diversity.

An example is how the quality of relationship can reflect the structure of the organisation. A bureaucracy tends to encourage a transactional style of leadership with a 'top down' approach generating hierarchy rather than equality in relationships.

In this scenario, the feedback conversation is likely to be formalised as part of an appraisal system encouraging a 'tell' and 'receive' relationship. Managers will adopt the expectation of knowledge champion, possibly encouraging dependency with direct reports being discouraged to use initiative despite company rhetoric declaring 'empowerment.' Direct reports are likely to adopt a laissez-faire attitude and depend on instructions from line management about task completion. Even the more enlightened managers may feel hampered by the systemic properties of the structure in their endeavours to release the constraints of company policy and procedures on business operations.

The more 'open' or matrix style of organisations with flatter structures and fewer reporting lines create a stimulating environment for a transformational style of leadership that encourages autonomy and creativity in the workforce.

We may be fully aware of our own 'contact matrix,' but how much do we know of others' awareness? Depending on the size of organisation, people can easily fall into the trap of thinking workplace relationships involve only those they interact with on a regular basis: team members, line manager and perhaps some internal and external 'customers.' A more realistic view of relationship is to acknowledge the impact of the wider system; everyone in and outside of the business and who bring their personal agendas. This gives us a clearer picture that every encounter on every day is an opportunity for feedback, whether this is implicit or explicit. This is a great practice ground for observing, reviewing and refining our exchanges with others.

The dynamics impacting on relationship

Interpersonal dynamics

'How are our relationships working?' is an important question to answer and is one to ask regularly and to reflect upon.

New relationships are susceptible to what we know as 'first impressions.' We know we make judgements about each other in the first few moments of meeting. This stems from our hard-wired neural pathways that reflexively activate when 'newness' enters our domain. We are hard-wired to make instant decisions about others and fit these to a range of stereotypes. Our evaluation incudes an intuitive response, as well as other signals we notice such as appearance, race, gender, age, tone of voice and accent. We can be consciously or unconsciously biased in our assessment.

This judgement of others metamorphoses as our relationships become more mature. Although we become more familiar with others' behaviour, values, beliefs and attitudes, we are just as likely to make a wrong decision about what we believe we perceive as we are when making a new acquaintance. We can easily make a wrong judgement about a facial expression or receive a comment not as intended by the giver. Complexity is probably not sufficient to describe the dynamics presenting when two people meet. It sounds complicated, and it is. All conversations have the propensity to unravel in an unintended or unexpected way. When we realise and accept that the other hasn't read our 'script' we can start to see the situation from another's perspective as well as our own.

Take a moment to look at the following common 'scripts' that we may internalise and reinforce in conversations and relationships.

How can you rephrase those that resonate with you to give a more positive and realistic script for experimentation in future conversations and relationships?

---

1. I don't know how I got promoted to this level; my fear is being found out
2. I think it's best not to show too much ambition as people will see this as egotistical
3. Forget asking for a pay award; it's bound to be rejected
4. I'll wait until others speak before commenting to see if my view is worth contributing
5. I'm not as good as other people
6. I don't seem to be able to say 'No!'

7.   'X' hasn't been in touch so I must have upset them
8.   I avoid giving my view in case people think my ideas are stupid
9.   I wish I hadn't said what I thought; I expect this will be held against me now
10. Everyone else just seems more confident than me.

We all want feedback to be welcomed and to add value both as a giver and receiver. Awareness of the dynamics and psychological contract we bring into conversations is fundamental when expecting to discuss existing or emergent sensitive issues. We each enter a conversation with our unique blend of personality, emotional state, expectations, experiences, biases, worldview and much more. We need to consistently attend to the potential potency of these in our preparation or 'in-the-moment' interactions. This doesn't mean being self-absorbed. It means recognising that we may not always express ourselves in a way acceptable to the other, but we will be authentic in a way that others appreciate as respectful and caring.

Capability dynamics

We will already have developed skills fundamental to productive conversations through life experiences and we may also have 'blind spots' about our level of competence. The Relational Leadership WAY© assumes proficiency in these essential skills. Take a check on these essentials – you may like to ask another to share a feedback exchange on how you view each other's skills in these areas:

Active listening: this is more than 'hearing' what the other person is saying. Deep listening skills are developed by being totally focused on the other and being conscious of everything that can be observed beyond the dialogue; body language, tone of voice, energy, ability to maintain eye contact and so on. Active listening means:

- avoiding being drawn into the other's dialogue when we can miss salient words worthy of exploration
- trusting we will know what question to ask or statement to make when the other has finished speaking as our brain can only cope with one action at a time and active listening avoids us missing what may be vital information
- noticing what the system brings to the conversation in which the relationship exists; what we notice that is helpful to share.

Questioning: how effective are we at using a range of questions that encourages transparency, openness and willingness to disclose barriers to progress?

Summarising: are we remembering to regularly review what is being said to check understanding and intention?

The challenge/support continuum: are we practising a mix of developmental challenges to raise self-awareness and support to encourage a safe and secure environment for improving sustainable performance?

Power in relationships

One of the study participants described 'connection' between practitioner and client and felt that power held the key: 'I guess it's hard to describe it because it definitely feels for me where the power is, it's really, really hard to describe.'

Power can be described as 'power over'; having control over what others want, need and aspire to. Power over devotees are likely to abuse power to reinforce rather than alleviate any discomfort about and perhaps fear of feedback. This is synonymous with treating others as inanimate objects that are void of feelings and unworthy of respecting us as human beings. The most productive relationships are those where each is valued as collaborative and equal contributors to a constructive discussion.

'A confronting intervention unequivocally tells an uncomfortable truth but does so with love in order that the one concerned may see it and fully acknowledge it ... this has nothing to do with the aggressive, combative account sometimes applied ... confrontation is about consciousness raising' (Heron, 1975).

Being aware of how power in relationships is adopted by or bestowed upon us helps us to calibrate advantageous and relevant postures in feedback dialogue. Let's be aware, for example, that unsolicited feedback can cause anxiety.

The combined complexity of human behaviour and types of relationship become an intoxicating cocktail fuelling a myriad of feedback approaches.

The position power

Jenny is Managing Director of a pharmaceutical organisation. She started her career as PA to a department head and has enjoyed the challenge of widening her skills and knowledge within the business. Every opportunity for promotion was taken by Jenny. She became appreciated and respected for her ambition and willingness to accept the challenges of facing rejection when being unsuccessfully appointed to new roles. Her perseverance and resilience eventually took her to the top of the organisation.

So how does the 'Jenny as PA' differ from the 'Jenny as MD?' In her eyes she earns more, she's enjoyed the excitement and fulfilment that each role has brought on her journey to the top of the organisation. Jenny still sees herself as the egalitarian, democratic, caring, positive and empathic person she's always been. In her mind she's no different and continues to be surprised when people attribute her with different qualities belonging to her role rather than her. To others Jenny is very different.

A director within an organisation is likely to have attributed power (status) based on job title and seniority in the business. By the very nature of the position, feedback offered at this level is often received unquestioned. Having this inherent power relies on a sensitivity to understand how others may react and to adjust leadership style.

The intimidator power

Jay Jay is a 'dominant' person; in company role, in stature, in personality and in behaviour. Jay Jay's idea of 'getting things done' was to manipulate people into fulfilling expectations by use of 'threat': 'if you don't complete this by the deadline it won't look good on your annual appraisal' and 'punishment': 'well, you didn't secure that client contract we needed so I can't agree to the promotion we discussed.'

Jay Jay harasses and intimidates direct reports and colleagues to achieve expected outcomes. Feedback, although regular, is aggressively delivered with undermining comments sapping confidence and self-esteem in others. Leaders within the business respect the outcomes achieved and ignore the behaviour to gain these results.

This type of behaviour can achieve short terms goals. The longer term effect, however, is likely to be disengagement, demotivation and eventually increased employee turnover. Being aware of the cost of recruitment and damage to business image provides an easy formula to assess whether 'intimidator' behaviour is worth nurturing.

The 'motivator' power

DD works the hours that appear in the terms and conditions of employment for the business.

DD genuinely cares about others in the organisation; this is not just another banal statement on an unread laminate of organisational values.

DD commits to fulfilling additional activities whenever these are commercially essential.

DD daily role models the behaviours expected for the organisational culture that emulates the 'way we do things around here.'

DD exerts influence because people are eager to deliver what's wanted.

DD is the CEO.

This power gains respect and engagement and is noticed in leaders who respect employees as people and who work at seeking ways for continuous improvement both for themselves and others. These leaders make efforts to 'meet' with everyone throughout the organisation even when – depending on the size of the business – there's only time for a daily salutation. 'Use of self' is key in encouraging engagement and 'self' needs to be seen by others as leadership that listens, empowers, appreciates and develops people and the organisation as socially responsible and ethical as well as successful in business operations.

Feedback from these leaders appreciates the efforts of others and inspires, motivates and energises people to push their performance levels to new and greater heights. These leaders will actively welcome feedback about how they can improve themselves, working conditions and opportunities for increasing the wellbeing and engagement of the human capital in the business.

Accepting that work is a community of people contributing and reacting to social relationships, the use of power will influence behaviour far more than any strategic planning, company handbooks and policies and procedures. If one person sees an issue or wants to leave, others will probably feel the same; people talk! Increase in employee turnover is a potent and tangible signal that 'something needs fixing' in the organisation. There may be many reasons within the complex social structures prevalent in organisations. One of these may be feedback and the many related factors such as: lack of feedback, style of delivering feedback or failure to deliver promises made in feedback discussions.

The cultural perspective

Here we review the macro and micro elements of culture: the relational dimension emerging from globalisation, business culture and virtual team working.

Clutterbuck et al. (2016), sourcing a range of references, say that culture:

– Is created over time through the interaction of people and their environment
– Creates consistent patterns of meaning and behaviour that bind people together and make them unique as a group
– Is a combination of visible and invisible elements that exist on multiple levels
– Is a unique, shared set of beliefs and assumptions that are adopted over time and which lead to consistent patterns of meaning and behaviour.

Culture, in a word, is complex! As an introduction to the topic I cover what's immediately on the horizon of relationships and that impact on the feedback conversation:

Challenge: demographics

We are predicted to have five generations in the workplace by 2020 (Shah, 2015). Changes in life expectancy are likely to increase this number as people stay in employment longer.

How might this number of generations coexist where we have newcomers entering employment with a preference for digital communication – the native digitals – and mature employees – the immigrant digitals – generally preferring social interaction? How this evolves will be revealed in time as organisational development specialists forecast potential scenarios. Who knows, people may prefer to have feedback from a humanoid robot programmed to be non-judgemental and bias free!

Opportunity: cultural diversity as a business resource

Globalisation opens new horizons daily as organisations expand markets and technology liberates communication boundaries. Cross-cultural working is becoming the norm for many businesses recognising the benefits of leveraging diversity and capitalise on increased human potential. Being aware of our own culture already brings challenges to the feedback conversation – imagine this multiplied on a global platform. Developing this exponentially shows the challenges that businesses are likely to face.

Converting challenges to opportunities offers exciting prospects as we enter the cultural mix with the realisation that self-awareness and appreciation of others is paramount. This awareness goes beyond emotional and social intelligence to embrace the essence of what it is to be human. Cultural assumptions we make and that exist within our relationships are a natural phenomenon arising from individual socialisation and experiences. Being more than culturally aware and becoming culturally intelligent are bonuses of self-reflection.

Summarising this entry into the cultural perspective as it relates to feedback:

- We are the product of where we are born, the society in which we live, the nature of our education and our experiences as we develop from child to adult
- We may not be aware of our prejudices, unconscious bias and stereotypical judgements
- We may avoid discussing barriers within the relationship based on fear, shame and vulnerability.

Table 4.1 Becoming culturally intelligent (Lewis, 2014b)

Cultural awareness	Cultural intelligence
• Builds cultural knowledge relating to race, customs, social class, religion, gender balance, generational hierarchy	• Evaluates influence of own ethnicity in creating judgements and uninformed stereotyping
• Develops awareness of culture-based values, beliefs, attitudes	• Self manages impact of personal values, beliefs and attitudes • Remembers we're all human beings
• Determines how to create understanding of boundaries/confidentiality/safe environment	• Actively encourages relationship building and seeks equality in conversation • Avoids making assumptions and stays curious
• Is able to communicate in a shared language	• Is alert to the propensity for using colloquialisms, metaphor and regional variations that may distort understanding
• Researches corporate culture and organisational norms of behaviour	• Compares the research with own perception of corporate culture and adjusts approach.

Awareness, openness to learning and accepting we may make mistakes without intention will help us move beyond our own cultural limits and accept diversity to foster mutual prosperity in these times of unprecedented geographical mobility.

More information is available on organisational culture from the authors:

- *Trompenaars and Hampden-Turner's Seven Dimensions of Culture* model helps you work better with people from different cultures
- Geert Hofstede: The 6-D measure of national culture
- Phillippe Rosinski: *Coaching Across Cultures.*

The common features of productive relationships

Trust is frequently referenced as the most important feature of productive relationships. Without trust our relationships exist at a superficial level of lightweight conversation, with neither person willing to be truly transparent and both looking for signals to reinforce perception of whether trust exists.

In his research on the 'Neuroscience of Trust' Zak (2017) tells us that because 'experiments show that humans are naturally inclined to trust others – but don't always' he hypothesized that there must be a 'neurological signal indicating when we *should* trust someone.' Previous research tells us that oxytocin is shown in animals to signal that another is safe to approach. Oxytocin appeared to do just one thing – reduce the fear of trusting a stranger – and the more we trust, the more oxytocin we produce when we interact. Zak's work builds on existing knowledge about the production of oxytocin between a mother and their newborn baby; the human 'love' hormone.

An extrapolation of research into the effects of oxytocin together with Zak's longitudinal studies identified 8 management behaviours that foster trust. Once trust is well established, the confidence to give and the acceptance to receive feedback becomes easier:

1. **Recognise excellence.** This had the biggest impact on trust when praise is given immediately after a goal has been met, when it comes from peers, and when it's tangible, unexpected, personal, and public. This endorses existing theory showing that recognition is the highest motivator
2. **Induce 'challenge stress.'** When a manager assigns a team a difficult but achievable job, the moderate stress of the task releases neurochemicals, including oxytocin and adrenocorticotropin, that intensify people's focus and strengthen social connections. I take from this that we all like

a 'stretch.' Being offered opportunities for development of this kind reinforces that care is being extended to our wellbeing at work

3. **Give people discretion in how they do their work.** Being trusted to figure things out is a big motivator. Absolutely! Most of us respond well to being trusted to take responsibility for what we produce and tend to find more creative ways of working

4. **Enable job crafting.** When companies trust employees to choose which projects they'll work on, people focus their energies on what they care about most. This approach is gaining popularity where people are now working in 'self organising groups' selecting the skills and knowledge that are needed for a particular project and then re-forming in a similar way for the next project

5. **Share information broadly.** Openness and ongoing communication are key. We all like to know what's 'going on' and when we don't we usually fill in the gap – not always correctly. Sharing information good and not-so-good is a strong reinforcer of demonstrating that people will adapt to expectations

6. **Intentionally build relationships.** The trust and sociality that oxytocin enables are deeply embedded in our nature. Zak's neuroscience experiments show that when people intentionally build social ties at work, their performance improves. A Google study similarly found that managers who 'express interest in and concern for team members' success and personal well-being' outperform others in the quality and quantity of their work

7. **Facilitate whole-person growth.** High-trust workplaces help people develop personally as well as professionally. Numerous studies show that if you're growing as a human being, your performance improves. High-trust companies adopt a growth mindset when developing talent

8. **Show vulnerability.** Leaders in high-trust workplaces ask for help from colleagues instead of just telling them to do things. Asking for help is effective because it taps into the natural human impulse to cooperate with others and cultivates trust.

I think with a little creativity we can adjust the research of Zak to reinforce existing quality relationships and improve those in need of attention.

Revisiting what we can learn from psychotherapy text and Mearns and Cooper (2005) with their concept of 'relational depth' is 'a state of profound contact and engagement between two people, in which each person is fully real to the Other, and able to understand the value the Other's experiences at a high level.' This sense of 'profound contact' was 'not all the time, but at some moments.' Evidently, this 'profound contact' happens from a 'sense' of being 'engaged, enmeshed, intertwined' as if 'when I turned I affected my clients, and, when they turned they affect me' (Mearns & Cooper, 2005). At these times, the 'pace of work is much slower' and the experience is a 'profound sense of genuine human contact' created by meeting the (other) 'on their terms' (Mearns & Cooper, 2005).

'Meeting others on their terms' featured regularly in the research study. An example cited 'pace is not a technique; it's a result of interest … [thinking about the subject] when their pace will slow; when … more interested … they start reacting … interested in what the coach … says next; [then] the pace picks up.'

Another feature in relationship is acknowledging the way we perceive ourselves and others. We are reminded by Gilbert (2009b) that people who experience 'self criticism … may struggle to feel … reassured or safe' which has an effect on their sense of well-being. This 'gives a sense of creating an environment conducive to people being kind to themselves, enabling a healthy approach to personal development.' This means being responsive to the client in showing 'empathy … an emotional skill that allows us to respond to others in a meaningful, caring way' (Brown, 2007). However, Scott (1984) refers us to the work of Hackney (1978b) with the caution that 'someone highly capable of empathic experience cannot necessarily communicate that experience' to a client.

Mearns and Cooper (2005) feature in their work a perspective that is reminiscent of the phenomena I can sense when working with clients: 'those moments of connection and intimacy … when each person's words … flow from the other's and all self-consciousness is lost? [This] can feel beyond language, and to put words on to the moment can feel like cheapening the depth and profundity of the experience.' Research participants gaining this same sense of connectivity also experienced the difficulty of articulating this sensation, real but inexplicable.

When looking for an explanation of the phenomena, 'the next step was to explore the circumstances where the client might bring it out' and to realise that 'the client only brought the really important stuff out when they experienced relational depth with their counsellor or therapist' (Mearns, 2004c). Also observed is 'the corollary to the discovery that much of what "normally" happens in counselling and therapy hardly scrapes the surface' (Mearns, 2004c).

A later example and similar reference to engagement with the client is Barrett-Lennard (2005) who termed a 'client-centred relational psychotherapy' as an approach to person-centred therapy. The primary focus of the work is on 'encountering the client in an in-depth way and sustaining a depth of relating.'

Describing this in-depth approach from a Gestalt perspective is 'a wide ranging and holistic vision focused upon "direct perception" and what a person is sensing, feeling and projecting out upon the world, rather than what they are thinking or interpreting' (Barber, 2008). Here, we are encouraged 'to work alongside … within a relationship which is authentic, valuing of openness and focused upon the clarification of meaning … and … open to guidance from the energetic field relationships create' (Barber, 2008).

The Gestalt approach emphasises 'applying self' rather than using 'techniques' and to 'let the here and now, (another's) inner wisdom and own intuition guide them' Barber (2008). 'Its root meaning (intuition) is to guard or protect, and so intuition should serve as an invaluable tool' (Cox, 2013).

The immersion of both (in the relationship) is emphasised again in the description of Yalom (1980) who suggests that we 'must approach the (other) phenomenologically: that is, enter the (other's) experiential world and listen to the phenomena of that world without the presuppositions that distort understanding.' A more tangible explanation compared to that from psychotherapy for connecting with clients comes from a coaching reference by O'Neill (2000) who talks of bringing 'values, passion, creativity, emotion, and discerning judgment – to any given moment with a client.'

Recognising the significance of engaging with clients – being client-centred and the client having a 'voice' – is 'a relational model meaning therapists work *with* rather than *on* clients. In a with-therapy, clients have the most important voice about what they want and how they prefer to get it' (Duncan et al., 2004, p. 51).

Sourcing information on neuroscience and its potential contribution to relationship uncovered the way mirror neurons facilitate the mapping of the mind of another person (Iacoboni, 2009). In an interview with Scientific American entitled 'The Mirror Neuron Revolution: Explaining What Makes Humans Social,' Iacoboni (2008) talks of mirror neurons being essential for social interactions. When we interact, we use our body (gestures, facial expressions) to 'communicate our intentions and feelings; the way mirror neurons likely let us understand others is by providing some kind of inner imitation of the actions of other people. This leads up to "simulate" the intentions and emotions associated with those actions.' He gives the example of us 'initiating a cascade of neural activity that evokes the feel we typically associate' when we see another smile.

Siegel (2010) refers to this phenomenon as the 'physiology' of empathy and how the 'neurobiology' of 'we' is what we 'feel like when we are joining with someone, not just understanding somebody, but really connecting … as a "we."'

This apparent innate ability to create relationships may assume that we are 'one part of a larger network ... we are all interconnected and interdependent' and through 'realizing we are all a part of the interconnected whole, it's not that we lose *the self*, but we actually expand *the self* to include a much larger sense of interconnection' (Siegel, 2010).

Creating productive relationships

Drake (2011) reminds us of the need for learning 'agility that enables more engagement with the knowledge and evidence' that people bring to the conversation and to what 'emerges in the relational field in conversations, and that is present in the larger culture.'

We've seen that much is referenced about how we need to be more engaged with others' perspectives and, may I suggest, less concerned with our own. This is not to advocate that our needs go unmet, just to remind us that productive relationships really do mean equality of 'airtime' for both and to be proactive about how we contribute to introducing, accommodating and cultivating the common features of productive relationships.

In parallel with creating The Relational Leadership WAY© by theming the rich data generated from the research study a complementary resource emerged defining the common features of productive relationships:

- Trust
- Security
- Authenticity
- Transparency
- Interest
- Passion
- Creativity
- Equality
- Connection
- Self disclosure.

A research study by de Haan (2008) also mentions qualities for building the relationship:

- Courteous
- Approachable
- Available

- Attentive
- Responsive.

I suggest we add the work of Goleman (2007) on Social Intelligence to the mix for creating productive relationships and who also cites the following key findings from neuroscience:

'Our brain's design makes it sociable and capable of brain-to-brain connection whenever we interact with others ... [the] emission of a stream of hormones [regulating] our biological systems ... can have a positive or a negative effect.' An external indicator for noticing our impact on each other is to notice changes in our breathing when in contact with different people or in different relationship settings. Have you noticed how our pace of breathing slows when we feel relaxed with another and speeds up when we feel nervous or perhaps excited in the company of others?

Through Goleman's work we are introduced to the concept of 'a two-person psychology: what transpires as we connect.' He reinforces along with others and the research findings how we sense another person's feelings that invokes empathy and subsequently encourages rapport. He identifies that 'empathy is an individual ability, one that resides inside the person whereas rapport is between people and emerges from their interaction. These interactions take on a deeper consequence as we realise how, through their sum total, we create one another.'

To cultivate a relationship that gives a deep sense of trust and safety has been shown in this chapter to be a joint responsibility where both have a desire for the same outcome. We have to abandon our own agenda and be willing to work towards reciprocity. Each of us will know and have the innate ability of recognising when there is genuine transparency in wanting the best for both without judgement from either. Accessing this ability means going within ourselves, stilling our busy minds and listening to what every part of our being is telling us; total concentration. At a cognitive level we will be aware of any implicit goals we have and put them to one side – to bracket them (Spinelli, 2005) and reengage with the actuality of emergent experiences. We have to meet each other from a place of naivety and genuine curiosity; the beginner's mind that was our gift when we started out in life.

You want to maintain a natural way of being in relationships. Don't wait until appraisal time to give feedback; the reaction to this is covered earlier in this text. If you've built a mutually respectful and trusting relationship where strengths are recognised and how these can be valuably applied at work others will look forward to feedback because it's a regular pattern of working together. Both feel included in this example of developmental dialogue.

To support you in embodying a 'way of being' and to become proficient in the skills to create this level and quality of relationship it's time to introduce The Relational Leadership WAY©. Without being formulaic in its application you will create the productive relationships that will enhance your working and extended relationships.

I introduce you to this unique framework created from evidence-based research (Lewis, 2014b) in the next three chapters. Here's a graphic illustrating the framework to give you an overview of what to expect.

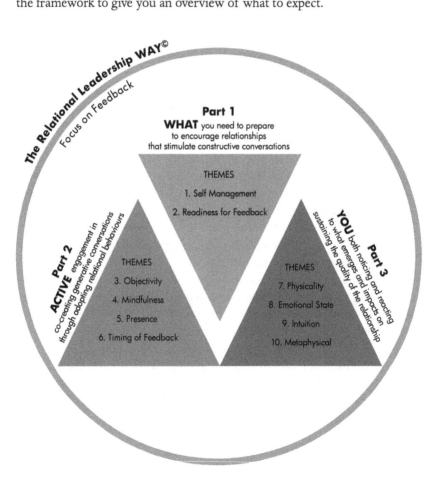

Figure 4.1 The Relational Leadership WAY©

Part 1 of The Relational Leadership WAY© **5**

What needs preparing to establish relationships that stimulate constructive conversations

Being part of a tribe or society generally means we're regularly in conversation with others. This is a natural function from the time we learn to talk, it's a way of life and essential for being a member of the human race. What's so special about the feedback conversation when we're such practised conversationalists? Just take a moment to reflect on your conversations today, over the last, week the last month and ask how many of these benefitted all and were pleasurable, how many were just OK and served some purpose and how many were a waste of time. You get the picture. Most conversations – even planned meetings – happen spontaneously often with a serendipitous outcome.

Demonstrating an understanding of how to adopt a 'relational way of being' means that whatever our role we realise how essential it is to fully prepare for important conversations. Preparation is a vital habit to adopt; however, with the everyday pressures of working this can be easily overlooked. How often do we experience the unexpected when underestimating what can emerge in any conversation? Then imagine how this omission can ignite emotion when feedback intermingles with the unknown relational mix. Without constructive reflective thought, we become complacent in anticipating what others may say or how they will react to what we say. How often have we heard the phrase 'they didn't read the script,' meaning *our* script, when conversations fail to meet expectations? We obviously can't plan for every interaction and spontaneity is often the key to conversation flow. However, the 'difficult' feedback conversation does need special attention. Preparation is essential, especially in business cultures where the practice of 'often and regular' feedback is absent.

The work of Thach (2002) cites 'Creating a good environment consisting of being Open, Positive, Empathetic, Trusting and Supportive.' This finding was based on research into the 'chemistry' between a coach and coachee. Similarly, the premise of the **Preparation Element** is to take time to reflect on how best to accelerate connection and create that good 'relational environment' between us and another, especially when feedback is part of the meeting agenda.

There may be a variety of information sources available when preparing for a feedback conversation. The themes in this chapter emerged from my own research and accentuate the relationship as worthy of specific attention in enabling feedback. There may be other themes that you wish to add to your preparation routine depending on the intent of the feedback discussion.

The function of the **preparation element** is to set the scene for feedback as the foundation for the 'relational way of being,' and this is the distinctive signature of The Relational Leadership WAY©. The first theme of 'self-management' guides us in the practice of preparing ourselves; being mindful of how our emotional state and behaviours contribute to the scene-setting scenario. The framework asks us to assume a mutuality in the relationship and a mindset of respect for anticipating how feedback will be delivered and received; this is the second theme of 'readiness for feedback.' The philosophical view is that both people are responsible for entering the conversation as their best possible self and to acknowledge good intention as the underlying principle of information shared.

John knew his annual appraisal was due and was keen to impress his line manager with how he was working, and to talk about some ideas he had for future development of his role.

He accessed the company scheme online and gave a lot of thought to the best way of completing the appraisal discussion documentation. John had several conversations with key company personnel, fact finding and gaining opinion on how the business might grow for the future. Comparing this with any information he could find about others in the same sector, John felt confident he would make a good impression at interview time.

His big day arrived, he met with his line manager and was greeted with, 'I hope we can get through this meeting quickly as I have another one to attend. I think you're doing a great job, continue doing what you're doing and perhaps you can encourage others in the team to show the same motivation for work as you do.'

John left and is now working for a competitor.

We may assume that the line manager entered the conversation with positive intent. However, he clearly underestimated the expectations that John had for the discussion.

Part 1: *What* needs preparing to establish relationships that stimulate constructive conversations.

Part 1 has 2 themes:

1. **Self-Management** with the sub-themes of **Confidence** and **Compassion**

   - Identifying and managing our 'state': tired, stressed, frustrated and how we manage these before and during the conversation
   - Recognising and managing our personal biases or critical thoughts about the person we're giving feedback to
   - Reflecting on our level of self-esteem and how to be confident about our behaviour in the feedback discussion
   - Difficult feedback is not easy to give or receive; how we generate ease by demonstrating compassion.

2. **Readiness for Feedback** with the sub-theme of **Impactfulness**

   - What we know about our willingness to participate in a feedback discussion, how this informs our propensity for engagement, and what we can do to prepare for this
   - We can't anticipate the impact of feedback and how the other will react; however, we can visualise potential reactions and plan ways of managing these.

How to adopt each theme and sub-theme is demonstrated through evidence-based research, literature review, case studies and learning bite extracts from the on-line webinars available at www.liselewis.com.

Theme 1 of The Relational Leadership WAY©: Self-Management with the sub-themes of Confidence and Compassion

The research data suggested setting aside 'biases or criticism' and delivering feedback '**confidently**, non-judgementally and with **compassion**.'

Preparing ourselves for the feedback conversation has several features. We need a heightened level of self-awareness to be able, for example, to notice our emotional state and extent to which this is activated by the anticipation of a feedback conversation. How well do we manage these feelings for ourselves, and what attention do we give to the recipient's feelings? If we feel nervous about sharing our thoughts with another this is likely to 'seep through our pores' and be noticed. If emotions escalate, how will we manage our own and displays of emotions from others? Self-management is prerequisite to being relational and is a condition essential for accommodating the emotions and regulating the behaviours that emerge in our conversations.

Confidence is a key resource for managing those conversations where we feel unsure or uncomfortable about how we may present and also what to say to another. Flexing our belief in ourselves is vital in enabling us to deliver our message coherently, with conviction and objectively. Similarly, being authentically relational in our way of being with another is demonstrating a willingness and encouragement for transparency in feedback exchanges.

The research data gives an example of a client's preferred approach to feedback endorsing the preference for transparency: 'she [coach] moved closer to me and my "stuff". she took a risk and I like that. I liked the way that on these occasions it confronted the issue head on – never avoiding or skirting round it.'

We recognise good practice and accept that requests for preferences about the giving and receiving of feedback can elicit clients articulating a willingness for such direct and 'transparent' interventions. However, the *actual* impact of feedback may not fall in line with assumptions and remains unpredictable until the point of delivery.

Aitch listened to the applicant recounting his achievements and sensing feelings of anxiety and discomfort. He recognised the mismatch between his and the client's values. This client's rendition of how successful he was in gaining contracts was not a surprising claim at interview. However, the supposition that his team couldn't function without him clashed resoundingly with Aitch's values of collaboration and respect for others.

How can we anticipate Aitch will react in this scenario:

1. Express his discomfort through 'disapproving raised eyebrows' and bring the interview swiftly to a close?
2. Challenge the supposition and request an explanation of the assumptions being made about the team?
3. Manage his discomfort, remain curious and encourage the applicant to think more about the truth of the supposition?

Option 3 demonstrates an honouring of personal values and managing self to support another's raised self-awareness; we can control our reactions (Green, 2014). A choice we may not wish to take; however; the outcome may be of service to others with underdeveloped emotional and social intelligence.

Compassion was intriguingly identified by the research as relevant to both people in the feedback conversation; expected from the receiver and advocated for the 'giver' whose discomfort may go unrecognised.

Theme 1: self-management and the sub-themes of **confidence** and **compassion** are now expanded to give a deeper understanding of the intended application in the feedback conversation.

Self-management is achieved through informed self-awareness, enabling us to responsibly manage ourselves both in preparation and during our conversations with others.

Confidence is believing we can deliver the feedback message effectively with transparency and authenticity in a way that achieves the intended outcome and is accepted and acted upon by the receiver.

Compassion is promoting wellbeing and mutual respect. Both are critical factors in relationship management, with compassion deserving the lion's share of this chapter in recognition of its significance and currency to today's workplace of increasing demand, pressure and uncertainty.

Self-management

This section draws from a range of views on self-awareness and self-management and takes a deeper dive into emotional intelligence as pivotal to self and relationship management.

The theme of **self-management** is multifaceted when preparing for a feedback discussion. Pelham (2016) gives an example of 'self- and relationship management – addressing ingrained patterns of behaviour.' I believe we first have to be *aware* of our reflexive responses and recognise the impact on others, both positive and negative, before we can begin to calibrate our behaviour and negotiate the complexity of relational management. If these behaviours are 'ingrained' I believe we need support to identify what are likely to be 'unknown' facets of how we interact. Perhaps a salutary reminder of when a feedback conversation about our own level of competence helps before we venture into the relational maze!

The EMCC Competence Framework offers guidance on 'self-management' with capability indicators underpinning the competence of 'understanding self':

- awareness of own behaviours, recognises how these affect their practice
- identifies when their internal process is interfering with client work and adapts behaviour appropriately
- proactively manages own 'state of mind' to suit the needs of the client
- responds to client's emotions without becoming personally involved.

This competency acts as guidance on behaviours demonstrating professional practice in coaching and mentoring and can equally apply to relationships in general. The International Coach Federation (ICF) code of ethics describes the style and approach of the coach in relation to their client in building relationships. Our attention is drawn to having a 'positive belief in the qualities' of the other being 'capable, creative, wise and good' and to 'choose conscious creation over reaction.' I think both examples from professional bodies give support to the power of 'being relational' and what we bring of ourselves into conversation.

Grossman (1984) talks of The Rule of Epoché that asks us to set aside our initial biases and prejudices of things, to suspend our expectations and assumptions, so that we can focus on the primary and immediate data of our experience, and impose an 'openness' on our immediate experience. Being non-judgemental is fundamental to creating the conditions for disclosure based on trust that each has the other's best interests in mind through reciprocal feedback.

An extract from Spinelli (2005) suggests that:

> phenomenology ... asks us first to consider ... possible assumptions and biases that [lead] us to our conclusions ... true reality is ... both unknown and unknowable to us. What we perceive ... exists [is] through the meanings that each of us gives them.

This implies that for each of us, reality is dependent on our own interpretation and validates the complexity operating within us and between us in conversation. This phenomenological approach also accepts that many of us share similar interpretations of reality.

Meaning making is implicit in our experience of reality. Our brain seeks what we believe to be true based on life experiences combined with our current view of reality. This includes interpretation of the 'signals' we receive from others. Each of us constructs a unique interpretation of the world: 'as a result of the unique experiential variables in each of our lives, no individual experience can be fully shared by any two people. In this sense, each of us experience a unique and solitary phenomenal reality' Spinelli (2005). The philosopher Immanuel Kant states what has since become a perceptual truism: 'we see things not as *they* are, but as *we* are' (Kaufmann, 1980a) and will likely transfer our worldview onto others. At best, our communications and interactions with one another allow us to produce approximations of each other's experience of the world. If we apply the principles of phenomenology not to challenge or question an individual's interpretation, how might this relate to feedback? We can respect the other's view of a situation as their reality; this at least acknowledges another's perspective. However, we may think, where does this lead us in fulfilling the intended outcome of feedback? If an organisation has expectations for specific behaviours and performance levels, the conversation has to extend beyond respecting another's worldview. Organisational norms at some point need satisfying, and the more enlightened business cultures will encourage the integration of both agendas.

What appears to be happening is that our perceptions of others are intricately and intimately bound up with our perceptions of ourselves. The better we come to know ourselves, the more able we become in 'bracketing' the self from our perception of others (Spinelli, 2005). The use of the descriptor 'bracketing' suggests we can 'set aside' our prejudices, biases, values, beliefs and attitudes that may be accurate but that we don't allow to filter into another's narrative; self-management as a 'relational way of being' is achieved.

When Bluckert (2006) talks of 'self-interference' he reminds us to remember that a function of a conversation where feedback exists is to develop greater awareness in each individual. We are reminded to be aware of when personal material, patterns and issues obstruct the learning process. An example is 'knowing whether your typical response to authority is challenge, compliance or avoidance of contact [and which] alerts you to whether our response in the here and now may be more to do with you than your client.'

Self-awareness is therefore a prerequisite in informing self-management that leads to productive relationships

Knowing more about ourselves, what others think of us and how we can adapt our style and behaviour is the key to gaining traction in achieving productive relationships. Börjeson (2009) reminds us of the value of self-awareness and that often we neglect to check – what we know about ourselves and what others think of us. Lacking this knowledge is likely to lead to a lot of unnecessary misunderstandings.

Börjeson (2009) offers this 4-quadrant model of 4 easy ways to improve self-awareness:

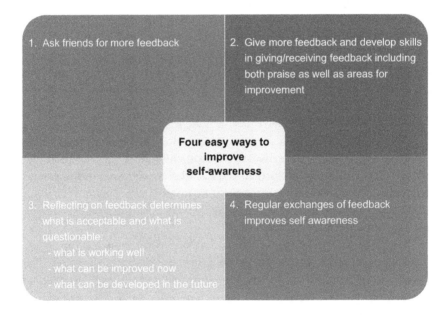

Figure 5.1 Four easy ways to improve self-awareness Börjeson (2009)

Emotional intelligence

Managing our emotions is often the tough part of relationship management. We enter conversations carrying emotional baggage gathered during a moment, during a day, during a lifetime. Let's just take a day as an example:

– We forget to set the alarm so wake later than intended
– The kids are squabbling over the giveaway in the cereal packet

- Your partner is having a long phone conversation
- You get stuck in a traffic jam and arrive late for work
- You're late for a meeting and the agenda item you've taken hours preparing for has been covered and agreed
- Today is your appraisal meeting and your preparation is left at home.

This may be interpreted as an exaggeration of the start of the day; however, it illustrates the emotional state that evolves as we journey through a 'day in the life of...'

No small wonder that tolerance levels can be low, impatience high, empathy left at the door, energy drained and it's only 10.30am; all contributing to an emotional highjack.

Emotional intelligence (EI) is now widely recognised in guiding us to understand more about how we manage our own and others' emotions.

A UK BBC Radio Four broadcast (1999) advising on 'learning to learn in our everyday lives' and – still relevant today – encouraged us to know how we feel and how others feel and what we do about our feelings and their feelings. Knowing what feels good and what feels bad for us and knowing how we can get from one emotion or mood to another creates an inbuilt emotional sensitivity and experience in managing our own and others' emotions.

EI is important because we have to interact with people appropriately. There is sufficient recorded and empirical evidence (Goleman, 1995) to suggest that the higher up in the hierarchy of business we go, the more important EI becomes in conveying and gaining acceptance of ideas, given the need to achieve results through relationships/others. If we are constantly angry our brilliant ideas may be dismissed when judged on the kind of person we appear to be.

When we are agitated this interferes with our ability to learn and interrupts the learning experience. We are offered 5 basic skills for better managing our emotions:

1. Self-awareness – aware of our own emotions as they are occurring and being able to identify and label feelings in ourselves and in others
2. Able to discuss emotions and communicate them clearly and directly
3. Ability to empathise and feel compassion towards others. This includes the ability to motivate, inspire, soothe or react to how others are feeling
4. Ability to make decisions by using a balance of both intellectual and emotional information
5. Displaying self-management is the ability to manage and take responsibility for our own emotions. When we're upset by the actions of others we are responsible for how we manage that.

EI connects continuously in interactions. We may not always be aware of this when connecting at an unconscious level. During a conversation we listen to the verbal content and may miss processing signals from another. However, we tend to know when to start and stop talking in a conversation from the facial appearance of our conversation partner, unless we are an inveterate interrupter!

Neuroscience tells us that we have an inbuilt emotional sensitivity to help someone who appears distressed. EI is learned from past experiences, learning about our own emotions and from dealing with life events.

The first key step in developing EI is to become aware of our own emotions. We start by labelling how we feel and can use a scale of 1–10 to gauge our level of emotion. For example, to gain perspective on our emotions – do we feel less or more upset about a current situation when compared with a previous one? This helps us notice patterns of emotion which drive our behaviour and how to deal with future similar situations that arise by calibrating actions to be the same or to act in a different way.

EI is about using our natural emotional sensitivity and the experiences accumulated throughout our lives to be more aware of our emotions and others in our lives. This understanding improves communications and helps to avoid misunderstandings. Our emotions offer valuable and factual information in helping to make sure we best use them and are able to control them.

Goleman (1995) dispels the popular belief that IQ (Intelligence Quotient) is largely responsible for success when reporting that really successful companies clearly want smart people who also need to have high EI – the ability to get along with others and understand how one's own mood and feelings impact on others.

We know that when we are under stress and emotionally raw we are more prone to be reactive, irritable, and insensitive (Kabat-Zinn, 2009) – not great for maintaining healthy relationships. So as stress goes up, EI goes down.

Stress is therefore a key factor in enabling or disabling EI.

How we cope with stress is individually determined and is increasingly referred to as 'resilience.' Some of us thrive and some of us feel debilitated. Those of us who welcome some stress and exhibit resilience in response often explain this as 'I work better under pressure'; usually meaning having the ability to meet 'just in time' deadlines. Those who prefer a different way of working are likely to prepare the lead-up to meeting a deadline and may wish to work towards a detailed plan that guides them smoothly to completion of a particular task or project.

Self-awareness helps us to label stress as a potential barrier or enhancer to our effectiveness and what levels of resilience we possess as a coping mechanism. However, stress seems to be a barrier to relationships that are

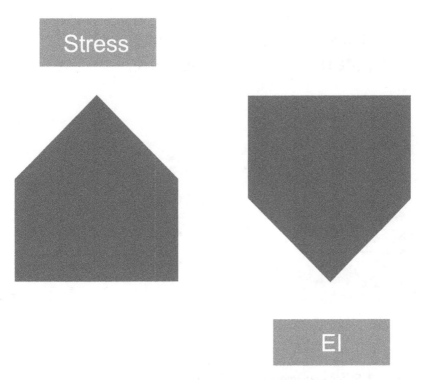

Figure 5.2 The stress/emotional intelligence barometer

'worse off when people are under stress' (Falconier et al., 2014). There are helpful and unhelpful levels of stress and when interacting in a relationship we are working and dealing with the collective stress load. Joining any conversation when stressed is, therefore, unlikely to gain best results. Feeling stressed when we're in a feedback situation is likely to invoke feelings of anxiety leading to one or either of us possibly withdrawing from the conversation or – at the other end of the range – we may become aggressive. Neither of these behaviours or similar reactions are of service during feedback.

Our ability to regulate feelings of stress and to recognise when our performance is impacted by these feelings is a key factor of self-management.

Stress was not identified as a primary theme for The Relational Leadership WAY© so will not be expanded further in this text. You may find, however, this diagram informative as a 'provocation guide' to self-management.

The key to self-management is knowing the triggers that ignite and fuel our negative behaviour and that 'use of self' as a resource in the feedback conversation is complex, fascinating and a continuous source of self-learning data.

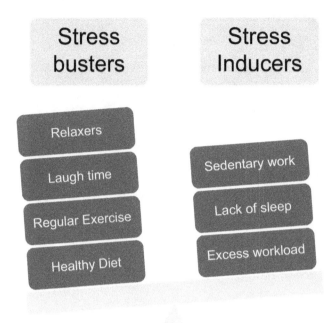

Figure 5.3 Self-management provocation guide

Confidence

It's not surprising to hear that confidence is a contributor to positive self-management. However, observation from the research data shows specifically how confidence enhances coach practice and facilitates a relational approach when entering the feedback conversation:

> 'So the conditions have to be, well I know they have to be right for feedback, but it depends on the individual doesn't it what those conditions are, is that fair to say? ... when I'm coaching my self-esteem is very high – my confidence is at its highest, as anywhere else I've ever been in my life, when I'm not coaching my self-esteem is probably sort of average.'

Building on this pre-condition and strengthening this sense of confidence comes from Bluckert, 2006: 'the ideal is for a substantiating event to emerge in the conversation as immediacy of giving feedback at the time of the incident is reported as being the most effective.' Through attending, observing and sharing observations of what we see, hear and feel, we use ourselves as a 'mirror' for the other person and we raise 'the most pertinent observations to raise awareness' in others.

Growing confidence to feel capable and comfortable develops with the 'knowing' of what is relevant to share as feedback; Bluckert (2006) cites 'self-awareness' as giving us the ability to 'assess when your inner radar screen reads own personal material or client's personal material.' We are reminded in this statement to understand what we, ourselves, may experience in this type of situation. This enables us to differentiate whether what we're 'picking up' is self or client generated. Can we really assume how the recipient is reacting or will react to feedback based solely on observation? What we may be noticing is our own nervousness grounded in a learned sense of how we would feel when receiving this type of feedback. The recipient may have the same feeling. Alternatively, they may have an entirely different perspective and will possibly welcome being alerted to an incident noticed by the giver, especially when reinforced by appropriate evidence noticed 'in the moment.'

Although Bluckert (2006) refers to 'use of self' as a research tool which he suggests 'usually seems like a risky thing to do,' his observation may be relevant in the feedback discussion. He believes that use of self 'is possibly the highest value intervention you can make'; believing this approach can deepen the relationship.

My observations are that there appear to be mixed views about the use of self. Gestalt practitioners similar to Bluckert (2006) reinforce his view about the practitioner actively disclosing in the conversation. Others prefer the practitioner to avoid biasing the conversation through 'use of self.' The Clean Language (www.cleanlanguage.co.uk) questioning framework used to help clients gain insights into their chosen topic uses a prescriptive set of questions created to remove practitioner bias. My experience of beneficial 'use of self' is where disclosure is in the form of 'I am noticing my reaction to hearing that is' rather than making a directive statement that discloses a personal opinion.

Mutual trust is a well reported 'prior condition' for increasing a sense of security and confidence to feel safe in working with whatever may emerge in the feedback conversation.

Building trust in relationships

We know that trust does not necessarily spontaneously manifest in a relationship and usually, although not always, has to be worked at to stimulate the type of confidence needed for feedback.

A Gestalt tool helps us with a planned approach to building trust by using components of trust based on observations from coaching practice. There are a number of values and assumptions that most practitioners appear to share according to Zinker (1994):

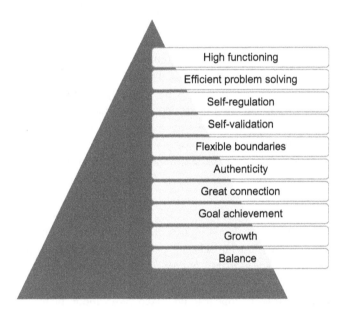

High functioning

Efficient problem solving

Self-regulation

Self-validation

Flexible boundaries

Authenticity

Great connection

Goal achievement

Growth

Balance

Figure 5.4 Values and assumptions for building trust (based on Zinker, 1994)

Kosfeld et al. (2005) offers an alternative by directing us to 'oxytocin' as increasing trust in humans. The claim is that 'trust pervades human societies and is indispensable in friendship, love, families and organizations.' Gregory (2012) agrees that oxytocin is increasingly shown as triggering a wide variety of physical and psychological effects in both women and men. The hormone's influence on our behaviour and physiology originates by being produced in the hypothalamus part of the brain. The oxytocin transfers to the pituitary gland for release into the bloodstream. Oxytocin receptors are found in cells throughout the body and similar to antennas picking up a signal. Levels of the hormone tend to be higher during both stressful and socially bonding experiences; it's like a hormone of attachment and creates feelings of calm and closeness.

A stream of studies in the last decade has focused on oxytocin's effects on body and mind with a similar quest for improving relationships. We can now add 'acceptance of feedback from generative relationships' to the list. A mix of biological stimuli, emotion and cognitive reasoning come together as a powerful cocktail for developing the confidence to feel relaxed and competent for what may be difficult discussions. Oxytocin is a natural resource within us, so why not use it?

Strozzi-Heckler (2009) of the Strozzi Institute in the USA believes we can identify tendencies we have in relationships and train ourselves to recognise motivations, dreams and fears in others. When our body is congruent with our story we are in harmony, at our best and create trust. 'Silent messages' between our bodies generate feelings of why we trust someone or not. This activity is reinforced in neuroscience, discovering the connection we have between our own and others' brain and body and through the recognition of the capabilities of oxytocin. In this approach, known as embodied learning or somatics, the belief is that when we're under pressure our 'history' presents. This history is learned and can be seen in our bodily movements.

JR's perception of feedback developed through experiences within the family. His mother – a perfectionist – expected JR to excel in everything. She repeatedly punctuated his efforts with the words 'you can do better.' Limbic resonance registered with JR that 'he wasn't good enough.'

Similar experiences embed in our nervous system and mould our shape in a single moment; this accumulates over time.

JR became very successful in his career through continuously striving to improve himself and become the 'perfect' person he believed was essential to gain acceptance. Although all this hard work paid off in career success JR's self-efficacy went down a different track. JR was anxious about being 'found out' as 'not good enough' and consequently not deserving of the position he worked so hard to achieve; a situation we now know as 'impostor syndrome.'

We have all been 'conditioned' in some way; if the result works for us, great; if not, and this goes unobserved, this negative conditioning controls us.

The Strozzi Institute (http://strozzinstitute.com) gives examples of how we may receive and transmit signals and their impact on whether we feel trust:

- 'Moving away' from pressurised situations means a person may disconnect physically by moving to a space where they feel safe
- 'Moving against' and resisting the pressure gives individuals a feeling of safety in connection
- 'Moving towards' is making friends and acquiescing to feel safe.

According to the Strozzi Institute, if we can feel our centre of gravity we can make a preferred choice about how we react.

Picture the image where a leader's conditioning manifests in behaviour demonstrating 'holding self back' or 'holding breath' in the presence of others. The leader is likely to move into a state of control and 'move away' (disconnect) and remain unconnected to people unless this state is recognised. This is clearly not ideal for fulfilling a leadership role of fully engaging and motivating employees to deliver their best work.

Transferring this work to the feedback conversation and by being 'connected' we are better placed to observe and learn what we notice in the 'body' of the other. This enables us to act purposefully through reacting appropriately, builds trust in the relationship and creates more efficient conditions leading to emergent change.

Practising 'being centred' – more on this in Chapter 6 – enables us to overcome some of the obstacles we may feel about discussing feedback. By removing any barriers created by limbic resonance creating learned reactions we have more effective conversations. Although not impossible, it is difficult to 'think' ourselves different. We can, however, become more aware of our embodied learning and take steps to 'undo' the past. One way of doing this is developing a 'centred presence' and habitually bringing ourselves back to this state.

Developing a 'centred presence' can be achieved, for those of us preferring a physical routine to effect personal change, by practising body work routines using a 'Jo' staff and based on Aikido Lomi Body Work. During this practice 'felt' senses alert us to notice habitual patterns and through this awareness we are able to notice our mood and to change our patterns. This enables us to have more choice about the way we act out in situations and encourages others to do the same.

If this approach appeals to you get more information from the Strozzi Institute: https://strozziinstitute.com

Recognising how we react, centre and respond to situations builds trust!

Compassion

What is compassion, why is it important in feedback and how does it materialise within us? There are two schools of thought about compassion in the workplace:

Table 5.1 The upside and downside of showing compassion

The 'upside' of showing compassion	The 'downside' of showing compassion
• Enhances working relationships	• Reduces the 'toughness' of resilience needed for these turbulent times
• Diffuses the frustration, discomfort and anger caused when mistakes happen	• Dilutes accountability
• Easier to identify learning opportunities	• Slows operations needing agile responsiveness
• Motivates people to be responsible for own learning	• Viewed as weakness and eroding the role of leadership
• Allows the brain to restructure and develop	• Overcompensates for lack of competence.

If you are already questioning the efficacy of empathy and compassion in the workplace – think again!

Seppala (2015) raises the question: 'How should we react when an employee is not performing well or makes a mistake?' Frustration is acknowledged as a natural response to the traditional approach of reprimand. This action releases our tension and may send messages to other team members. However, an alternative response route is suggested in this text; one of compassion and curiosity. This chapter uses research to show that 'compassion and curiosity produces more powerful results and increases employee loyalty and trust. Feelings of warmth and positive relationships have a greater say over employee loyalty than the size of their pay check.'

We know feedback makes sense and can be rewarding when well delivered. At work we like to know we're doing a good job and that our contribution makes a difference. What seems reasonable with this mindset is that we can assume our work is at least acceptable and at best valued in the absence of being told otherwise.

Unfortunately, we know of many instances where feedback is ignored, withheld or given without sensitivity. We've all probably had life experiences when feedback has been mishandled in our judgement and when feedback has been handled well.

Brené Brown (2016) is well known for her work on 'vulnerability' and quoting from her research exposes what 'blame' is:

- 'Blame is simply the discharging of discomfort and anger
- People who blame a lot seldom have the tenacity and grit to actually hold people accountable because of spending energy raging for 15 seconds and figuring out whose fault something is
- Blaming's very corrosive in relationships.'

We hear of the more enlightened approach of 'seeing mistakes as learning opportunities' which is clearly aligned to accepting that sometimes things don't turn out as anticipated, and only by reviewing the event do we identify what to do differently another time. Basic learning theory pivots on the formula: Plan – Do – Review – Adapt; an encouraging motivator for people taking responsibility for their own learning.

However, the 'carrot and stick' theory of scientific management created by Taylor (1911) continues over a century later! Clearly, a different agenda operates in those needing to blame rather than taking the more rational approach of learning theory. Whatever the motives or unconscious drivers of this behaviour, the result is the same – debilitating when present in feedback conversations.

Gregory (2012) combines shame with blame as being evident in many educational, family and social systems. Shame being an existential feeling that can become toxic and block development by changing brain structure. Approaching feedback, therefore, through a 'blaming/shaming' lens of passing the responsibility for errors to another with the purpose of evoking shame will likely discourage rather than encourage learning potential. A more beneficial approach comes from neuroscience, demonstrating that compassion opens the channels of empathy, allowing the brain to restructure and develop; therefore, encouraging a will to learn through feedback.

Giving feedback tagged with a 'blame and shame' label does not resolve the issue. Exercising compassion opens our minds to caring about the other who may not even be responsible for the action attracting blame. Adopting this mindset encourages discovery of the root cause(s) of mistakes, and stimulates seeking possibilities for new ways of working, new design, new innovations. The challenge is how to remain present, exercise compassion and not slip into a closed mindset 'blamer' mode if this is a practised and reflexive mode of being.

What is compassion?

Green (2014) believes that showing compassion is not about 'softening the blow with false praise, but by giving bad news straight and then offering some breathing room.' She advocates giving the rest of the afternoon off when delivering some particularly hard-to-hear news. I wonder what effect this has on nurturing an authentic relationship between the giver and the receiver?

We are prompted by Gilbert (2009b) that people who experience 'self-criticism may struggle to feel reassured or safe,' affecting a sense of well-being. A tangible act of compassion 'gives a sense of creating an environment conducive to clients being kind to themselves, enabling a healthy approach to personal development.' Maintaining a place of safety means the giver of feedback being responsive to the client in showing 'empathy, an emotional skill that allows us to respond to others in a meaningful, caring way' (Brown, 2016). However, it's not sufficient to feel empathy; we also need to acquire the skill of applying this to another.

You may have noticed 'compassion' and 'empathy' used interchangeably. There is a difference. Compassion is generally viewed as being more dynamic than the competency of empathy. A simple explanation of empathy is recognising hurt or distress in another. Demonstrating compassion is taking a more proactive step to act and give tangible support to someone we see as 'suffering.' Gilbert (2009b) talks of 'creating conditions for compassion' in a way similar to plants needing specific conditions to grow. Perhaps we can adapt the 'plant' metaphor into nurturing the practice of *feed*back.

The Association of Psychological Science (USA) defines compassion as the 'emotional response when perceiving suffering and involves an authentic desire to help.'

'Compassion and altruistic love have a warm, loving and positive aspect that "stand alone" empathy for the suffering of the other does not have,' suggests Ricard (2015), whose work merges the Eastern Buddhist wisdom and Western sciences.

The Dalai Lama says, 'Compassion is the radicalism of our time.' The quality of compassion has been emphasised by every spiritual leader and philosopher over the ages but rarely practiced (Khuna, 2017).

Neff (2009) reminds us that there are two people in the feedback conversation deserving of compassion:

'Having compassion for oneself is really no different than having compassion for others. Self-compassion involves acting the same way towards yourself when you are having a difficult time, fail, or notice something you don't like about yourself.' This definition encourages us to acknowledge our feelings of hurt or even distress and to reposition our thoughts into focusing on how we can comfort and care for ourselves as well as another in this moment.

We all know the inner voice that harshly judges and criticises us for our shortcomings and inadequacies. Neff (2009) tells us that 'self-compassion means we are kind and understanding when confronted with personal failing. Having compassion for ourselves means that we honor and accept our humanness.' We can remind ourselves that mistakes and failures are learnings – every day is a school day! The more we take and share this view of the human condition, the more we encourage the same approach to compassion in others. In a TED talk Neff (2013) reinforces his concept of self-compassion as including ourselves in the 'circle of compassion' and treating ourselves as we do our friends; as he says, 'we're allowed to be nice to ourselves!'

Accepting ourselves as being human through practising self-compassion enables us to offer compassion to others and to receive it from them. Next time you take a flight, notice how the cabin crew encourage us to first affix our own air mask before attempting to help others with theirs in the case of emergency. We can't take care of others before we take care of ourselves.

Why is compassion important in the feedback discussion?

The influence of demographics and the generational expectations predicted to change the way we relate in the future are likely to demand more of us than our ability to demonstrate emotional intelligence. It won't be enough to understand and manage our own and others' emotions. The interaction between the five anticipated generations in the workplace inevitably brings a deeper level of complexity to the future of work. A broader understanding of capabilities and motivations will be essential for informing and managing the expectations of both management/leadership and of each age group. A strong dose of compassion will inevitably smooth the path of generational interplay. Paradoxically, we need more compassion to cope with increasing demands in the work environment, yet the same environment can create the barriers to stop this happening.

Growing evidence is emerging that younger generations, beginning with millennials, are welcoming and have the expectation of receiving feedback (Sveen, 2015). This is undoubtedly progress for changing a negative image about feedback where this exists and a rejuvenation of obsolete performance management systems. What still remains is the human factor and how we relate; it's not what we say, it's how we say it, and the intent driving our observations.

COMPASSION

Compassion for the client	.... I'm a great believer that a coach has to have compassion for the person they're coaching, and also when I coach somebody for them to have compassion for themselves and also compassion for other people .. it's something that comes up a lot,
Compassion for the client	... when I use softer focus it's something to do with, it's something to do with the eyes .. and finding something in them to be compassionate about I think.
	.. definitely a sort of compassion... I hesitate to use the word love .. and the way you look at somebody so that you see the whole person and you're engaging, it feels like I'm engaging all of me in that.

Figure 5.5 Extract from *Creating the Conditions for Receptivity of Feedback* (Lewis, 2014b)

Showing compassion for ourselves and others means we accept the reality of life that none of us is perfect and that generally we're all striving to do our best. We can advocate that by nurturing this attitude we also improve the activity of feedback.

Similarly, my own research gathered observations clearly indicating a willingness and need to show compassion during the feedback conversation.

Extract from *Creating the Conditions for Receptivity of Feedback* (Lewis, 2014b) (see Figure 5.5):

Accepting that compassion attracts reciprocity, the act of caring about others continues to be lacking in the workplace (Seppala, 2015). This is despite an emergence by more well-informed employers who introduce the word 'compassion' into the organisation's business speak and implement wellbeing resources.

Anecdotal comments from my practice suggests that people are too involved with their own survival in fast paced environments to be concerned too much about others.

A glimpse into a manager's familiar 'self-talk' when preparing for the feedback discussion.

Manager's first thought:
'How am I going to get the message across to "J" that the behaviour they're displaying in the team is disruptive and having a negative effective on others?'
Impact of this thought on the giver = Feelings of anxiety
Impact of this thought on this receiver = Not considered

Manager's second thought:
'I can give examples of what team members are complaining about but I don't feel comfortable about giving this type of criticism and naming names.'
Impact of this thought on the giver = Rationalisation of feedback content and conjecture of anticipated negative reaction by 'J'
Impact of thought on this receiver = Not considered

Manager's third thought:
'A better approach may be to organise a team coaching event and brief the facilitator during the diagnostic phase of the programme on the shortfall in J's performance.'
Impact of this thought on the giver = Relief of feelings for self. Abdication from responsibility
Impact of this thought on receiver = Not considered

As we can see, this scenario neither recognises compassion for the 'giver' who experiences anxiety at the prospect of starting this conversation nor empathy for the receiver's feelings. The assumption is that the feedback will be received as criticism although there is no evidence to suggest this will happen. The individual 'J' may welcome knowing that he can improve his performance as a team member and be prepared to discuss ways of achieving this. We don't know until we have the conversation to check it out.

A solution is to ask a few preliminary questions for preparation and to foster the good relations that encourage receptivity of feedback:

• Do we assume understanding of others and believe we can predict underlying causes of behaviour?

- What do we know about the person who irritates us or those who give us a sense of dislocation?
- When we offer feedback, is our motive to support and help improvement or abandon and inflict punishment?

Ideally, the goal of feedback integrating compassion is to create dialogue that transcends ego and generates a fertile environment for change. How do we measure up?

Knowing that we all experience disappointment, rejection and pain at some time in our life seems to imply an easy route to understanding others. However, experience tells us it can be difficult to move beyond our personal agenda and put ourselves in the shoes of others. This is assuming that we're interested in doing so in the first place – a reminder that toxicity still exists in dark corners of some organisations!

Capacity for tolerance depends on the cultural environment informed by leadership style – and by us – we generally need to feel we 'fit in' with expectations! Organisational culture infiltrates relationships and inevitably impacts on performance discussions. Endeavours to display compassion are, therefore, likely to reflect the cultural norm.

We all have the capacity to be unkind, and we also have the ability to be compassionate. We can choose how we react to others. Being non-judgemental and 'not labelling' others is true compassion, argues Tolle (2013), who believes that some people can only show compassion for people in their immediate circle, tribe or family. He believes this happens 'if we conceptualise others in our mind' and develop a 'screen of conceptualisation' which we transfer to all those we consider to be the same, for example, a particular race. The British always talk about the weather, Germans are always punctual, the Dutch are direct in their speech. Conditioning our mind in this way recreates situational relationships which can only be released with self-awareness to transcend these patterns. We have to work harder at building compassion for those lacking membership of our 'immediate circle.'

A simple approach to showing compassion for ourselves and others is simply to mirror beliefs of how we treat ourselves and project these as beliefs on how we treat others (see Figure 5.6).

This diagram invites us to see ourselves 'as a good person' and view others through the same lens. Nurturing these positive views about ourselves and others helps us to be confident about our capability and that of others. The cumulative effect for the giver of feedback is a strengthening desire to lessen any anxiety emerging in the receiver. This relaxes the receiver and triggers

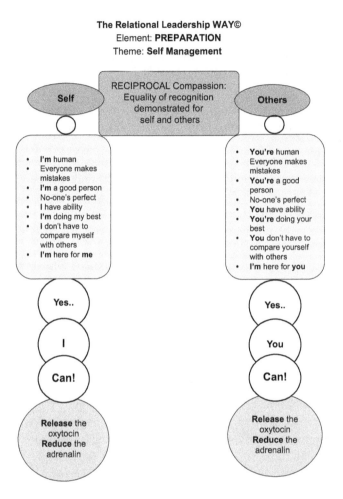

Figure 5.6 Demonstrating reciprocal compassion: The Relational Leadership WAY© Part 1: *What* needs preparing to establish relationships that stimulate

a biological reaction that releases oxytocin and diffuses the body's natural reaction to produce adrenalin when in a situation where feedback is causing anxiety.

Where does compassion come from and how do we develop it?

Neuroscience tells us compassion is already within us!

Siegel (2009) talks of the brain as a social organ that links internal and external experiences. Our brain stem connects neural pathways throughout our bodies with the limbic region enabling us to 'attach' to a caregiver. Our social brain or prefrontal cortex integrates with the neo-cortex which is the thinking or cognitive part of our brain.

Siegel describes the 'Nine Functions of the Prefrontal Cortex of the Brain':

1. Balance body functioning
2. Attunement – crucial for compassion
3. Emotional balance – regulates emotions
4. Response flexibility – ability to pause – mediates impulse and action (act of will)
5. Calms fear – fear modulation
6. Develops insight – self knowing and awareness
7. Empathy – ability to imagine what it feels like for others
8. Morality – for the larger social good
9. Intuition – instant connectedness to all body systems (heart, gut, spleen, brain, etc) – creating integration.

An article by Keltner (2004), reporting on the findings of a study of the biological basis of compassion, indicates that we're 'wired up' to respond to others in need.

Subsequent studies from neuroscience record areas of the brain showing activity when responding to others' suffering and affirm that compassion is an innate human response. The science behind this claim shows that when the hormone oxytocin is biologically released into our bloodstream this promotes nurturing behaviour that lies at the heart of compassion. In studies performed by Keltner (2004), people demonstrating behaviours associated with compassionate love – warm smiles, friendly hand gestures, affirmative forward leans – produced more oxytocin. This suggests that compassion may be self-perpetuating: being compassionate causes a chemical reaction in the body that motivates us to be even more compassionate.

Another signal that compassion already exists within us is the non-verbal cues in facial expressions seen as a concerned gaze. A conversation is more than an exchange of dialogue; we are programmed to be sensitive to non-verbal cues when we are open to address these at a conscious level. More on non-verbal cues features in Chapters 7 and 8. Evidence suggests, therefore, that compassion is deeply rooted in human nature; it has a biological basis in the brain and body.

Other studies indicate that the brain structures involved in positive emotions like compassion are more 'plastic' – subject to changes brought about by environmental input. We can assume, therefore, that compassion is a trait that we can develop further over time and in an appropriate context.

For example, there is evidence that growing up in a nurturing family promotes the development of compassion. We see that compassion is deeply rooted in our brains, our bodies, and in the most basic ways we communicate. What's more, a sense of compassion fosters compassionate behaviour. Simply realising this is not enough; we must also make room for our compassionate impulses to flourish.

We all have the ability to display both positive and negative behaviour: we can be helpful, critical, inspiring, undermining – we choose. In developing compassion for self and others the key is to be aware of the emotions and thoughts that drive these behaviours. Remember the references to flight or fight. Are we feeling threatened by the other and therefore becoming evasive, withdrawn, defensive or aggressive? If we experience these behaviours in ourselves at the thought of impending feedback, we need to calm these and activate the opposite behaviours to nurture and mobilise self-compassion. If we sense or detect that the other in the relationship is feeling or exhibiting these, it's time for us to trigger our compassion for them. The practice of mindfulness supports us in our endeavour for being our compassionate selves; more on this in Chapter 6.

Drawing on the work of Gilbert (2010b) helps us outline the skills for compassion:

Table 5.2 Skills for compassion (based on Gilbert, 2010b)

Skill	Effect in the feedback conversation
Attention: how we observe, listen, remember	Shows genuine interest and helps to balance negativity with positivity; a 'can do' culture
Reasoning: objective thinking	Demonstrates willingness to refocus and find a way to move from dilemmas to productive solutions and outcomes with honesty and transparency
Caring: being kind to self and others	Being transparent about change being painful, not always easy and demonstrating a willingness to help others flourish
Positive intent: well meaning conversations	Shows sensitivity and interest in retention of employees
Tolerance: celebrating diversity	Demonstrates tolerance in respecting a range of cultural norms with being judgmental

Figure 5.7 An awareness spiral of self towards compassion and being human (Gregory, 2012)

All this talk of empathy and compassion may leave us thinking – well, that's all very well but how do we fit in all this soul searching and caring for others into the complex and volatile world in which we operate? There just isn't time! Whilst not entirely agreeing with this premise, Hinsliff (2017) takes the view that we are overdosing on empathy and suggests that 'kindness can, in some senses, be a weakness. Feelings aren't everything. Empathy might be making the world a worse place, not a better one. Kindness can, in some senses, be a weakness.' He does, however, shift his views on reading Bloom (2017), who favours social intelligence as a way 'to understand why other people feel as they do even when the feeling is completely alien to you.' Bloom's (2017) main theme seems to be 'less heart, more head; less gooey emoting, more objectivity and distance, allowing for a fairer assessment of who really deserves our compassion. Don't just feel. Use your brain, and think.'

The ability to strengthen our resolve and show resilience in the face of adversity comes to mind, with the suggestion of moving away from being empathic towards brain power. The proliferation of available text and trainings seems to reinforce the antidote of resilience as the solution to coping with our turbulent times. My question is, does this mean we're no longer able to show that sometimes we find it difficult to cope and that we must always be able to 'bounce back' and be resilient, whatever obstacles life puts our way?

Being compassionate does not mean avoiding engaging with painful behavioural tasks such as delivering difficult feedback. It is about being courageous. Helping the client to have courage requires clear collaboration on 'the new behaviour' as a compassionate intervention (Gilbert, 2010b).

Basically, in this preparation stage of feedback let's remember that both are human beings in this relationship. We each have our feelings and our ego to protect. If the feedback is particularly difficult to deliver for us with the potential of being received negatively, emotions will run high, and this is not the time to point score or assert a particular position. If we wish to nurture positive and caring working relationships, then feedback empathically and compassionately prepared – if not given or received as the proverbial gift – can become the breakthrough solution for reaching a joint winner's podium.

How we do what we do is more important than what we do!

Theme 2 of The Relational Leadership WAY©: Readiness for Feedback with the sub-theme of Impactfulness

Readiness for feedback

Gauge the gravity of the feedback and plan to match!

The definition of the **readiness for feedback** theme in the context of this text is the ability of the giver of feedback to gauge when the other is likely to be receptive to hearing opinions based on others' perceptions of them; both affirming and developmental.

> Harriet may know she gets irritable when under pressure to deliver, but she doesn't necessarily want to hear that from someone else, however well-intentioned the feedback may be.

Impactfulness as a sub-theme of 'readiness for feedback' determines how the feedback may be received by asking us to reflect on possible scenarios that signal how the other may react. The suggestion is not to assume we know how it will be received as this is likely to reflect our personal lens of how we might react. We may unconsciously be projecting this view on to others. Having awareness that the receiver can react in various ways to feedback is sufficient – without determining what the scenarios may be – to give us a sense of preparedness for whatever emerges in response to what we have to say.

Richie lacks confidence in his ability and is likely to react negatively to anything but praise about his performance. He assumes everyone thinks and feels this way and as he 'likes to be liked' will actively avoid giving anything other than praise to others.

Regular and frequent feedback conversations enable changes to be made before they become too big to be easily remedied. In situations other than this ideal we need educative strategies. A classic example and a cause of 'early leavers' is the failure to support and provide feedback during the induction period. New entrants lacking understanding of what's expected and how to gain support feel disenchanted with the onboarding process. Extending this beyond induction and finding performance management lacking from corporate vocabulary or neglected in its delivery will inevitably colour people's willingness and readiness for feedback.

The ideal for guaranteeing a reciprocal attitude or 'positive readiness for feedback' really depends on making feedback part of the cultural fabric of the organisation. If we know that feedback emerges routinely in conversations, we know to expect it, we already have experience of it and we recognise the benefits.

People will be used to sharing expectations, celebrating impressive successes, feeling motivated to excel and taking responsibility for personal development. We can encourage a climate of continuous improvement culture even if we remain mindful that feedback is not relished by many!

The easiest way of determining **readiness for feedback** is simply to ask the other party what their thoughts are about this activity. Usual practice in coaching/mentoring is to cover the topic in the 'contracting' conversation which has the advantage of alerting each to the prospect. Whether this reveals a true sense of how each is feeling may remain unknown until feedback occurs.

We need to know that we're both as curious as each other about what will be revealed in the conversation. This willingness for reflection and introspection determines the 'availability' or 'coachability' of the receiver of feedback. When this is lacking, a feedback conversation may be more damaging than developmental.

However, the experience of an unprepared conversation, when feedback is not anticipated, can reveal unexpected surprises. If unanticipated feedback does emerge, either or both may feel reluctant to venture into what may appear as unfamiliar territory; fear of the unknown. Revealing an unwillingness to participate in feedback when the conversation is in flow can be both embarrassing and time wasting.

An unprepared feedback conversation:
The manager may say following a request for change in behaviour: 'I'm really pleased you agree with me about the need for change,' and at the same time may be thinking: 'I notice you nod in agreement, but I'm not convinced you mean this and I don't feel confident about challenging what I'm sensing.'

The direct report, noticing hesitancy in the line manager's statement, may be thinking: 'I've shown I agree but I'm not seeing this is good enough; what else am I supposed to do to convince them I'm fine with the changes needed?'

Some possible outcomes from this scenario:
Line manager thinks

- I wish I hadn't started this conversation
- Maybe I should have predicted feedback might come up and been more prepared
- I feel more disengaged now with this person than I did before
- I don't trust this person will behave any differently

Direct report thinks

- I feel put on the spot
- I wish I'd been given some notice that we were going to talk about this
- I don't seem to be able to do anything right
- I don't feel trusted and I don't trust this manager is looking after my best interests.

Each person has to be prepared to play a part if feedback is to add the intended value. Sensitivity, transparency and clarity in managing expectations all encourage positivity for feedback exchange and represent the best we can do to avoid surprise and resistance once the conversation has started.

Giving feedback can be stressful for both parties. Including both participants, therefore, the 'preparation' stage makes it a prerequisite to explore feelings about feedback and evaluate perceptions and willingness to participate.

Similarly, gauging the receptivity to feedback during the discussion means focused attention by both to sustain the quality of the relationship as the conversation unfolds. Missing these cues and ending a conversation with, 'By the way, several complaints have been made from team members about your unresponsiveness to requests for support; take a look at it,' is likely to be a 'conversation stopper' and counterproductive to encouraging improvement. What is absolutely unacceptable is giving individual developmental feedback in the company of an audience.

The practice of feedback and co-creation of the relationship are not explicitly referenced in 7 conversations for the coaching conversation offered by Clutterbuck (2008). However, he introduces the practice of *preparation* to 'ensure the coach and client are mentally prepared':

'Conversation 1: My dialogue with myself before the session;
Conversation 2: The client's inner dialogue before the session.'

The concept of 'preparation and setting the scene' for coaching appears again in Jarvis et al. (2006), who state that 'coaching works best when the individual is both a willing and an informed participant.' We can include feedback, although it is not explicitly referenced. An extract of data from my own research endorses this view: 'it's about the readiness to do the work, a readiness to learn something about themselves' and to 'engage in something that I don't know quite where it's going to go but am quite willing to get something from it.'

Similarly, David et al. (2013) remind us in their reference to coaching that 'it's easy to assume that a ... client is ready... that isn't always the case.' They suggest a 'readiness spin on the initial getting to know you conversation with the client' by acknowledging that much can be gained from 'observing physiology, language and motivation.' Feedback is not included in their suggested questions for this conversation. However, they do ask 'what is your energy level for coaching right now?'

Grant (2006) suggests we 'need to explicitly assess the [other's] readiness for change.' Similarly, for 'successful change to occur the individual needs to be willing to believe that the target behaviour is important' (Passmore & Whybrow, 2008).

When comparing Locke and Latham's theory (1990) with other research, David et al. (2013) found that people with 'learning goal orientations' are 'more likely to seek and benefit from feedback than those with a performance goal orientation' (VandeWalle et al., 2000). They believe that even people with a strong learning orientation will make judgments on what feedback to listen to, on the basis of receptivity, the perceived credibility of the ... source, individual differences (e.g. openness to experience, curiosity) and emotional skills (David et al., 2013 p.14).

Attachment styles (Bowlby, 1973) refer to a person's internal working models of relationships developed in childhood, and comprise three different categories: anxious, avoidant, and secure attachment. This theory suggests we subconsciously hold this model in mind even as an adult, and as such consideration of the relationship between the giver and the receiver in feedback conversations can be very complex. Being given feedback by someone who reminds you of or you associate with a 'voice of authority' in your past and who you perceived as controlling and suppressive is unlikely to engender a positive reaction to any comments received, however well-intentioned the giver. Any hint of being reminded of the teacher who vomited a red pen across your homework or the bully who saw you as sport for ridicule is unlikely to persuade you to their opinion of you. *The SAGE Handbook of Mentoring* (2017) offers a range of studies examining the influence of individual attachment styles on mentoring processes such as feedback seeking, feedback acceptance and the willingness to mentor.

The willingness to engage in feedback is determined by several factors open to question.

Emotional capacity

- How do I cope with the feelings that feedback may elicit in me?
- How do I manage the impact the feedback may have on the other person in this relationship?

Knowledge capacity

- What do I know about giving | receiving feedback?
- What is the purpose of giving | receiving feedback?
- What do I see at the value?
- How ethical is the source of feedback?

System capacity

- What is likely to happen as a result of engaging with feedback?
- What are the repercussions of avoiding this feedback conversation?
- How will feedback affect ongoing relationships beyond the immediate feedback discussion?

Timing capacity

- How do I know when to give feedback?
- Is giving feedback at the point of observation always good practice?
- What do I need to consider before I offer or receive feedback?

Figure 5.8 Factors affecting the willingness to engage in feedback

Impactfulness

The research data identified that clients increasingly expect feedback to be integral to the coaching conversation. At the same time, the data gave indicators of reactions to the feedback content. These reactions informed the sub-theme of **impactfulness** highlighting the rationale for recognising the personal challenges and emotional pressure intrinsically intertwined in feedback:

> 'I like to win people's approval. If I'm going to give hard feedback that's counter to my natural inclination to stay in rapport and to seek their approval, there's some discomfort around 'he's not going to like this' and 'he's not going to like me.' Giving feedback is quite a courageous thing to do I think and it's a bit scary. So – there's all this wrapped up in it that's all put at risk, but the coaching is about them, not about me, and you have to stay with it and stick with it.
>
> So, I strongly suspect the fear will always be there. I think it's the deep psychological need for human beings to want to gain approval from each other. That obviously varies from person to person but as human beings we all have a need to be socially approved of. And if you're going to give feedback to somebody, they might not like you for it.'

This co-researcher's observation demonstrates the emotion generated by the prospect of giving feedback and also concern for the impact of that feedback for both the giver and receiver. The impact of feedback can be 'felt' by those with a strong level of self-awareness able to detect changes in 'body language.' Being relational is how we relate to others, how we relate to ourselves and how we relate consequently to feedback.

Creating 'readiness for feedback' and being sympathetic to 'impactfulness' acknowledges our social and emotional needs, as illustrated by Kline (2017) referring to 'Thinking Enhancers' and 'Thinking Inhibitors':

Table 5.3 Thinking enhancers (Kline, 2017)

Thinking enhancers: We think best when...
• We know we are respected
• We trust our own intelligence
• Our minds are free of fear

(continued)

Table 5.3 *(continued)*

- Our ideas will affect a specific outcome
- We are seeking the best idea, not trying to win
- People show interest and delight in us
- We have accurate and complete information
- We are in charge and not being exploited
- We are not rushed
- Our questions are welcomed
- We are asked incisive questions
- We are engaged in work that expresses our values
- We are in active pursuit of our dreams and goals
- Stereotypes and oppressive attitudes are not tolerated
- We are at ease
- We think well of ourselves
- Everyone in the group is given a chance to think and speak
- We know specifically how we are appreciated
- The physical environment says back to us, 'You matter'
- We are encouraged to think beyond the usual
- Our physical bodies are comfortable and respected
- We are in caring relation to others.

Table 5.4 Thinking Inhibitors (Kline, 2017)

Thinking inhibitors: We think least well when we are in the presence of...

- Ridicule
- Competition
- Intimidation
- Perfectionism
- Cynicism
- Criticism
- Powerlessness
- Self-doubt
- Formality
- Physical discomfort
- Seduction
- Low expectations
- Addiction
- Stereotyping.

A client of mine gives an example of 'best intentions' for feedback not meeting the reality of receptivity. A leading financial services organisation intent on escalating performance management introduced the concept of a feedback culture. The virtues of espoused willingness to give and expect feedback on capability, influence on others and future expected performance was communicated throughout the business. Amazing result! 'Everyone accepts hearing what others think whatever their role in the organisation.'

Discreetly digging deeper with the client revealed a reality of individuals declaring unhappiness with what was described as 'anything goes' in what people think they can say about you. This was generating anxiety, defensiveness and retaliation depending on psychological reactions.

A story of good intention, undermined by a subculture reacting to an underestimation of the emotional impact on some of this free-flow feedback climate.

How many well-orchestrated projects fail because of lack of attention to the emotional impact of leading change without sensitive feedback on the human agenda?

Dedicating preparation time pays dividends in exploring 'readiness for feedback' and how individuals are likely to react to the impact of what they may perceive as criticism, however well intended the dialogue.

I think this case study is a reminder of the advantages of predicting without assuming what the likely impact of feedback may be AND we also have to be mindful of the 'after-effects' once the feedback is given.

Referencing the work of Kubler-Ross, & Kessler, (2005) based on emotional states of terminally ill patients offers a framework for transposing feedback to each stage and evaluating the possible outcomes. The model has received criticism about the lack of empirical evidence and nevertheless is useful as a concept informing how people *may* react to the prospect of feedback:

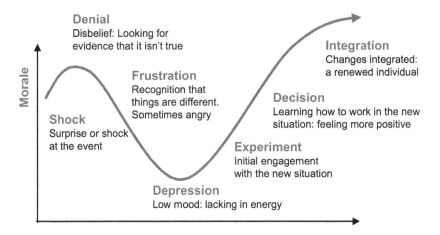

Figure 5.9 Kubler-Ross change curve

Table 5.5 Using the Kubler-Ross change curve to demonstrate reaction to feedback

1. Denial	• At this stage the recipient believes the feedback is 'wrong' and prefers to hold on to their own perception of reality, or they can just ignore the feedback
2. Self-pity	• When the recipient reflects on the 'evidence' supporting the feedback and realises 'denial' is no longer an option they become frustrated and adopt a 'victim' stance: 'it's not fair' – 'I always get the blame' – 'people just don't bother to try to understand me' – 'why is this happening to me?'
3. Rationalising	The recipient realises that to move on they have choices including: • withdrawing completely and ignoring the feedback • starting to believe there may be some truth in the feedback • seeking further clarification about the feedback
4. Exploring	• Gathering further information about the feedback
5. Moving on	• I think what's best for me is to leave the organisation • I now understand what I need to do to work at the level expected for my role • I want to seek support to help me improve my performance at work.

Giving sympathetic attention to the 'preparation' stage of the feedback conversation is the foundation stone for effective feedback. We may believe we don't always have time for this, and that may be the situation, especially for emergent feedback conversations. Sometimes short-term gains create issues in the longer term and may be more time consuming and damaging to working relationships.

Part 2 of The Relational Leadership WAY© 6

Active engagement in co-creating generative conversations through adopting relational behaviours

Themes in this chapter

1. Objectivity:
   - How we develop the ability to 'step outside' and objectively assess what's happening and the quality of the relationship through being non-judgemental and aware of personal biases.
2. Mindfulness:
   - Maintaining and sustaining awareness of connectivity through total focus on all aspects within the relationship and in the conversation without prejudice or judgement.
3. Presence:
   - Being fully 'in the moment' with each other to create a stronger relational connection
   - Working together and staying 'connected' in the relationship and knowing when 'interrupting' this flow produces a different dynamic for different results
   - Generating 'balance' and being 'grounded' to avoid distraction and maintain focus in the conversation.

4. Timing of Feedback:
   - 'Tuning in' with the other to predict when to introduce feedback and when it's appropriate to move the conversation forward to create an entry for feedback.

Introduction to Part 2 of The Relational Leadership WAY©: taking the initiative and activating a 'relational way of being'

The Scout motto 'Be Prepared' was created in 1907 by Robert Baden-Powell, the founder of the youth movement. The motto has stood the test of time in encouraging 'a state of readiness in mind and body' for every eventuality. This sentiment is equally transferable and meaningful for the first level of The Relational Leadership WAY©. The intention is to prepare ourselves as best we can for all eventualities in the feedback conversation – we cannot assume how each of us will react to what is said!

Once we've completed the **preparation** enabling our state of readiness for a feedback conversation, how else can we behave to lubricate and ease the real or perceived tensions triggered by the prospect of feedback?

In this chapter I introduce the next group of themes surfacing from the research (Lewis, 2014b). These combine as Part 2 of The Relational Leadership WAY©. These themes detail what enables us to **instigate** and **activate** within ourselves a 'relational way of being.' By applying these themes within the conversation we cultivate conducive conditions for creating and sustaining a trusting environment. This stimulates us to *really* want to talk to and encourage generative dialogue with each other. Our common goal is to gain new knowledge about ourselves. We can become more conscious of how others perceive us and what expectations are reasonable for workplace performance. This springboard of security encourages us and others to work with feedback without fear of being judged, intimidated or daunted by the prospect of what may emerge as the dialogue unfolds.

Next you have a short overview of themes as introduction to the deeper examination of each that follows:

Objectivity is demonstrated by constructing feedback impartially and controlling our biases without speculation or judgement. This means leaving out of the conversation any interpretation of how we see a situation or making a supposition that feeds our ego. A colleague recently shared with me how a member of a selection board said in a deprecating tone after being interviewed as an internal candidate: 'You could have done better; we expected more of you.' Our commitment to behaving in a relational way is established in how we encourage others to bring perspective to the topic discussed. We achieve this by viewing feedback as a cooperative activity with dual responsibility. Any hint of power dynamics erodes objectivity and destroys the ethos of a learning partnership!

Practising **mindfulness** is now popular as a technique for improving our concentration in the continuously changing complex world in which we strive to function and to be the best we can in the moment. Mindfulness gives us a welcome break from our 'brain busyness' and helps us focus on a reflective space that re-energises our brain function. With practice we avoid being distracted away from conversation when the other may be rather more elaborate in their delivery than can hold our attention span. We may not want to hear every detail of every moment of another's recollection of a workplace conversation. 'I said … and then he said … to which I replied … and then they said … which made me say …' You get the picture. There may be times when we do need to be fully aware in a similar dialogue and practising mindfulness helps us relax and concentrate with full attention.

How we activate **presence** is to be openly available for others and as we speak to notice and engage with what is happening 'in real time' moment by moment. When a behaviour shows up that is indicative of the topic being discussed we draw attention to this and use this powerful resource of immediacy to guide the conversation. An example from 360 profile reporting may show a tendency towards volatile behaviour. Sharing this with the individual may incite just such a volatile reaction, paradoxically disputing any behaviour of this type. We can immediately work with this 'in the moment' behaviour as an illustration of what others may perceive as aggressive behaviour. How the conversation evolves depends on how well both fulfil a 'relational way of being' that verbally deescalates emotion to a level for constructive discussion.

There is a range of strategies that develop the ability to work 'in the moment'. We can create **flow** enabling us to spontaneously 'clear our mind' and **break flow** when a change in dynamic facilitates different thinking.

Encouraging **flow** will 'reap great reward' in generating information to 'draw on when choosing to give feedback,' said one of the research study participants. There are also occasions when we serve our clients more effectively by discouraging harmony (**breaking flow**) and that this state may actually be necessary for feedback to effect change. The proposal of creating 'disharmony' causing 'discomfort' supports the claim that without this 'there'll be no shift' (in behaviour). Clients of study participants recorded the sensation of 'breaking flow' as being 'slightly uncomfortable' and generating 'inner resistance.' We don't welcome the forced move away from effortless dialogue to the disruption of staccato discourse. Perhaps this testifies to the claim that change happens when we step out of our 'comfort zone' and is an alert for us to work with this state.

The research exploring knowing when the **timing of feedback** has optimum effect elicited diverse suggestions from either going to source and 'asking the client when the time is right' to acting on conjecture and 'reacting to a signal from the client.' 'Asking the client when the time is right' does seem the obvious approach. However, experience tells me that this response comes from a rational state that can easily be disrupted at the prospect of feedback that may be less than favourable: a rose by any other name may *not* smell as sweet after all. Clients of the study participants generally preferred to rely on their coach 'knowing' when to provide feedback, reinforcing the predilection of some coaches for 'judging' when the time is right. Whether this suggests waiting passively for feedback or dependency that there is trust in the strength of the relationship remains unclear. What is clear is the lack of overt agreement about the inclusion of this fundamental contribution to people development, reinforcing the recommendation for being **proactive in the timing** as this stage of the framework suggests. Being decisive about when to give feedback also encourages preparation for delivery.

With the prerequisite that feedback is transformational, 'the data point to the inevitable conclusion: the engine of change is the client' (Bohart & Tallman, 1999) and who consequently activates the desire leading to new learning of self. The implication is that we spend our time more wisely gaining experience on ways to employ the client in the process of change (Duncan et al., 2004). How prepared really is the client to receive potentially unsolicited 'in the moment' feedback – 'learning occurs through the examination of here and now experience' (Bluckert, 2006) – and how does this affect the relationship as a vehicle for improving performance? Similarly, if 'coaching cannot take place unless there is a high level of trust ... and ... needs to account for the level of risk that both parties take ... how you conduct yourself will set the tone for the meeting' (Morgan, 2013 e-conference). We cannot, therefore, assume that the client will actively or routinely engage in feedback; we know the maxim 'you can bring the horse to water but you can't make it drink!' These references suggest a need for fostering the right conditions and engaging both parties in strengthening the probability of creating a trusting relationship. If this sounds effortless, we should remind ourselves that a highly developed sense of self-awareness is needed to self-monitor for any indicators of compliance with the conversation flow and being led away from challenging it and neglecting feedback!

Given these potential hurdles to overcome, a parallel seems to exist between how each *approaches* feedback and the *expectations* of both from the conversation. A coach has to 'bring her own presence (bringing yourself) in order to be a contributing partner' (O'Neill, 2000). My curiosity is about how we manifest this reference to 'presence'; what prompts us to know when the time is right to offer feedback, in what format will it be delivered and how do we 'know' the client will be responsive?

Theme 3 of The Relational Leadership WAY©: Objectivity

Dilthey (1976) wanted to know, 'How can an individually constructed consciousness reconstruct – and thereby know objectively – the distinct individuality of another?'

A good question! Are we expecting too much of ourselves to truly practice impartiality towards another? This section recognises that being human means we cannot be totally objective in the way of programmed robotics. The text seeks to inform some of the pitfalls that being human creates and how we can counteract these to lessen any damaging effects from the subjectivity inherent in our human condition.

We know that reality means different things to different people. Take the example of friends discussing a shared incident that happened a while ago; possibly a trip taken or a conversation about a shared memory. Accepting that the event is well-remembered, both will have a vivid recall of what they believe happened or was talked about. The surprise comes when the discussion recalls different stories! Of course, each person believes their recollection is the right one, and well we know how the rest of the conversation goes! Difference in recall of friendship stories may not have too many repercussions. When we're dealing with feedback we need facts and to check out what fit our sense of reality has with another's. As always, it's best not to assume we know the full story and to enter a feedback conversation with curiosity about another's viewpoint; the first step to demonstrating 'objectivity.'

Objectivity is probably unachievable in its purest sense. We have to make judgements about others to satisfy our innate survival need for safety. However, we are able to become aware of our personal biases and prejudices that are likely to encourage us to be judgemental and display stereotypical behaviour. Different value sets, beliefs and attitudes will propagate different agendas. If we sense dissonance with another the source may well be conflicting values. We now have a choice of whether we step into self-management mode and 'park' our differences or whether we disclose our observations and discuss together how perceived differences may impact the relationship and the action to take. This helps us prepare for using our differences as a resource that achieves a positive and useful outcome through working with, and not against, the relationship.

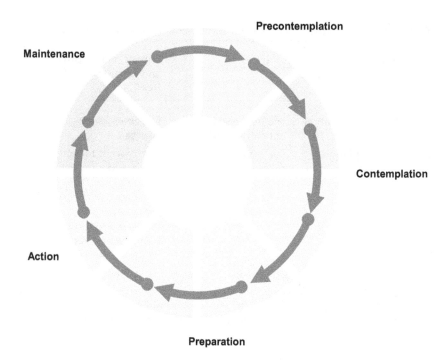

Figure 6.1 Stages of readiness for change (Prochaska and DiClemente, 1992)
Adaptation of 'stages of change' model

Easier said than done, you rightly challenge! Well, if we're conscious that this phenomenon is likely to occur or is already occurring this is a further step towards 'objectivity.' Prochaska and DiClemente's Transtheoretical Stages of Change model (1992) suggested behaviour change as a dynamic process that occurs in a sequenced and cyclical order (see Figure 6.1).

My view of this model is not to expect change to occur immediately after feedback is given. As humans we need time to ponder on the need for change and to come to terms with the discomfort that change generates. Only when we start to accept that change is inevitable within a given context can we begin to test out and adopt new behaviours. Both as givers and receivers of feedback, another solution to being objective is to have patience and belief that change will happen, given space (see Table 6.1).

Being objective can sometimes create a sense of tension in relationships. The research illustrated this with a co-researcher's definition of how the pendulum swings to strike a balance between subjective personal needs and objective professional practice:

Table 6.1 Applying the Prochaska and DiClemente model (1992) to feedback

No	Stage	Effect	Impact on receptivity and acceptance of feedback
1	Pre-contemplation	The new behaviour is not considered	Feedback is initially rejected
2	Contemplation	The new behaviour contemplated	Feedback is reflected on driving information seeking about the behaviour to change No other action towards adopting a new behaviour is taken
3	Preparation	Efforts are made to prepare for change	Thinking time about what changes are needed to change a behaviour
4	Action	Initial change is made	New alternative behaviours are attempted
5	Maintenance	Change in behaviour is maintained over time	Feedback accepted and integrated as new behaviour Situations are avoided that are likely to initiate a relapse to the old behaviour.

'So I want them in that way to like me but in other ways I don't so I don't mind being very blunt in giving feedback to them or challenging them or saying exactly what I think about some of their issues and the way they avoid them and stuff like that but I do want them to know that I really try to understand them.'

Systematically promoting the conditions to create a fertile relationship doesn't necessarily mean striving for maintaining harmonious exchanges. Clutterbuck (2008) asks if in fact we have the 'conditions for sustained connection – the right mental frame and whether the impact of the disconnect can be ignored or explored and if so, [when] is the right time to do this.' Sustained concentration and attention to the relationship by both is to be anticipated as energy draining. I suggest that both recognise this and be willing to disclose any feelings of fatigue or lack of focus as they emerge. This avoids any subjective thinking that either is losing interest in the conversation and recognises that working with change can be taxing and possibly exhausting. Working with connection and disconnection can be consciously maintained and encourages a verdant playground for stretching both mental and emotional agility in seeking new possibilities. There will be more on this later in this chapter with exploring 'challenge when in flow and arousing the client to be out of their comfort zone gains them access to the area that most people learn from' (Csikszentmihalyi, 2013).

Objectivity as a concept is multifaceted, with components not always obvious or visible. I want also to remind you about what we can experience from 'transference' and 'countertransference' and how these can affect objectivity.

Transference

- Transference stems from a person's unconscious struggles that are causing them inter- or intrapersonal issues
- Person A unconsciously transfers their feelings and attitudes about an influential person or situation in the past on to Person B. Person B may behave similarly towards Person A
- This may be a positive or negative transference
- A negative example can be the anxiety about rejection leading either person to seek approval from the other
- A positive example can be anticipating unconditional positive regard leading either person to expect total acceptance from the other whatever their behaviour
- The act of transference may impact on who we decide to choose for close relationships.

Countertransference

- Is generally defined as feelings evoked in one (A) by the other (B)
- These feelings may be associated or not with the source of the original transference. Person B will also have their own internal models of influential others and ways of behaving that will evoke emotions in addition to those evoked by transference from Person A
- Countertransference surfaces as a constant process of monitoring by Person B of what is happening between them and the client

- Countertransference is not an impediment or negative as long as Person B reflects on it and uses it constructively within the relationship
- Examples where countertransference remains unnoticed and affects between Persons A and B is where either in the relationship experiences feelings and/or is acting differently to how they usually feel or behave
  - giving the other more time than they would for others
  - colluding with a person's reasons for avoiding the action they agreed to take.

This basic knowledge of 'transference' and 'countertransference' acts as a reminder of how each influences the others in relationships. We maintain objectivity by noticing when we get drawn into the world of the other, noticing how we react and *actively* working with the emotion evoked in the relationship in support of each other (see Figure 6.2).

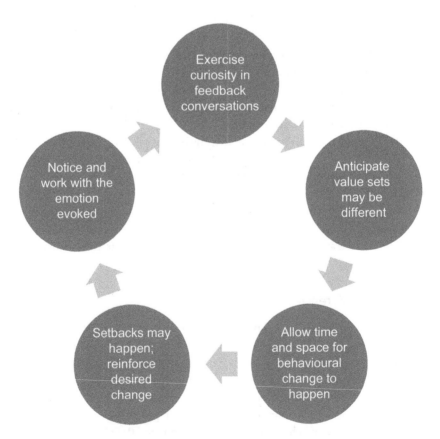

Figure 6.2 Top tips for introducing objectivity into feedback

Conscious bias

How does bias affect our actions?

'Most of us believe that we are ethical and unbiased. We imagine we're good decision makers, able to objectively size up a job candidate or a venture deal and reach a fair and rational conclusion that's in our, and our organisation's, best interests,' writes Harvard University researcher Mahzarin Banaji in the *Harvard Business Review* (2003). 'But more than two decades of research confirms that, in reality, most of us fall woefully short of our inflated self-perception.'

Yes, in reality our biases affect us and our decision-making processes in a number of different ways:

Table 6.2 How personal biases affect decision-making

Bias affects:	Decision making process:
Our perception	how we see people and perceive reality
Our attitude	how we react towards certain people
Our behaviours	how receptive/friendly we are towards certain people
Our attention	which aspects of a person we pay most attention to
Our listening skills	how much we actively listen to what certain people say
Our micro-affirmations	how much or how little we comfort certain people in certain situations

The fact is that we all have biases! Some have a survival function. The human brain is hard-wired to fulfil this role for keeping ourselves safe. The days of 'fight or flight' in the original sense of fleeing dangerous animals or defending ourselves from marauding tribes may not be as relevant in our modern world. Nevertheless, we are programmed to continue 'defending' ourselves in our everyday interactions. Allport (1979) tells us that 'bias is a human trait resulting from our tendency and need to classify individuals into categories as we strive to quickly process information and make sense of the world.' To do this, we mould our worldview to 'fit' the situation and ignore what doesn't. Even though we're unlikely to be fully conscious of what 'doesn't fit,' it's probable that we cut the edges of the pieces to make our personal puzzle complete. This action is known as 'confirmation bias.' So, we may overlook shortcomings in the performance of those we relate to and not be as tolerant of, or even magnify, similar shortcomings when the closeness in relationship is lacking.

Being objective means scrutiny of our approach. If we're harsh on ourselves then we may be harsh on others. We all have biases and these can lead us to become judgmental. Whatever our biases, these will 'show up' in conversation unless we're prepared to recognise and 'park' them to avoid inappropriate exchanges.

A braver move is to disclose and talk about our prejudices and how they make us think and feel. The more we accept the prevalence of biases, the easier they are to manage and enable us to make wiser and more ethical decisions. Organisational culture will feature hugely in our willingness to declare these inner prejudices. It's a courageous person who jeopardises the security of a position that pays the bills. It's an enlightened organisation that accepts the reality of bias being part of the human psyche and encourages openness and transparency in managing the consequences.

It's usually easy to recognise and be conscious of our biases, even if we find it difficult to manage them. We can like people for supporting the same football team and dislike the same people for using plastic straws and not being environmentally friendly. The more we reflect on our reactions to others who have the same value set, and therefore don't present 'danger,' and to those with different values sets who are potentially 'threatening,' the easier it is for us to distinguish and calibrate our behaviour.

We can identify our biases by noticing how we behave with others. What do our family relationships tell us about ourselves? Are these the same as those with colleagues or do we behave differently at work? How do we react and interact socially? Much can be learned, as an example, about our propensity for displaying and exercising compassion in our immediate circle of relationships.

Unconscious bias

We develop 'unconscious biases' at an early age. These are prejudices we have but are unaware of. They are mental shortcuts based on social norms and stereotypes (Guynn, 2015). So, how do unconscious biases manifest in the workplace?

Unconsciously, we tend to like people who look like us, think like us and come from backgrounds similar to ours. We like to think we're naturally objective; however, our brains rapidly categorise people instinctively. The way we speedily process information takes us beyond what we immediately absorb about others; age, height, gender and race. We also compute our perception of social background, education and accent. We form a judgement spontaneously that influences our relationships with others. We can experience a 'halo' effect and look for what's positive in another or we can classify using a 'horns' effect and look for negative signals that reinforce our belief.

Unconscious biases impact our decisions and actions without us realising this is happening. We may not be aware of these views or their implications. This universal tendency toward unconscious bias exists because bias is rooted in the brain. Scientists have determined that bias is found in the same region of the brain (the amygdala) associated with fear and threat. However, bias is also found in other areas of the brain. Stereotyping, a form of bias, is associated with the temporal and frontal lobes. The left temporal lobe of the brain stores general information about people and objects and is the storage place for social stereotypes. The frontal cortex is associated with forming impressions of others, empathy and reasoning (Henneman, 2014).

In other words, our brain evolved to mentally group things together to help make sense of the world. The brain compartmentalises the barrage of information and tags each section with general descriptions to ease speedy data storage. Bias occurs when those categories are tagged with labels like 'good' or 'bad' and are then applied to entire groups. Unconscious bias can also be a result of conditional learning. If a person has a bad experience with someone they categorise as belonging to a particular group, they often associate that entire group with that bad experience (Venosa, 2015). From a survival perspective, this mental grouping into good or bad helps the brain with making quick decisions about what is and isn't safe and what is appropriate or inappropriate. It's a developed survival mechanism hard-wired into our brains – and this makes it far more difficult to eliminate or minimise than originally thought (Ross, 2008).

Unconscious biases are indiscriminate when formed and develop from our socialisation, education and empirical experience (see Figure 6.3).

If we accept these citations, they offer little hope in surfacing and managing these unconscious biases.

The beliefs, attitudes and values we inadvertently project or transfer on to others can and probably will be damaging to the quality of some of our relationships. If we've had a negative experience with an authoritarian figure in our past, we can unconsciously project resistance onto another who reminds us of this person even though the comparison may be totally speculative. Someone may also unconsciously transfer their thoughts onto us in a similar way. Consequences for the feedback conversation in these situations are helpfully illustrated by Transactional Analysis, which was originated by Eric Berne (1964) (see Figure 6.4).

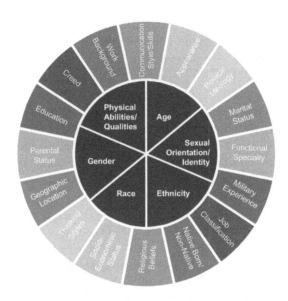

Figure 6.3 Sources of bias

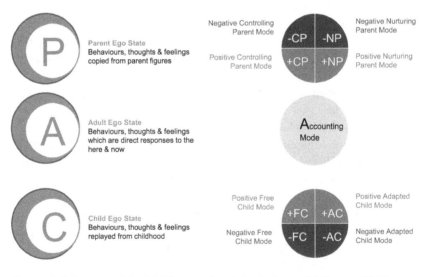

Figure 6.4 Parent-adult-child Transactional Analysis model (Berne, 1964)

By developing the 'authoritarian figure' scenario and applying the model where the giver of feedback reminds the receiver of a particularly critical teacher (Parent Ego State), this unconscious recollection may incite the receiver to adopt a 'Child Ego State.' The giver is likely perceived as a 'Negative

Controlling Parent' resulting in the receiver adopting a 'Negative Adapted Child' state. This is not the best platform for creating a relationship of positivity towards feedback. The giver also being unaware of the unconscious bias in the receiver may perpetuate, and even escalate, the unravelling breakdown in relationship by perceiving the receiver as unreceptive. The ideal scenario, as you can see in the model, is that both the giver and the receiver adopt the stance of the 'Adult Ego State' facilitating objectivity in conversation.

I believe that one way of counteracting the conditioning that fuels 'unconscious bias' is reflective practice. Developing this habit encourages us to make time to reflect on relational interactions, especially those where we've experienced disengagement. Regular reflective practice can familiarise us with behaviours identifying our conscious biases. Banaji and Greenwald (2013) reinforce this suggestion that 'unconscious biases' are malleable and that we can take action to minimise the impact of unconscious bias. Neuroscience helps by showing that the brain is capable of reworking the hardwiring in the brain to create new neural pathways. Neuroplasticity is the ability of the brain to change. With practice we can strengthen or weaken the synapses that build neural pathways and that inform the way we react to stimuli. Behaviour, thoughts and emotions can cause neuroplastic changes. We can neglect to nourish thoughts and emotions about people who are slow to respond and nurture thoughts and emotions that show empathy for differences in cognitive reactions. This weakens the neural pathway expecting fast flow in conversation and strengthens the neural pathway that appreciates that some people need thinking time before responding. Reflective practice helps to recognise patterns of behaviours suggesting unconscious bias, and of course we can always ask for feedback to help us identify neural pathways ripe for change!

Until we notice our patterns and ways of behaving, our unconscious biases will continue to drive our behaviour (see Figure 6.5).

'If you change the way you look at things, the things you look at change,'

Wayne Dyer (Dyer, 2007)

Eradicating biases and stereotyping is a major step in growing our 'relational objectivity muscle' to:

- Be courageous and authentic in approach and speech; as human beings we value being respected
- Show integrity by sharing honest and transparent feedback; we may not like what we hear; however, reflection on what's been said often brings rewarding new insights

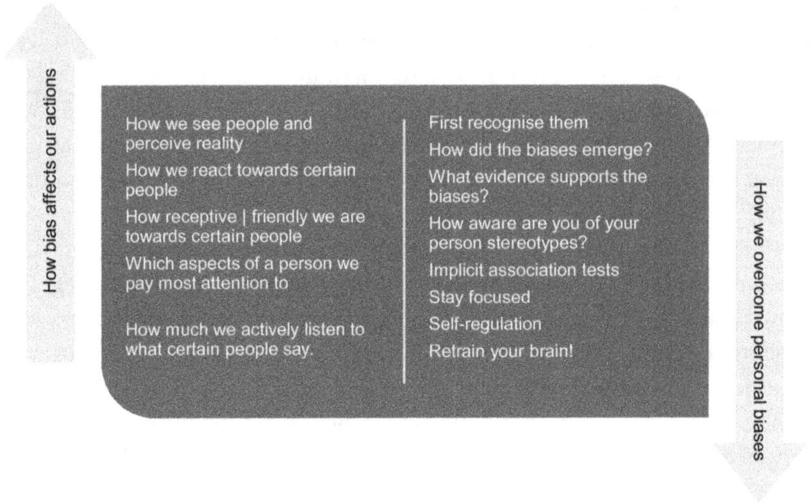

How bias affects our actions

How we see people and
perceive reality

How we react towards certain
people

How receptive | friendly we are
towards certain people

Which aspects of a person we
pay most attention to

How much we actively listen to
what certain people say.

First recognise them

How did the biases emerge?

What evidence supports the
biases?

How aware are you of your
person stereotypes?

Implicit association tests

Stay focused

Self-regulation

Retrain your brain!

How we overcome personal biases

Figure 6.5 Overcoming our personal biases

- Be curious and work creatively to find a way forward; feedback can be fun!
- Encourage self-responsibility for continuous development and be free of blame by genuinely reassuring others that mistakes are rich sources of new learning
- Show observable interest in wanting others to achieve transformational and sustainable change.

We achieve a balance between support and challenge through feedback that is motivational and helps with recognising strengths, what's working well and what needs to change. Being objective is primarily managing the 'interferences' we subjectively bring to the discussion and genuinely focusing on generative feedback, on good practice and on areas for improvement. Both scenarios work best when reinforced with explanatory data illustrating observed behaviour. Tell the person what they did to demonstrate good practice and ask for their thoughts on how improvements can be made before offering your own suggestions! People usually know best about how to improve the processes they work on routinely.

Theme 4 of The Relational Leadership WAY©: Mindfulness

The practice of **mindfulness** is now well established as a way of improving concentration and helping us to focus on what it feels like to be present.

There are several texts, exercises and training courses promoting the merits of mindfully practicing, say, meditative breathing as a way of balancing and centring ourselves to be 'present' in the moment for self and others. This section seeks to adapt the principles of mindfulness that encourages presence as an essential component of a relational 'way of being' and is not necessarily advocating an in-depth study of the practice.

Achieving presence is in the sense of 'the awareness that emerges through paying attention on purpose, in the present moment and non-judgmentally to the unfolding of experience moment by moment' (Kabat-Zinn, 2003). Mindfulness advocates the act of observation as highly important in being in the moment with self and others; noticing words, breath, pace and somatic reflexes. Think of the important contribution that these observations about each other make to informing how each may or is reacting to feedback. Is speech fluent or hesitant, are there signs of discomfort or a relaxed state, is the breathing rapid or slow?

Our wider attention on the other rather than ourselves may be directly what contributes to our own presence. Cox (2013) refers to 'mindfulness being seen as a necessary precursor to presence.' The findings of the research suggested that practice over time creates an embodied state of mindfulness that activates presence in the moment. Proficiency in mindfulness accelerates our ability to summon 'presence' as a conscious state of being in the moment with others.

Siegel (2010) talks of interconnectivity between two people through referencing empathy (Brown, 2007) as 'trying to sense the inner world of another' and then to 'really understand that world'; as 'human beings we have a whole system of neurons that are detecting the intention of another person.' The emphasis is that the one becoming aware of the empathy will feel care as well as a 'sense of connection' leading to trust and feelings of safety; a 'sense of security.' Demonstrating mindfulness as a relational 'way of being' encourages this 'sense of security' by being 'really present in an open way … to what's going on inside of you as it's happening [without] judgement' and provides a 'gateway to being open and present to other people' as well as yourself. 'The more you are aware of your own bodily sensations, the more you could be aware of other people's internal emotional states' (Siegel, 2010). In his WABC article Ehrlich (2011) tells us that mindfulness training increases empathy and the ability to read (observe) others' emotions (Goleman, 2003) as well as increasing compassion and igniting positive emotion in our brain. The observations engendered by being present take us to this deeper level of witnessing emotional connection. How best can we transform alerts signalling fear of feedback into a relaxed anticipation that feedback will be in our best interests? Read more on working with emotion in the next chapter.

The holding environment that mindfulness gives is uninterrupted thinking time through silence for thinking and feeling that gradually enables others to reveal and accept themselves.

Silence is a powerful tool to gift to others and enables reflective space for sourcing new ways of thinking and finding new possibilities. Perseverance with overcoming the discomfort that some dislike when sitting in silence is well worth the rewards gained. We know the best way of facilitating sustainable change is for each of us to reach our own decisions about what to change and how we want to do it. Acknowledging that feedback informs desired change is insufficient alone to make change happen. The feedback message needs help and providing the space for reflection enables the brain to access all the information that helps us to reach a conclusion and make decisions about the expectation for change. We have to resist the temptation to interrupt the other's thinking space, believing that nothing is happening because nothing is being articulated. What we articulate is only a fraction of the information our brain is actually computing; give the brain a break and give space to think!

Below is a 'taster' for mindfulness practice to introduce you to the power of focus. The best way to try this activity is for someone to read the practice to you. I find this a particularly helpful exercise to practice with clients who come to coaching straight from a busy schedule. These few moments of mindfulness practice take us away from the rigours of business demands and towards the space of creativity that 'being present' offers.

Mindfulness practice encouraging the state of 'being present'

- Make yourself comfortable
- Relax and release any tension in your shoulders. Do this by raising your shoulders slowly up to your ears and then let your shoulders slowly drop
- Gently close your eyes
- Take time to 'scan' your body and notice any areas that need attention – if you feel any areas of tension, take a long breathe in, and focusing on the area let the tension go as you slowly breathe out
- Now, fully focus your attention on your breathing
- Simply pay attention to what it feels like in your body to slowly breathe in and slowly breathe out

- Bring your attention to your abdomen. Notice your chest rise as you breathe in and your lungs fully inflate as you take the breath down until you feel your abdomen rise and expand. Now as you slowly exhale, feel your belly fall, your lungs deflate and your chest fall
- Continue to breathe with the same rhythm – slowly in and slowly out
- Focus your attention on the full experience of breathing. Immerse yourself completely in this experience.
- Anytime that you notice your mind wandering away from your breath, just notice the thought, simply accept it and let the thought pass from your consciousness – then gently bring your attention back to the present moment – your breathing
- Continue for a few minutes to breathe with the same rhythm – slowly in and slowly out
- Now gradually bring your breathing back to your normal pace
- When you're ready, gently open your eyes and come back into the room.

Theme 5 of The Relational Leadership WAY©: Presence with the sub-themes of flow and breaking flow

We may believe we're good listeners and pay attention to others in conversation. However, being human means that we have a propensity for our minds to wander. Our brains like novelty, and when this is lacking it's easy for our concentration levels to lower and seek new stimulus. Keeping fully focused is, therefore, difficult for us – it's hard work even when the conversation is scintillatingly interesting. We also have biological interruptions that weaken our concentration when we're tired or perhaps experiencing stressful times.

However, the effort to maintain focus on others reaps a huge reward. This third theme in Part 2 of The Relational Leadership WAY© that encourages 'active engagement' in co-creating generative conversations is having the conscious ability to summon 'presence.' We know from the previous section how we can achieve this by using the practice of mindfulness. Presence enables us during the conversation to use what is happening 'in the moment' as a resource. When noticing a behaviour that is indicative of the topic or feedback being discussed, this can be shared. 'In the moment' observations provide tangible data to explore, to build self-awareness and to illustrate behaviours for change or dispel preconceptions about observer perceptions and/or bias.

Tolle (2017) brings many years of mastery in accomplishing presence. The belief is that if we think we have presence we can forget this thought as we've made it into a concept; presence is a way of being. This is a powerful way of reinforcing the loss of presence as soon as we start thinking! He talks of 'being completely open to whatever happens in this moment; as we only have this moment.' A profound if unobvious statement; we do only have this moment, and how often do we dwell on the past and worry about the future, both of which take us away from the only time we have; the present? When Tolle talks of the 'complaining mind' we can easily relate to this in ourselves and notice it in others; the voice(s) that gives us the 'shoulds' and 'coulds.' Noticing this behaviour and use of vocabulary alerts us to pathways for exploring transformational change. This trait is noticeable in the 'perfectionist' who 'should' meet every deadline and grumbles about never having any time for social activities because there's so much to do. Tolle encourages moments of being in the now, when in the silence of being totally present – focusing in the body and not in the mind – the solutions for transformational change emerge. Sharing what is happening for you and what you are noticing in the other at the moment, you hear the perfectionist bemoan their fate. Encouragement to relax and ponder the location of the 'should' and challenging any assumptions to encourage reality to emerge is the support we can offer by being present.

Sounds simple, doesn't it? However, the true art of being present is much more than showing up! Presence involves how 'grounded' we are in ourselves and our work and how able we are to connect with others even when they are difficult to reach. How 'present' we are alerts others – and not necessarily consciously – to what they choose to reveal to us. We are much more likely to disclose and share even intimate personal details with people we feel connected with and who show a genuine interest in us; the bedrock of beneficial relationships. We also have a responsibility to respect this deep level of engagement.

Much can be learned about relationship from the world of psychotherapy and adapted for the business world without fully adopting the discipline. Gendlin's (2003) work on focusing, known for its concept of 'felt sense,' was refined and expanded into the article 'Inner Relationship Focusing' by Cornell and McGavin (2008). The relevance to this text is 'allowing all aspects of the personality to be held in acceptance and awareness, new insights and shifts can emerge.' The approach relies specifically on the ability to be 'present' through friendliness, gentle curiosity, and being non-judgmental (Cornell & McGavin, 2008), enabling the other to experience and navigate their inner world. This quality of engagement is likely to elicit a greater level of realisation and self-awareness than a barrage of questions disrupting productive thinking space.

The benefits of accepting and implementing change through the ability to express and 'listen to' feelings and thoughts and finding solutions for oneself is well documented in coaching literature.

Clutterbuck and Megginson (2009) refer also to **presence** as a practice that we can **activate** similar to the advocacy of this Part 2 of The Relational Leadership WAY©. They talk of

> how 'grounded' you are in yourself and your work, how able you are to 'reach' the client, even when they are difficult to reach … to be aware of what is going on within him or herself and between him/herself and the client in the here and now, and be prepared to articulate some of this to the client as one way of making contact.

If being fully present is the starting point for building good connections and this requires you to be authentic – to be who you are and use your presence creatively (Bluckert, 2006) – how can we detect when we lose interest or when we become more engaged and innovative in our dialogue with another?

Noticing our energy level is usually a fairly accurate barometer for gauging how enthralled we are with a conversation. We may experience monotonal delivery as soporific, but if the topic excites us, we are likely to overlook the speech delivery. An entertaining monologue delivered with passion may not hold substance; however, we can still be enthralled by enjoying the energy created. We recognise the signals motivating us to stay connected, but how do these moments of presence convert to opportunities for spontaneous 'in the moment' feedback when this is the purpose of the conversation?

A Gestalt (Barber, 2009) perspective encourages us to 'expand and raise our awareness, attend to everything, dismiss nothing and to establish a robust and intimate dialogue with what is unfolding in our immediate environment – right now.' If I recall and disassemble observations made of past conversations, what becomes evident is that we are less than conscious of what is happening right here, right now. Many conversations – especially at meetings – spiral into a cacophony of clashing voices, each competing for airtime. How is it possible to notice what is happening in the moment when one is scrambling to be heard or too busy thinking about what to say next? Moments of spontaneously noticing what is happening in relationships beyond the conversation are lost and probably overlooked.

We're back again to practising being 'in the moment' to attain the art of 'presence.' Gestalt theory also adopts a relational framework by advocating a 'way of being.' Exploratory questioning invites a situation into the present in place of relying on interpretations of past events:

Thinking about the situation right now:

- What are you experiencing?
- What sensations are you aware of in your body?
- What are you thinking?
- What are you feeling?
- What are you hearing?
- What are you seeing?

Gestalt practice encourages deeper exploration leading to a great understanding of what a person is experiencing 'in the moment':

- 'When you speak of this situation I notice you tense your shoulders' (*mirror the action to keep focus on the activity rather than what is being said*)
- 'What happens if you tense your shoulders even further?' (*mirror the action*)
- 'What are you experiencing now?' (*thinking, feeling, hearing, seeing?*)

The Gestalt approach is to respond to and deal with *what is* rather than *why it is* or what it *should be*. Working with the Gestalt approach encourages us to be who we are and who we want to be; to achieve internal validation rather than be influenced by external expectations that are detrimental to our well-being and self-efficacy. Through achieving this we achieve the capability of being authentic in our relationships; the precursor to meaningful feedback conversations. 'Change occurs (paradoxically) when I fully become what I AM, rather than trying to be what I am not, and that lasting change cannot be attained through coercion or persuasion' (Beisser, 1970).

If the aim of Gestalt theory is to attend to everything, dismiss nothing and to establish a robust and intimate dialogue with what is unfolding in our immediate environment, right now, we have to manage our relational behaviour. We have to notice what we're sensing, feeling and what is going on in the conversation and resist the temptation of seeing our own worldview as reality and using this to form what we say next. The only way we can cultivate an authentic relationship of inclusivity and joint respect is to focus on what is actually happening in the dialogue by embodying non-judgmental presence.

These references, from both psychotherapy and coaching texts, emphasise the rewards of presence in relationship. We get a sense of proximity that enables the closeness for unguarded conversation. Perhaps a willingness for vulnerability and honest exchanges.

Extrapolating these interpretations of 'presence' into a business context, what can we learn that aligns with the demands on leadership today and expectations for the future? The anticipated role of leadership and how leaders are perceived remind us that the quality of presence affects how others form their reality of relationship engagement:

What leaders do

- Your personal impact is immediate
- You are always watched and everything is noted
- Your personal power is your attributes, not force
- You are an inspiring role model
- You are willing to show vulnerability
- You operate with passion, clarity and humanity
- Your energy is always contagious
- You structure your ideas clearly and allow others around you to be clear
- You speak with passion
- You speak with an optimistic tone and range
- You use language that embraces not alienates the listener
- You encourage open dialogue
- You listen, don't interrupt and interject purposefully
- You respond well and articulately when challenged
- You provide effective feedback using a coaching style to empower and develop.

The purpose of this text is to propose relational leadership as meeting the dependency of business success on continuous improvement. We can't achieve this without feedback. I increasingly hear the prediction that technical expertise defers to the relevance of relationship as the leadership focus of tomorrow and feedback moves up the ladder of fundamentals. Leadership is more about personal attributes – a key one being presence – and less about competencies.

I refer to the work of Rodenburg (2007) as an exemplar of the benefits of 'presence' making available the 'experience, and all the messages and tools required to survive physically, intellectually and emotionally.' Basically, we all have access to resources enabling the co-creation of relationships that help us with the less attractive features of feedback.

Training with Patsy Rodenburg demonstrated to me that totally being present takes practice, practice and more regular practice! However, the rewards are worth the effort as we project ourselves in a way that instils confidence in others about us and to work with us.

I offer a brief introduction to Patsy Rodenburg's work with this exercise that focuses on voice projection as the enabler of personal presence and complements the recognition of personal attributes or 'self' as a 'way of being':

Table 6.3 Use of voice in creating presence (Rodenburg, 2007)

1. Prepare your body

A centred body frees the voice, reduces tension and creates a more impressive presence:

- Your feet are on the floor almost parallel and under your hips
- Stand or sit with your weight slightly forward on the balls of your feet and your knees released
- Your spine is straight, neither rigid nor slumped
- Your head is balanced at the top of your spine
- Your jaw is relaxed.

2. Prepare your voice

- Breathe as deeply as you can without sound
- The more you breathe naturally, the more present you will be
- Stretch the sides of your ribs
- Stretch the back of your ribcage
- A gentle breath with a push against a wall places the breath in its lower and powerful place
- Speak on the breath – the equivalent of the readiness of breath that you feel the moment you throw a ball.

3. Speaking

- Presence is harnessed when fully physical; breath, voice and speech energy are focused to specific places outside you
- When you feel the voice is forward practice clear unrushed speech
- Always maintain eye contact
- Give full attention through the breath to a group or individual and to the voice actually reaching the listener. This is generous and impressive.

'What Leaders Do' can be learned and understood through the **Three Circles of Energy**, which were created by Patsy Rodenburg and appear in her book *Presence* (2007).

We can see the relevance of presence generally and specifically in leadership. Maintaining this level of focus can only come with practice and more practice! We have to build the neural pathways that we want to create and repeat as habitual behaviour. A way of achieving this is through practising **mindfulness**, which was covered in the last section.

Being present enables us to hold the space for others to address any issues emerging. We become more effective in feedback conversations when we remain more present rather than distancing ourselves when strong emotions emerge (Drake, 2011).

Mearns and Cooper (2005), in their reference to 'relational depth,' describe 'a sheer sense of connection ... not all the time, but at some moments, I would have this sense of my client and I being deeply connected to each other: engaged, enmeshed, intertwined.' I believe the reference to 'not all the time' offers a more realistic assessment of what is achievable in terms of sustaining 'presence.' However, working to achieve presence in its truest form is well worth the effort in creating productive relationships.

Let me give the final word on this section on presence to Waitzkin (2007) who quotes:

> Much of what separates the great from the good is deep presence, relaxation of the conscious mind, which allows the unconscious to flow unhindered... The Grandmaster looks at less and sees more, because his unconscious skill set is much more highly evolved.

Flow

A product of being fully present in relationships is to create 'flow' in the conversation.

This concept of 'flow' described here is 'intense, focused concentration on the present moment with merging of action and awareness and a loss of reflective self-consciousness' (Nakamura & Csikszentmihalyi, 2009). 'Flow' involves focused, absorbed concentration in the moment, says Cox (2013). When feedback is difficult to say, this intensity of concentration creates a closeness, enabling each in the conversation to notice then react.

We often link the idea of flow with athletes and musicians who are 'on the ball' or 'in the zone.' Picasso's later refinement of his art was the ability to paint on glass his representation of a bird with one continuous brushstroke; a visual representation of 'being in flow.' What we observe with the phenomena of flow is that activity and performance appear effortless: we know what we're doing, what to do next and react instantly to what we're noticing.

Csikszentmihályi's (1997) work is widely referenced on the 'components of flow' (see Figure 6.6 represented as challenge level and skills level).

These are the 9 factors he describes as accompanying an experience of flow:

1. Clear goals: expectations are clear, goals are attainable through aligning with a person's skills set and abilities and the challenge and skills levels are high
2. Concentrating: a high degree of concentration on a specific activity

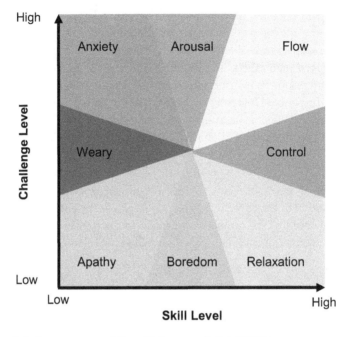

Figure 6.6 Components of flow (Csikszentmihályi (1997)

3. A loss of the feeling of self-consciousness: the merging of action and awareness with no attention to self
4. Distorted sense of time: one's subjective sense of time is altered
5. Direct and immediate feedback: success and failure are obvious so that behaviour can be adjusted immediately
6. Balance between ability level and challenge: not too easy and not too difficult
7. A sense of personal control of the situation or activity: leading and not being led
8. The activity is intrinsically rewarding: action is effortless
9. People become absorbed in the activity, focusing fully on the activity itself.

Not all of the factors need to be in place to experience 'flow'. The very nature of 'flow' can come from realising you have 'enough' of one factor to move on whatever activity you're engaged in.

We know when we're in flow with others; conversation is effortless and with a sense of equality and shared responsibility in the relationship. The application for ease of feedback conversations for improving performance management is an easy connection to make; the practice of flow is perhaps more difficult to achieve.

However, we do know when we're in flow and know when we're not! I remember attending a training with Tim Gallwey, who wrote *Inner Game of Work* (2001) based on his professional career in tennis. He demonstrated to the group how we could improve a tennis serve and putt a golf ball by applying the concept of *Self 1* and *Self 2* to create a sense of flow:

Self 1 is the inner critic we all have who knows better than we do and who is continuously telling us what to do and how we can do things differently, while another part of us remains quiet and subservient to the dominant voice! Gallwey (2001) calls this inner critic *Self 1*, while *Self 2* is the silent doer. Basically *Self 1* doesn't trust *Self 2* to achieve anything without help and takes over by moving the body, tightening muscles and signalling the brain to move the limb in the direction it thinks it should go. As all the muscles are now taut and our body tense, the result is usually a mis-hit – another sense of failure for *Self 2*.

Gallwey (1998) created the formula:

$P = P - I$, meaning Performance is equal to Potential (*Self 2*) minus Interference (*Self 1*)

The belief is that our bodies are perfectly capable of adjusting to make the perfect putt if there is **no** conscious interference. We've all noticed that our best performances, whether this is in sport, making a powerful presentation or offering a convincing argument, come when we are at our most relaxed. Every part of us connects; muscle work in unison without tension, our breathing is regular, neither too deep not too shallow, and oxygen flows effortlessly throughout our body and energises our brain function.

The Inner Game approach encourages this relaxed state that achieves full potential:

1. Gradually build a trust in our innate ability to learn and adjust to improve performance. Don't consciously try to *make* it happen, just *want* to make it happen and let *Self 2* be responsible.
2. Quiet the mind! The capacity to perform at our highest potential is in direct proportion to the *stillness* of our minds. When the mind is noisy, anxious and distracted by *Self 1* it interferes with the neurons that send signals to other cells which cause chemicals called neurotransmitters to be released at junctions called synapses. A cell receiving a synaptic signal from a neuron may be fearful, excited, or modified another way. The connections between neurons form neural pathways that determine behaviour. We can see how easily we send unconscious instructions to our muscles and create tension. The Inner Game aim is to *quiet the mind* to what is essential.

Using the analogy of relationship, if the interfering *Self 1* gets absorbed by focusing on being present, then *Self 2* is free to concentrate on what's important to take notice of the phenomena occurring and emerging in the conversation. What is the physiology of each other displaying; comfort or discomfort – pleasure or dissatisfaction – engagement or disengagement?

In this way *Self 2* is now in control of *Self 1* and is able to use it as a tool when messages are meaningful and worth acting on. This take practice, as *Self 1* is so active that it clouds our judgements and germinates doubts. The Inner Game approach increases awareness of what 'is' and to take one step at a time to make the desired change.

3. Learning is gained through awareness of our own experience and to be able to fully experience ourselves we have to be non-judgemental. Non-judgemental appears again as an attribute of maintaining presence and maximising our learning.
4. Being non-judgemental means not placing a value on something and defining is as 'good' or 'bad.' Labelling in this way stops us noticing information about what happened. Developing the habit of reflection avoids this judgement making and involves us taking a deeper dive into events that created the current situation or perhaps performance. In this way we can learn and adjust our approach the next time we wish to repeat the same or similar activity. Being judgmental about our performance slows or even stops growth and learning. If we decide we're no good at creating effective relationships that facilitate feedback we will gradually believe this and avoid interacting in conversations involving feedback. We can choose if we want to make these debilitating connections in our minds. The Inner Game approach suggests a state of acceptance of events and of ourselves, resulting in the freedom to make rational choices.
5. In a flow state we have a sense of control that feels effortless and eclipses our everyday awareness. We relinquish our insecurities, any feelings of unease, lack of confidence or feelings of embarrassment and simply 'be.'

Breaking flow

Clutterbuck (2008) invites us to 'recognise and cherish moments of disconnect' or 'breaking flow.' This 'breaking flow' or disconnect is to 'feel they're not with you or you with them – this can be a wonderful learning opportunity for both ... feeling comfortable with the silence.' Speaking of this break in flow, he asks us: 'Who's aware of disconnect – you, them or both; where is the disconnect located – in you, them, the environment around you?'

When the concept of breaking flow is applied to feedback, I think we can see how 'breaking flow' and disconnecting from the other may reintroduce the full extent of the power of objectivity into the conversation. Creating a binding attachment in the relationship may have served to create a sense of deep connectivity conducive to flow and ease of conversation, when now a different dynamic may be more effective for feedback. Optimising performance in others can be achieved when the tension caused by 'breaking flow' is constructive, calibrated and dynamically adjusted.

Above all, I believe we can be 'present' both 'in flow' and when 'breaking flow'; we just have to be mindful that we know this and the appropriateness of each state.

Theme 6 of The Relational Leadership WAY©: Timing of feedback

Creating the right conditions for feedback ideally results in *knowing* 'when to engage' or at least having a strong sense of the best time and place; a bit like predicting the weather forecast when atmospheric indicators are available but not infallible. How can we make our best estimate, then, through a 'way of being' in the relationship?

Asking the other when and how they prefer feedback seems obvious and can be effective in some situations. What is critical for sustaining the quality of relationship is having informed insight into how each person *really* thinks and feels about feedback. Individual reality at the prospect may be very different for both the giver and receiver. Whatever a person's preference, I encourage you to be aware of empirical and recorded evidence that feedback is recognised by most as necessary. However, not all relish the possibilities of what's to follow when they hear the word 'feedback' entering conversation. We are by now very familiar with what some may refer to as the '3F's' 'fearful feedback fiend.'

Feedback features in many texts offering tools and techniques as facilitating the activity. What appears to be missing is how we gauge the 'best' time, accepting that the 'right' time is likely to remain elusive. Waiting for the 'best' time may not be ideal either as we can easily fall into the trap of procrastination and avoidance waiting for the perfect moment to become obvious. This is especially true when it's not our most welcome action on the 'to do' list.

This section draws heavily on references and empirical observations from my own and others' interpretations of working with feedback to inform what's possible to extrapolate and apply in the quest for gauging the timing of feedback. The concept of the 'best' time applies for both a planned feedback conversation and also an emergent feedback opportunity.

Let's begin with some introductory dialogue from the research informing this text. 'Creating the conditions' as the gateway for introducing feedback was the challenge for co-researchers: 'we can't make people responsive and ready if they don't want to be; we can only help people to be more curious to explore further.' We discussed the pitfalls of 'manufacturing moments for feedback' when two 'dynamic organisms' come together, which are likely to disrupt any prepared 'script.' This co-researcher thought it 'would be arrogant to think we could make that happen [create the conditions for feedback] each time.' We agreed that there will be certain conditions conducive to co-creation and possibly leading to increased receptivity, but cannot be conclusive about predicting such an outcome.

Another co-researcher's opinion was that it was not 'possible to create the conditions because you have to work with the moment that the client's experiencing'; this gained the response: 'you have to go with this, although in this case I could have let it go, I think I could have but I would have withheld a useful challenge to her.' A difference of opinion; one coach resists the opportunity for encouraging feedback, while another grasps the moment.

The research elicited a range of responses for assessing the 'best timing of feedback.' As expected 'asking the client when the time is right' was a popular choice based on the premise that the client *must* know what's best for them. I identified earlier in the chapter potential flaws in assuming this to be a reliable predictor when the brain selects a rational response by overriding the signals generated by emotional needs. However, we know that humans can be irrational in this way, and that decisions are ultimately made on knowledge gained from emotional experiences. This is why sometimes we say one thing and actually mean something different!

Other responses suggested 'reacting to a signal from the client' which is probably a more convincing hypothesis. Clients contributing to the research relied on their coach 'knowing' when to give feedback, reinforcing some coaches' predilection for 'judging' the best time. Given the ambiguity of actually knowing the 'best' time, a question asked of the co-researchers in the study was: 'In the moment, what happens to evoke the need to give the client feedback?'

First reactions were 'not knowing; the time just seemed right.' Further probing revealed that the 'knowing' came from a place of 'sensing' and 'feeling.' The co-researchers who were in 'flow' conversations experienced a somatic sensation: 'a tingling in my fingers.' This, combined with interpreted 'invitation' signals from the client, prompted the timing to be gauged as 'good' and even the 'best' time for feedback.

Clients of co-researchers were asked a similar question in an attempt to validate the findings from the question asked of co-researchers: 'What do you think prompts the coach to give you feedback?'

The most popular response was, 'We trust our coach to know when's the best time for us'; a strong validation of how 'trust' in a relationship facilitates meaningful and sometimes difficult conversations.

As the research developed, my own experience of 'knowing when the timing was best for feedback' was emergent: 'something's happened, it's time for me to say something [a prompt to give the client feedback]... and then it *felt* right to say something....'

My embryonic thinking at the start of the research was being curious about what gives us that feeling: 'Whatever that sensation is, whatever the thought is... I can't even put a label on it, whatever it is that feels right in that moment, and then from the client's perspective, their level of awareness about receiving feedback... so they are expecting it to happen ...' Recalling this early thinking now holds echoes of a rambling flow of bewilderment about the 'knowing' I labelled as 'something,' and illustrates the motivation for gaining a sense of certainty about when feedback is at its most productive. Is it as simple as saying we're relying on our 'intuition?' There will be more on this in the next chapter!

Mezirow (1981) suggests that 'insights gained through critical self-awareness are emancipatory in the sense that at least one can recognize the correct reasons for his or her problems.' Habermas (1970) suggests 'reflective learning leading to perspective transformation'; which if clients can take responsibility for self-reflection can lead to transformative action (Askew & Carnell, 2011). Ideally the client will adopt reflective practice to elevate self-awareness and inform the desired change. Coaching literature recognises the value of reflecting, 'but detailed examination of why it is beneficial and how it operates in practice has been lacking' (Cox, 2013). Let's acknowledge that personal reflection is the ideal for raising self-awareness and at the same time accept the scarcity of this practice. This void offers the coach and the manager a critical role in closing the gap in learning and development for clients and direct reports through effective and timely feedback.

Feedback is referenced in 'Enabling Insight and Learning' and 'Evaluating' two of the competences created by EMCC, a professional body internationally recognised for setting the professional practice standards in the mentoring, coaching and supervision industry:

- *Appropriate style for giving feedback:* the first hurdle to overcome – what might be an appropriate style? I believe the key rests in the way we present; our 'way of being' in relationships

171

- *Uses feedback and challenge effectively and at appropriate times to help the client and increase awareness, insight and responsibility for action:* How do we make sure that feedback and challenge are effective? I agree we need to gauge when are 'appropriate times,' and again, how do we make sure feedback delivers insight, encourages 'responsibility for action' and defines the purpose of this action?
- *Requests, receives and accepts feedback from client on coaching/mentoring:* Absolutely! This is good practice that role models the benefits and suggests a reciprocity for feedback exchange.

Accepting the EMCC Competency Framework guides us on professional practice 'readiness,' and therefore 'timing' for feedback must also influence our attitudinal choice that steers us towards – if not to – full engagement.

What can we learn from others who have explored this topic? We find in coaching literature reinforcement of reliance on processes (tools and techniques) as conduits for feedback, and where again the focus is on delivery rather than engagement with the client. There is, however, acknowledgement of both the donor and receiver in the process in this example:

'A useful way to begin to understand how to give appropriate feedback in content, style and tone is to consider how you feel when you ask for or receive feedback' (Parsloe & Leedham, 2009). I like how this reference reinforces the need to consider another based on our own preferences; however, I don't see a recognition for timing of delivery.

When **preparing** for feedback, Starr (2012) again endorses the concept of inviting us to 'think a little about how the other person is likely to respond' and to 'consider the best way to approach the person' and the possibility that 'you may choose not to use the word feedback.' I fully endorse changing the definer 'feedback,' although this may be too much of a stretch when this descriptor is firmly embedded in organisational speak and culture.

Clutterbuck and Megginson's (2009) suggestion that 'you can help the learner to prepare for and subsequently manage their reactions to unpalatable messages,' suggests early signposting of potentially controversial feedback and is unclear about whether the preparation equips the learner to manage their reactions or assumes competence in the giver of feedback to fulfil this role. My preference is to adopt Scoular's (2011) belief that introducing feedback follows having 'established a relationship of openness and trust with your client.'

The theory of Garvey Berger (2004) suggesting that the work of a 'transformative teacher is first to help students find the edge of their understanding, second to be company at that edge, and finally help students construct a new, transformed place' also addresses the concept of assessing the timing of feedback. She believes that ultimately this practice will help 'students find the courage they need to transform.' This 'edge of knowing' is central to her work, which she describes as the 'most precarious and transformative space,' the

> liminal space that we can come to terms with the limitations of our knowing and thus begin to stretch those limits. This makes the liminal zones between our knowing and not knowing both difficult to understand because they are constantly moving and being transformed.

Garvey Berger (2004) describes her experience of knowing how to recognise a student as being 'on the edge of her knowing – she stumbles, stammers, circles back. It is only after she says: "I don't know what to say" that her tone of voice changes.' Evidence of being on the 'edge of knowing' is 'that those at the edge cannot usually name their specific problem because they are enmeshed in the problem and cannot gain a vantage point from which to name it.'

Let's imagine for a moment that this waiting on the edge of understanding in this liminal space until the student self-diagnoses and rises to the challenge of change may be an issue of complicity; conscious or unconscious. What if the 'transformative teacher' is avoiding feedback without the certainty of the 'right timing' before acting. If this interpretation is also valid then the justification for predicting 'timing' for feedback enables the giver to accelerate the process of change. Through actively engaging in feedback at timely intervals, the receiver gets regular injections of feedback, fuelling a speedier transformative transition. This supersedes passively waiting while the receiver lurches along a solitary path to eventual enlightenment.

A similar explanation to that of Garvey Berger (2004) for the 'edge of knowing' is Palmer (1994) who talks of 'holding vulnerability' and 'not knowing' including the 'about-to-know state.' She uses the Buddhist word 'shunyata' to describe this 'emptiness' – as a 'pregnant space, the space or void from which all things come,' the 'about-to phase of experience … before some kind of knowing arises.' Palmer (1994) believes that if we can create a space by developing this 'not-knowing, then our timing will become more accurate.' Using this 'intuitive timing … where we no longer have to think' so that 'our doing arises naturally, spontaneously' is the time for engaging with feedback with clients. 'This knowing appears as an insight with accompanying sensations that are the basis of bodily intuition… we know or sense what is beyond words' Palmer (1994).

Palmer (1994) suggests that 'during the moments when we feel this profound connection, we know we belong in the universe.' The coach accesses the 'energetic field that can be intuitively sensed… as a kind of atmosphere or fragrance that surrounds us.' Awareness of this field makes us 'more present and know that it is part of the sensation of being.' Evidently, we communicate through our field 'to the outside world' and encourage others to 'come closer or don't get so close.' Palmer (1994) also describes 'open attention' as the state we experience with others and how we can 'expand to include the surrounding situation' and 'maintain balance and stay in our own working center.' The relevance to the timing for feedback is the suggestion that 'two people holding space for each other can allow powerful feelings to flow.' This co-creates the strength of relationship, arguably encouraging the conditions for receptivity of feedback.

Similarly, Brockbank and McGill (2006) identify with engaging clients 'at the edge of their knowledge, sense of self and the world.' Cox (2013) emphasises the positive outcome of referring to these edges as having 'a driving effect, motivating clients and moving them towards understanding, and ultimately transformation.' Wallace and Shapiro (2006) cite 'research has found that… interventions matched to a person's conative–motivational level are highly effective' (Prochaska et al., 1992). In coach practice, the 'coach is continuously making decisions about when to intervene, what to follow up, what to ask, whether to suggest an activity, whether to share a hunch and so on' (Askew & Carnell, 2011). I suggest that all four references imply a timing for feedback; do it when you sense and notice the client engaging energy, becoming animated and positively stimulated by the prospect and opportunity for change.

Timing of feedback that relates to coaches and the relationship is the concept of 'critical moments' de Haan and Blass (2007). A 'key aspect … discovered in all critical moments was … the coach questioning something about their clients, themselves or their approach, so that they experience some form of doubt.' By analysing the various doubts occurring as 'the critical moment,' this implies transition in the coach and the coaching relationship. These 'critical moments' are explained as 'potential breakthrough moments'; perhaps conduits for change. The 'more critical moments there are, the better the coaching' and without 'critical moments coaches cannot continue to learn.' Complementary research (de Haan & Nie, 2012) explains that

> results suggested in almost half of the descriptions, the coach and the client referred to the same moments as being critical in the coaching sessions. Although the coach mostly described moments of self-doubt as being critical, the client focused on moments of new learning and a positive change in the coaching relationship.

I propose that both research studies reinforce that feedback or the potential timing of feedback has impact when embedded within a relationship rather than a discreet or disconnected activity in itself.

In his reference from phenomenological psychology, Spinelli (2005) asserts that: 'Meaning is implicit in our experience of reality and we cannot tolerate meaninglessness.' This implies that in the act of meaning-making the client may likely be receptive to feedback from a desire to understand their own and other's perceptions. I suggest this noticing of desire and curiosity in others as a further 'prompt' for effective timing of feedback. The question 'What do you think colleagues would say about your contribution to the team?' may offer a timely segue to deeper exploration, when performance in the team is the feedback topic.

Bluckert (2006) defines the coaching relationship as providing 'the vehicle for here-and-now feedback based on how you experience your client's styles of interacting, communicating and connecting.' This is typical of Gestalt theory 'about how change takes place and that learning occurs through the examination of here and now experience' offering immediacy as the timing for feedback. This is a quick entry to feedback needing skilful delivery for predicting willingness to engage.

This 'here and now experience as calibration' and 'learning how to read another person's responses in an ongoing interaction ... correlating external behavioural cues to specific internal cognitive and emotional states' is also identified by Lawley and Tompkins (2011). They suggest this NLP technique 'is more sophisticated than those oh-so popular books that tell you how to read body language based on so-called universal tell-tale signs.'

A reminder when predicting the best time for feedback is to remember any reluctance obvious in the other when attempting to 'know' when the client is receptive to feedback. Rock (2008) graphically illustrates that 'In most people, the question "Can I offer you some feedback" generates a similar response to fast footsteps behind you in the night.' This may seem marginally dramatic although Hesketh and Laidlaw (2002) 'Identify several barriers to giving effective feedback in the context of medical education:

- *A fear of upsetting the trainee or damaging the trainee/doctor relationship*
- *A fear of doing more harm than good*
- *The trainee being resistant or defensive when receiving criticism*
- *Poor handling of a reaction to negative feedback can result in feedback being disregarded thereafter*
- *Feedback being too generalised and not related to specific facts or observation*
- *Feedback not giving guidance on how to rectify behaviour*

- *Inconsistent feedback from multiple sources*
- *A lack of respect for the source of feedback.'*

Timing of feedback in this scenario lacks priority when the practice itself appears as an obstacle to harmonious relationships. Similarly, I think we can downscale the importance of timing of feedback predicated on feedback being a routine and regular activity. Feedback becomes the norm, not the exception, and is more likely to be perceived as prerequisite to career progression. Remember, the competence of the giver is also key!

My experience of leading a global not-for-profit organisation operating with volunteer support is that feedback adopts a different complexion when people donate time that is necessarily deducted from fee-earning or personal leisure time. A psychological contract exists when people offer time willingly because they gain intrinsic motivation rather than extrinsic rewards such as the remuneration of pay. Feedback in this context balances in favour of appreciation for any level of work contribution and is usually given impromptu negating the consideration of getting the timing right. Reluctance to act wins out in this scenario for offering feedback that leads to desired performance or to disengagement – asking people to leave their role. This can be particularly frustrating when people accept profile positions then fail to contribute the anticipated volunteer time. Rather than 'grasping the nettle' of dismissal, hope prevails that support will be forthcoming at some time in the future. The opportunity for assessing timing of feedback is lost. Charitable organisations may have a similar feedback profile, although both not for profit and charities owe survival to the generous efforts of volunteers, and the capacity for absorbing a level of absenteeism is created.

All sectors are likely to have a prevailing position on the continuum of timing for feedback ranging from 'not applicable' as in the not-for-profit scenario where improvement feedback can be non-existent, to a 'need for spontaneity' when regular feedback is essential, for example safety in the nuclear industry. Where do you think your business plots on this continuum and what impact do you think this has on business forecasting measured against employee contribution?

In summary, we co-create generative conversations by proactively and actively engaging with relational leadership themes. This chapter has introduced us to a 'way of being' through the lenses of objectivity, mindfulness, presence and timing of feedback. The next chapter takes us to Part 3 of The Relational Leadership WAY©, where *you* both notice and react to what emerges and impacts on sustaining the quality of the relationship.

Part 3 of The Relational Leadership WAY©

You both noticing and *reacting* to what emerges and impacts on sustaining the quality of the relationship

Productive and sustainable relationships happen when we react in a way that evolves differences into a cooperative fusion.

Forget noticing what's happening in and around a conversation when we're totally focused on thinking what to say next – so focused that we unashamedly interrupt when we believe our worldview is the right one and, of course, the only one! In this mode of being, it's difficult, if not impossible, for us to quieten our eagerness to take over the conversation. I heard someone use the acronym WAIT – Why Am I Talking? How amazingly appropriate is that? It's a reminder of the power of listening as the absolute precursor for understanding what's really being said and before we even contemplate speaking out. Listening is well recognised and recorded as key to effective conversations, so there's no need to focus more on this here.

This chapter says there is more – much more – that impacts on the relationship beyond absorbing, analysing and evaluating conversational vocabulary.

Chapter 5 *prepared* you for managing relationships, especially when feedback is a primary feature. Before attempting to start a dialogue, you're reminded to reflect on how the feedback may affect you as the giver; do you feel confident, nervous or something else? What might the recipient think and feel when they hear what you have to say; delighted, devastated or something else? Priority is given to entering a relationship with a positive intent that creates an environment of reciprocity, and also to how we encourage others to do the same. The themes in Chapter 6 enable you to know what to *activate* to nurture, maintain and sustain the relationship: objectivity, mindfulness, presence and timing of feedback.

In this Chapter I guide you through the themes that *both* people in the relationship need to *notice* and *react* to when committed to productive relationships. Having this developed power of observation enables you to work with and give attention to what is impacting on sustaining the quality of the relationship.

Scoular (2011) tells us that 'feedback is distinct from hypothesis and interprets what has been observed' and believes that 'keeping the two separate can be a challenge.' One solution to good feedback is to avoid interpretation and confine it to the facts. Second, 'use only yourself – where you have direct evidence – if some consequences are to be drawn,' (Scoular, 2011). I think we can agree that feedback is ideally based on accurate observation and without the bias of our interpretation. This is a big ask! Remember the impact of unconscious bias featured in the last chapter? However, as we also know, awareness reduces the influence of subjective misinterpretation.

The vital component missing from Scoular's view is *how* we deliver feedback. Neuroscience and studies of the Unconscious which are visited later in this chapter make it clear that much more is going on in our interactions with others beyond the spoken word. As human beings we have many untapped resources available within ourselves, and it's time to take advantage of these!

Part 3 of The Relational Leadership WAY© has four themes:

Physicality: noticing levels of energy and somatic changes
Emotional State: observable fluctuations in emotional stability
Intuition: level of accessible 'brainpower' from conscious learned experience and unconscious channels
Metaphysical: paying attention to the sensation of feeling what may be impacting on the relationship from the wider system.

Physicality (Theme 7 of The Relational Leadership WAY©) reminds us that being alert to changes in our own and others' **physiology** and the embodied sensations generated at these times can provide valuable information. The research study found that the most common of these are 'feelings' in the stomach and throughout the body generally (somatic) including the sense of smell. Observing the other, at the same time as noticing changes in our own physiology, helps us to detect changes in energy, body language, skin tone and breathing. You need to check out these signals and decide if these offer good indicators of how the other is reacting to what is being said in conversation and how this may influence the quality of relationship.

We make generous use of the word 'feelings' to describe our **emotional state** (Theme 8) that 'comes' and makes 'connection' with the other. The 'energy' of these feelings can be powerful, giving huge strength and resilience to use this 'energy' flowing between both, or even 'step into the energy' of the other to gain connectivity. What can be spontaneously noticed as the state of the other? Notice if your 'breathing, pace and energy' are matched and generating and maintaining a shared **emotional** space, facilitating conversation. Next time you're people watching at your favourite café, notice people who are totally engaged in conversation, talk flows easily, body language is similar and being together appears effortless.

Emotional state asks you to be aware of your own and others' emotional state. This concept was touched upon briefly in Chapter 5 and this chapter takes a closer look at how to manage emotions that present 'in the moment' when in conversation.

When reacting to signals from **intuition** (Theme 9) possibly offering a 'green light' for the timing of feedback, we're responding to an emergent sense of 'instinctiveness' located 'somewhere' in us: a *hunch*. Reacting to 'instinct' seems to create a state of openness for 'sourcing' signals from others, from silence and also from the wider system. Research into how we access information from the **unconsciousness** suggests there is still much to reveal about the richness of data still inaccessible to us. However, science moves on apace and new learning emerges.

Metaphysical (Theme 10) emerged as the descriptor that best illustrates those moments of 'sensation' that seem to be present 'somewhere' in the wider system. Conjecture surrounds claims for metaphysical properties as a source of data that informs relational states; however, as this text brings new thinking, the topic has been researched for inclusion here.

There was a time when humans believed the earth was flat and that space travel to the moon was impossible; as we know, this is now history.

Theme 7 of The Relational Leadership WAY©: Physicality informing a 'relational way of being'

We ignore noticing what's happening in the physicality of others at our peril! We try to cope with the unreliability of the emotionally charged spoken word that creates misunderstandings. Add these unintended misinterpretations to the mix of communication interferences in both (values, beliefs, attitudes) and the result is message distortion. Think how quickly what we believe has been an innocent remark can escalate into a volatile exchange of accusatory snipes. Random statements like these can trigger a propensity to believe we can 'read' the direction of a conversation, and it's easy to see how often 'we get it wrong.' We have to rely on supplementary information to get nearer to understanding each other.

Our bodies offer boundless clues, both from reflexive unconscious reactions to external stimuli that resonate with suppressed memories of past experiences and conscious gestures that punctuate our spoken word. Notice how we shuffle in our seat when we feel discomfort about something we're hearing or the anticipation of what we believe we may hear. Of course, we could just be sitting in an uncomfortable chair and need to shift our position!

In either scenario the cause of noticeable changes in physicality are possible warning signals about the temperature of the relationship.

Somatic red alerts

How we move is more important than *what* the movement is states Batson (2007). Our bodily movements are an indicator of who we are as a person. Our emotions show up in our body and others will sense how we feel towards them without us uttering a single word. The body is a living metaphor for the life we lead.

These are somatic indicators that are likely to be exposed in uncertain, continuously changing and ambiguous times in the workplace:

Table 7.1 Somatic causal indicators of presenting behaviours with their underlying activators

Causal signal	Typical presenting behaviour	Activator

Under pressure	• Aggression and resistance to change
	• Withdraws from conversations and 'secures' safety by distancing from any perceived threat
	• 'Freezes out' what's going on around
	• Moves towards the pressure and tries to neutralise risks by being – for example – over-friendly and 'pleasing'
		• *We're hardwired for these reactions. We need or have help to recognise the onset. This keeps us present and helps to gain a sense of reality about how to cope and regain a sense of equilibrium*
		
		• *Actions by the other that may trigger 'pressure' behaviour:*
		  • *threat of exposure*
		  • *negative feedback*
		  • *increased workload*

Table 7.1 *(Continued)*

Causal signal	Typical presenting behaviour	Activator
Mentally unhealthy	Sequence of ailments: • stomach pain • back pain • pain in arms, legs, or joints (knees, hips, etc) • headaches • chest pain • dizziness • fainting spells • heart palpitations • shortness of breath • feeling tired or having low energy • trouble sleeping	• *feelings of inadequacy* • *fear of failure* • *lack of self-worth about value contributing to business operations*
Anxiety about performance at work	Cognitive symptoms: • fear • unease • repetitive negative thoughts • difficulty concentrating	• making presentations • expectation to voice opinion at meeting • impostor syndrome.

Noticing the onset of dysfunctional behaviour in the early stages is vital in avoiding a deepening situation. The capacity to be attentive to this type of altered state relies on your wellbeing, ability and willingness to stay alert to signs of changes in the demeanour of colleagues and direct reports.

Somatic responses

Being relational means that you move your attention between the other and yourself; an ebb and flow of data transfer that moves with the rhythm of a dance. Changes in energy and noticing blocks in communication are more readily noticeable with this degree of connection. You're able to make observations and share what you're seeing, hearing and feeling; you're achieving a 'way of being' in the relationship. Heightened attention to changing sensations in the body enables you to reflect on the meaning of these changes and anticipate that something similar may be happening for the other. You now have the opportunity for acknowledging somatic empathy even if you don't totally experience emotional/intellectual empathy with each other in the *exact same* moment. If you can achieve the state of sharing reciprocal somatic experiences, the relationship is enriched with a mutuality of experience.

When another is displaying closed body language with crossed arms, possibly legs crossed over and with palpable tension oozing from every pore, a likely assumption is that the other is carrying beliefs that are causing a block to communication. Only by releasing this block can we have a productive conversation. It may be a step too far to expect rational dialogue while the other's mind is focused on a perceived injustice. There has to be a release of the tension created by the block before body and mind can relax sufficiently to connect. The strength of thought fed by beliefs will depend on how much energy they've been fed; the more the thought develops and the more attention we give it, the more it begins to affect or shape our world and our relationships to it (Seto & Geithner, 2018). Creating a safe and trusting environment is essential in enabling movement from the stagnation of these blocking thoughts to one with a positive energy flow that stimulates a willingness to move forward.

You start the process of creating a fertile environment through yourself. Knowing what is happening somatically in your body means you can engage with the other through a felt sense that leverages cooperation. This is notably valid when feedback is perceived as a threatening experience to be avoided. Just because there's awareness in the other of a need for change, that doesn't necessarily make it happen. Releasing and exploring what we hold in our bodies helps us work with limiting issues to facilitate the desired change. This also means that giving feedback in the future is sustainable as we don't drain our energy through unrecognised tension.

When you take time to slow the pace of the conversation, possibly adding periods of silence to tacitly acknowledge the tension in the other, this may be sufficient for the other to feel ready to participate. You may feel confident in expressing what you're noticing in the other to help overcome emotional discomfort perhaps not yet confronted. Showing empathy and compassion can be a facilitative segue to helping the other release and discharge the disabling energy in the body. The question 'Are you feeling angry about this?' gives 'permission' for the other to express what they're feeling and thinking, and offers an opening for further exploration and productive discussion. Brené Brown shares a personal story in her Netflix series about an argument she had with her husband. Before she knew what was going on for him, she had her own 'story' playing in her head about what she thought was going on. She says they now share their 'stories' to help them get through the argument and hear the other person: 'Let me tell you what story I'm playing in my head right now...' I think this demonstrates well how we can avoid falling into the 'assumption trap.'

The recognition of therapeutic release speaks loudly of your willingness to help with genuine care in achieving beneficial solutions. The other feels listened to and respected. The result is a reduction in adrenaline levels in the brain as the tension caused by perceived threat lessens. The outcome is cooperation and takes the form of being together in a supportive relationship that replaces the isolation of being a solo traveller under scrutiny. Somatic exploration precedes work at a cognitive level every time. Showing vulnerability and compassion through speaking our truth is a strength to be celebrated and which purges the bestowal of shame. Embodying an authentic relational leadership presence cultivates the trusting environment in which change thrives and feedback receives a willing invite.

Case study

Vee is conscientious, responsible and cares greatly about the contribution made to team objectives. There has been a lot of pressure lately about meeting deadlines to complete a proposal for a contract that will make a huge difference to the business bottom line.

Somehow the creative juices just aren't flowing today, and as Vee stares out of the window seeking inspiration, in walks the team leader.

Vee's shoulders tighten and curve in to a protective arc, her breathing becomes shallow and rapid, and facial muscles tighten into the stony stare of statuary.

The team leader looks at Vee and interprets a vision of perceived inactivity as lack of commitment to the urgency of completing the proposal. The reality is that Vee is somatically alert and has 'frozen submissively' as protection against an anticipated threat of an outburst from the team leader.

The result is that lack of emotional intelligence equals inability to understand impact on others and to sensitively explore reactions in others before making assumptions.

A contribution from neuroscience

Brown (2018), a leading neuroscientist answering the question of how we can embed our experience into knowledge about organisations, says we do this by incorporating what we hear into what's really happening in organisations. Energy from humans creates what emerges out of the system in organisations. If we feel respected and are given autonomy and responsibility at work, we're likely to create energy in others and use positive language about our work experience. If we feel the opposite, we radiate lethargy, negative speak and the environment becomes toxic.

The key question is how we create relationships where energy flows to raise productivity. Brown states that we have to develop models of how we map and trap energy. Perception controls our behaviour, and if we can track how people perceive organisations, we can have an idea of the energy flow in the system. If you create enabling cultural values and trust your people as self-regulating systems without the need to be controlled, energy flow is likely to be spontaneous when people are freed from micro-managing constraints.

Brown (2018) also enlightens us about the energy flow in male and female brains. The brains are the same, although connections made within the brain are used differently. After puberty the brain changes and works in either the left or right. Men evidently make connections as 'either or' binary, 'this' or 'that,' whereas women make connections between both the left and right sides of the brain. If we ask men, 'What are you thinking?' the reply is, 'Nothing.' The brains of men 'stop' while women's brains are making links all the time. Organisations are missing out on the ability to adapt and make things happen arising from feminine energy because women are generally working to male 'rules.'

We have this opportunity for informing relational leadership if we learn more about how to harness feminine energy in organisations. This is not a question of equality; it's about difference and not labelling women in men's terms, says Brown (2018). You may like to reflect on how this feedback from neuroscience can be integrated into your organisation's working practices:

- What are the prevailing 'rules' that inform the way people behave and work in your culture?
- How liberating and how debilitating are these rules?
- Who made the rules and who can change them?

Theme 8 of The Relational Leadership WAY©: Emotional State informing a 'relational way of being'

I often find a reluctance in business to work with emotion. The reason often given is fear of and knowing how to manage emotion. Exploring the assumptions underlying the aversion helps to release anxiety and offers encouragement to speak openly with the other to create a dialogue about preferences when managing emotions.

Sometimes there is a more systemic avoidance of encouraging what can be caricatured as an 'outpouring' of near hysteria, neuroticism, 'bad temper' or similar negative label. The tone of voice describing these unwanted interruptions translates into a clear dismissal of any emotional display outside the range of 'feeling great' about working here. Basically, 'unwanted' emotional reactions only gain airtime when they become an issue and 'need addressing,' rather than being perceived as currency informing the health of organisational culture. A colleague shared a recent news item recalling how showing emotion was once the passport to 'not being heard and listened to.' The story now seems encouragingly the reverse for some: 'You have to express emotion to be taken seriously!' The same colleague recognised this shift during her career, how both directions can be overdone and how so often we get emotion 'wrong'; it isn't good or bad – it just is! The observation was also made that we may all be perceiving the relevance and impact of emotional expression differently because of age, experience and culture; all the features of diversity.

Emotional climate

How is the culture in your organisation impacting on willingness for emotional disclosure, and what would change if the culture changed? A reflection reminder that may be helped by reading on.

Some organisations continue to encourage a 'traditional' and 'conventional' culture – one that expects employees to park 'the emotional stuff' before entering the sliding doors of automaton towers. The reality is – and a growing number of organisations are realising – that emotion is part of and also integral to being human. This may sound obvious, and you may wonder about the need to emphasise this. However, any hint of encouraging emotional shutdown will ultimately be equivalent to removing a SIM card and expecting a mobile phone to be fully functional for making calls.

The ability to recognise a prevailing organisational culture may seem easy to predict. Seeing people smiling, chatting, laughing together and generally demonstrating harmony in working relationships can be indicative of a healthy organisation supporting the wellbeing of employees. The reality can be a different story. This surface ambience of bonhomie may be hiding an underbelly of blame and shame for displaying any cracks in the shiny façade of being corporate.

I once worked with a business where the leadership style had tendencies towards a culture of 'we value our employees' with the sub-text – 'as long as they fit the template of expectations.' Valuing employees didn't appear to be translated as welcoming suggestions for improving the wellbeing of employees. Walking into reception, a practised smile and courteous greeting welcomed you into the architecturally polished waiting area. Coffee machines and lounge sofas invited you to relax into sumptuous cushioning before being ushered to your appointment. Working as an external contractor was like

185

being a refuge for a catalogue of war stories recalling bullying and expectations of performance beyond what was reasonable to expect in a routine working day. Of course, no one was expected to work in this time-bound way, and hours that extended late into personal time was the cultural norm. This leadership declared a need for innovation and challenging behaviour but didn't encourage it. 'Don't speak up at meetings,' was the perceived reality of employees in this organisation.

The chances of anyone revealing how they really felt in this company was a big fat *zero*, as long as they intended to stay! Forget the performance management conversation as an opportunity for shared feedback when the expected script was that 'all was fine,' and establishing what else could be integrated into an already bulging workload. The result was that everyone played the charade of happy working tribes, eventually resulting in increased turnover, burnout or worse. This toxic environment doesn't apply to all organisations and any perception of exaggeration in the description is intended to alert you to the downside of urging more for less from employees, especially in these turbulent times.

The scenario illustrated is not only uncaring, it simply isn't effective for the workplace of the future. Uncertainty, ambiguity and increased competition contextualised within digitisation and artificial intelligence replacing routine tasks will become the norm.

We have to calibrate our engagement with human capital – read 'relationships' for this use of business jargon – to retain a sustainable workforce.

Add to this the demographic dimension in which younger people entering the workforce have different expectations from the previous generation, and the complexity of both – and possibly more – age groups being employed in the same organisation at the same time. The synergistic contributions from all generations is an untapped resource. Younger generations won't tolerate the 'tell and do' of outdated leadership styles, which diminishes and does a disservice in supporting readiness for the work of the future, much of which is yet to be discovered. Younger people have the expectation of wanting to be heard and to be respected for who they are. Senior generations have a critical role as buddy mentors focusing own and others' efforts in making this happen. Have you noticed how people work better when they can be themselves and not feel judged? We also need to get better at not critically judging ourselves based on self-manufactured irrelevant criteria: self-reflective feedback can be undermining!

Valuing employees and genuinely taking action to promote an ethos of wellbeing in the 'way we treat people around here' means genuinely promoting a holistic perspective. This means an integrated, systemically-applied strategy integral to all business operations and demonstrated through relational leaders who know and who promote that this goes beyond making sure the workplace functions at the optimum temperature! A great place to start is with senior leaders, who may not even know each other very well, let alone others in the business.

Creating the conditions championed by relational leadership doesn't necessarily mean that people will be willing to 'reveal' themselves or be prepared to be their authentic selves at work. This happens when people feel they can trust a system where people continue to be reliable and deliver what they say they will; a system where mistakes genuinely are seen as learning opportunities, and when things don't go as planned, reasons are creatively explored and changes emerge. We must remember the cultural dimension, which may reinforce the suppression of emotion in our expectation for disclosure; this is well covered in other texts.

When relational leadership is operating effectively, what you will notice is an atmosphere of excited animation, of people wanting to be at work; they are happy! Positivity is palpable in communications through a willingness for personal disclosure and 'bringing yourself' to work becomes the norm. Imagine what could be achieved if people truly felt their ideas were valued and felt accepting if they weren't necessarily adopted; the reward is the recognition of being heard. Imagine a performance management review becoming a reflective conversation with the manager asking the question, 'What sort of working relationship do we want together?' The manager-direct report relationship is critical in fuelling energy to activate and motivate. We notice who bothers to get to know us and find out what captures our enthusiasm. Take a look at social media, which offers thousands of daily glimpses into how our contacts are feeling and what emotional drivers stimulate them.

We all have the ability to react to what we 'pick up' as being the emotional state of others. You can observe where harmony exists in relationships; just people-watch for a while and you'll notice 'matching' of 'breathing, pace and energy' in a shared **emotional** space. Evidently, every time our heart beats we send out an electromagnetic field that connects us to others.

A 'way of being' generated by adopting The Relational Leadership WAY© encompasses the recognition of emotion as imperative for creating and sustaining enabling relationships. The EMCC competency framework (2015) for coaches and mentors suggests 'responding to client's emotions without becoming personally involved.' Gestalt coach practice suggests 'paying close attention to your own reactions to [others], what sensations are stimulated, and disclosing these to your client' (Clutterbuck & Megginson, 2009). This implies different perspectives between the intention of 'disclosure' in the Gestalt sense and not 'becoming personally involved' from the EMCC.

I believe productive relationships only exist when emotion is recognised as an enabling, rather than disabling, resource. Seligman's research (2011) into Positive Psychology tells us that 'happiness at work' strengthens the psychological contract between employer and employee. You have to have a different conversation and accept feelings of discomfort before you can progress to feelings of connectivity, build trust and improve the quality of your thinking.

When we establish a relationship of openness and trust with another, this is likely to encourage deeper engagement leading to more fertile dialogue.

A colleague shared a distressing story heard about a manager who had used the same style of management for many years. This manager became concerned about the lack of motivation in a direct report to the extent of contacting the person's husband – who they knew – to ask if 'everything was all right at home.' The husband confirmed that everything was fine in their domestic life, and took the risk of asking if the manager wanted to know what the real issue was. The manager was shocked and mortified to hear the problem was their management style, and that because of this the employee was unhappy at work to the point of considering leaving. Why did the manager react in this way? It wasn't because of an understandable big dent to their pride. It was because for 25 years no one had given them any reason to think any change in their style was needed. No big surprise, then, that they believed they were doing a good job as a manager, having had this reinforced by incremental rewards and promotions. This is not an unusual scenario. This is a disingenuous and disrespectful way of treating people and working on and with the relationship has to be given the priority to change this diminishing behaviour. Not giving developmental feedback doesn't avoid the unconscious validation of acceptable performance when the opposite is true.

Neuroscience and emotion

Brown (2018), a leading neuroscientist, tells us that as humans we're not naturally rational beings; we rationalise by making up our own truths and our thinking is steered by our emotions, not vice versa. Evidently our brain makes 'sense' by the way emotions have attached to experience so that our brains control us and not the other way around.

When this is true, you can see how easy it is to generate a feeling based on past experiences. If we're treated fairly by others, we are likely to be trusting in future relationships. Negative experiences will 'warn' us to think we may be in 'danger' and to be cautious. Being relationally aware means we can detach from what we 'think' is happening, take a deep breath and then check it out. This applies to both negative and positive scenarios. As reactive humans we will not always make a measured response. However, awareness of such phenomena arouses an emotionally healthy world lens that helps us to respond with a considered view, rather than react without thought. Emotion suggests a force that drives what we do.

Have you noticed how one person in a group gives an opinion or suggestion about a way forward and others readily follow and agree sometime without question? This seems a more prevalent event in teams, particularly those where the membership is stable with little turnover. This clearly influences decisions and outcomes and extends to the emotional climate between team members. A dominant mood in the team can be contagious. Listen to the team conversations, and notice whether patterns of positivity or negativity dominate. What are the levels of positive energy and engagement in overcoming problems? How often are people criticising lack of resources and complaining about what can't be done rather than what can be done? This propensity for transference and countertransference of emotion leads to reflexive copying of facial expressions, repetition of what becomes team jargon and can extend even to movement. Being relationally aware enables team members to counteract this tendency for alignment and raise a consciousness in the team that encourages avoidance of adopting emotional states from each other. Improvement in team performance culminates in improvements for business performance.

This concept of transference and countertransference is explained by 'limbic resonance.' Lewis et al. (2001) talk of limbic resonance generated from the limbic system in the brain being the source for sharing deep emotional states. These states include the feelings of fear, anxiety and anger, and also empathy that is generated by dopamine. The concept is that our brain chemistry is affected by those closest to us and our systems synchronise, enabling non-verbal social connections so that we become attuned to each other's inner states. You probably recall those occasions when someone calls when you were just thinking of them.

Add to this the findings on 'mirror neurons,' and we start to understand the interrelatedness of human beings. Iacoboni (2009) talks of mirror neurons providing some kind of inner imitation of the actions of other people. We 'simulate' the intentions and emotions associated with those actions. When you see someone smiling, your mirror neurons for smiling fire up, initiating a cascade of neural activity that arouses the feeling we typically associate with a smile. So, when we're greeted by a smile we reflexively smile back; all due to brain activity. Our interdependence and sense of collective agency that comes from social interactions gives us the ability for empathic resonance. This limbic resonance and regulation are also known as 'emotional contagion,' with some emotions, especially positive ones, being spread more easily than others through 'interpersonal limbic regulation' (Barsade, 2002). This is one explanation for the team behaviour described above.

Reinforcement of the concept of transference also sits with quantum physics! Just a mention here on this to illustrate there is still much to learn about transference of emotion. There's nothing new about the study of the collective human consciousness and the effect on others. Human beings also radiate electromagnetic fields from their brain and heart. If our psychological health and wellbeing are interconnected with that of others, this gives cause for us to be mindful of the electromagnetic waves or energy that we feed continuously into the global connected energy field. In the world of quantum physics, McCraty et al. (2012) argue that we are connected in a way that goes beyond our conscious awareness. There's a thought!

Back to what happens in your brain to regulate emotion:

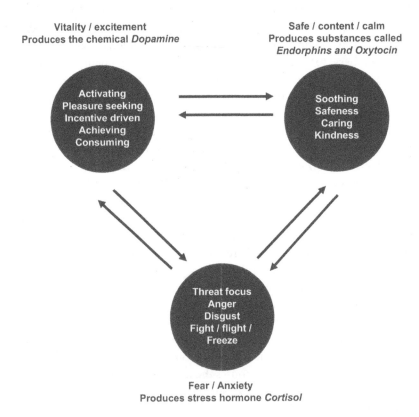

Figure 7.1 The emotional regulation system in the brain and body, based on the work of Gilbert, 2010b (Gregory, 2016)

How applying the 'emotional regulation system' into a workplace scenario may play out in a feedback discussion:

> Here is another workplace story shared by a disheartened client. What to say in an upcoming appraisal meeting was reflected upon, being well prepared and with a 'reward' expectation of praise for work well done, the perception was that an opening existed for requesting a salary increase.
>
> What happened was not as expected! The actual experience felt like one bordering on criticism about a shortfall in the quality of performance.

This person's brain, in anticipation of a positive appraisal experience, produces dopamine, one of the alleged four 'happiness' hormones. This releases endorphins in the brain instilling a sense of calm and a relaxed mood. When the expected event becomes a negative one, cortisol places the body in a flight, fight or freeze state of fear and anxiety about how the conversation will evolve. This reaction is well known as the old (reptilian) brain system creating anger that flows through the body and directs thoughts, actions and urges. This creates a desire for 'revenge' that clouds our 'thinking abilities' and may result in a fissure in this relationship if uncontrolled and unresolved.

Function of emotions

Understanding the causes and functions of emotion helps you to be more conscious of your own and others' behavioural drivers and patterns and how these can be managed:

Table 7.2 Causes and functions of emotion

Anger	Often accompanied by frustration: you have spent many hours preparing a report, your laptop crashes and you haven't backed up. You know you should have backed up and are frustrated with yourself because of the wasted time.
Shame	Usually an emotion about emotion: you are angry with yourself for feeling anxious about the way you reacted to a colleague. You felt justified at the time about your reaction to something they said. Now you're regretting it and feeling anxious that you've damaged the relationship.

(Continued)

Table 7.2 (Continued)

Love	This emotion reassures us that we have a positive relationship and that we are safe to be open in our conversations. The word 'love,' once absent from business vocabulary, is now emerging as a contributor to wellbeing in the workplace.
Happiness	An increasingly promoted emotion at work attracting conferences and businesses creating special breakout areas for employees, 'tech' allowances, on site spas and holiday parties.

Recognition that emotions are part of everyone's innate makeup, developed as the human race evolved, reminds you that the sensations aroused by emotion are present in us all. Emotions are evoked unconsciously and may be subconsciously in our body memory from past experiences. We are not unique or alone in enjoying the positive and wishing to avoid the negative feelings generated by the mix of emotions that are part of our daily life. Once accepted, you may want to ask some or all of these questions that help to release the thinking mind from keeping you stuck in an emotion causing discomfort:

1. Where is this emotion taking me and is that where I want to go?
2. Who's in control of this emotion – me or the emotion?
3. How often do I step back and reflect before reacting to my emotion?
4. What can I learn from accepting the emotion for what it is and moving on to a different experience linked to a different emotion?
5. How good am I at accepting that good and not so good emotions live alongside one another and are there for a reason?

The skill to practice is to find helpful mood-changing options that move you away from any negativity arising from disruptive emotions or when you catch yourself going over and over the same issue. When others see this in you, they are more likely to follow.

Emotions about emotions

Emotions are complex and can be cumulative. We can feel shame and satisfaction about being angry; we can feel happy about and also fear being contented. Sometimes emotions conflict with each other. Multiple emotions about the same event can be confusing. The good news is that we can control these events and gain balance in our feelings through being 'mindful'; a theme of relational leadership. In the same way as 'compassion,' another theme in The Relational Leadership WAY© reminds us of kindness and care for ourselves and others when we have confusion caused by emotional complexity. It's OK to feel happy about a promotion, sad that a close colleague didn't, and anxious that they'll be pleased for you in the midst of their disappointment. You don't have to avoid certain feelings because of being frightened of them or because they remind you of unpleasant things. Being relational is accepting ourselves and others as we are in the moment, and that the behaviour is not the person. We all have a need for being valued and appreciated.

So, how do these references help you with being relational? Hopefully this brief explanation of how the brain functions and is shaped by others has stimulated you to calm your feelings rather than allowing the feelings to control you. You can achieve this through practicing 'presence,' covered in the last chapter. The calmness you develop will be infectious, transferred unconsciously to others and lead to healthier conversations.

Even though we operate generally at a cognitive level in our daily operations at work, you will gain a greater understanding about human functioning through accepting we are emotional beings at *all* times and if you focus on the moods generated by emotion you can recognise the link with attitudes that may well be well entrenched in the way people behave.

We can also remind ourselves that we can choose whether we want to be happy or sad and whether we want to be positive or negative about the prospect of feedback.

If you want to learn more about emotional competence, read the texts of John Heron and Daniel Goleman.

Theme 9 of The Relational Leadership WAY©: Intuition informing a 'relational way of being'

'Intuition! Forget that soft skills stuff!' Relying on intuition has endured a 'bad press,' with business operations preferring to base decisions on logical rational thinking supported with evidence, preferably in a statistical format. We know that what is commonly labelled soft skill competency is far from soft, and that people issues are usually the most challenging to resolve. Think of the person who says, 'Yes, that's fine,' to whatever is asked of them only to fail to deliver, despite several reminders. Accepting this is a line management issue which often goes unaddressed, how helpful would it be to take time with this person and *really* zone in to what we're sensing may be the issue and sharing our thoughts to see where it goes? Worth a try, when other strategies have failed to connect.

Encouragingly, the trend now appears to be moving towards at least an acknowledgement that the 'feeling' we 'pick up' about others or a situation deserves attention. We're reminded (Tolle, 2004) that we've 'buried' the skills innate to human beings and created a dependency on cognitive thinking. As a primitive society, we honed our intuitive skills for survival (Harari, 2015) to ward off threats. Even today, no one is going to hang around trying to talk their way of out of a situation that spells trouble and makes us feel vulnerable. The caveman is still alive and functioning in our genes and trusting this primeval instinct as our ancestors did is likely to benefit our work, well-being and relationships in ways that surprise us!

'Dangerous' situations can be interpreted in many ways beyond the obvious of feeling personally threatened. I can remember in another 'career life,' holding interviews for a vacancy in my department. This person would be my deputy, so a close working relationship was essential. At selection time I consciously ignored my intuition guiding me to appoint the person I 'felt' most comfortable with. I gave full attention to the voice of rational thought by recruiting the person who appeared to complement my skills and 'fill the gaps' in my least preferred and weaker areas. Big mistake! This was definitely the worst recruitment decision of my whole career. As much as we both tried to find a compatible working relationship, progress was unsustainable. We were just so different in personality, working style and execution of tasks. What should have worked on paper couldn't survive in reality.

We can upgrade and regain this neglected resource of intuition by working at being consciously 'present.' This doesn't mean consciously *thinking* about being present. This means total engagement between mind and body, taking notice of what emerges from within and being curious about what this is alerting us to. We can judge whether this is a random sensation or a reassuring or a cautionary 'message.' It's the difference between the feeling after overindulging at a celebration dinner, the feeling of trust meeting close friends and the feeling of apprehension when your manager says those ominous words, 'Can I give you some feedback?'

We're not born with negativity, feelings of sadness or similar emotions; however, through life's events we attach these feelings with the causal memories and store this information in our unconscious. As these memories are unconscious, we don't realise or we're not aware of how they drive our reactions to situations and people. Unconscious reactions spontaneously ignite these past memories, which may evoke joy or manifest feelings of discomfort. If we have negative unconscious memories created by reinforced experiences our defences are up and our mind freezes as we put all our energy into 'protecting ourselves' from what we perceive as a threatening situation. Our unconscious mind is feeding our ego in this way – the ego that must be obeyed and crowds out thoughts of rationality in this scenario. We may have nothing at this stage to reinforce this thinking; however, the emotion has fed our cognition and this state of defence locks in.

Getting back in touch with our intuition may feel risky in a world predicated on logic. Can we really trust the ability to understand or know something with the immediacy available from intuition and based on feelings rather than fact? How can we rely on 'understanding' or 'knowing' the quality of a relationship without needing to think about it and without proof, evidence, or conscious reasoning, or without understanding how the knowledge was gained?

Well, Einstein reputedly said:

> I never made one of my discoveries through the process of rational thinking

The move towards giving credibility to intuition as a source of information gives a degree of validation for supporting the findings of the research study (Lewis, 2014b). Study participants were unclear about how they knew when to offer feedback; they just 'knew' it would be a good time. Through examining data together and exchanging experiences from practice what had previously been the 'mystery of knowing' gained a label. 'I notice my interpretation of feedback included intuition. I've been doing more living with my intuition than I was before and letting it happen much more.'

Barber (2008) describes this 'knowing' as 'being guided by the wisdom of uncertainty' or as he prefers: 'surrendering to the fertile void – something unknown and unknowable; when I can quieten my own desires I find intuition calls to guide me.' Barber develops his thinking by 'encouraging in myself and others the cultivation of "spaciousness" and a willingness to be informed by something beyond ourselves.'

These moments of connectivity symbolise relational leadership at its most potent. My reflection on this phenomenon is, 'You know it when it's there (connectivity) and you know when it's not.' The ability to make such connection comes through practice and giving attention to adopting a way of being. We are bringing into consciousness what we achieve intuitively in creating our most intimate relationships and adapting this in service of fertile working relationships. Take a moment to reflect on the relationships you have at work, how they differ and what makes some more effective than others.

We have words of caution, however, from an article in HBR by Locke (2015) who writes that 'Intuition Isn't Just about Trusting your Gut.' He believes that 'using our intuition is usually fine but only under certain conditions [with the] most important condition being expertise.' The article focuses on accruing domain-specific expertise over time – 10 years is quoted – to make accurate intuitive judgements.

Translating this research finding into making judgements about an ability to determine the quality of relationship perhaps makes it safe to say we can make predictions based on our feelings of whether a relationship is healthy or needs attention. Attempting to prove a subjective feeling with objective data is likely to be more challenging in a relationship situation than for a problem-solving situation. However, over time and with emotional intelligence we can look for supporting 'evidence' to enrich or exclude our feelings of whether relationships are working or whether they need attention. If we feel there is 'something in the air,' this intuitive metaphor is telling us it's time to talk!

The location of 'intuition'

Is what we familiarly call intuition as mysterious as it seems, or is there a perfectly reasonable rationale to explain its existence?

Researching the source of intuition, this definition comes from Encyclopaedia Britannica:

> **Intuition**, in philosophy, the power of obtaining knowledge that cannot be acquired either by inference or observation, by reason or experience. As such, intuition is thought of as an original, independent source of knowledge, since it is designed to account for just those kinds of knowledge that other sources do not provide. Knowledge of necessary truths and of moral principles is sometimes explained in this way.

The unconscious is regularly linked as the source of intuition. Sigmund Freud, known as the father of psychoanalysis, believed the unconscious to be the primary source of human behaviour and powerfully influence our feelings, motives and decisions. Like an iceberg, the most important part of the mind is the part you cannot see and only the tip of the iceberg, in this case the conscious mind, appears 'above the surface.' Freud (1915) claimed that our unconscious processes appear in dreams, 'slips of the tongue,' jokes, in our habits and in our 'intuition.'

Carl Jung (1953), a contemporary of Freud's, agreed that the unconscious determines personality; however, he proposed that the unconscious is divided into:

1. Personal unconscious: reservoir holding memory that was once conscious and now forgotten or repressed
2. Collective unconscious: deepest level inherited from the entire human species.

The concept of unconscious has also attracted controversy since Jean Paul Sartre (1943) disputed its very existence and firmly challenged Freud's theory of the unconscious. There doesn't seem to be sufficient evidence to conclusively prove these theories!

Kahnemann (2011) proposes his theory by sidestepping Freud with concepts:

Table 7.3 Kahnemann's Systems 1 and 2 theory

System 1 – intuitive response	System 2 – analytical response
This is the brain's fast automatic intuitive response that Kahnemann believes is more influential, guides and steers System 2.	This is the mind's slower analytical mode where reason dominates and which can be flawed.

Kahnemann puts into doubt the premise that decisions based on 'intuition' are irrational and suggests that the analytical response can be flawed. He also posits that the automatic System 1 responses can lead to flawed decision making or problem solving when System 2 thinking is ignored. Although the approach appears to have limitations, there is an argument that the distinction between the two helps to clarify thinking style.

Moving to more recent times, findings from cognitive neuroscience claim that most of the decisions we make – especially regarding people – are 'alarmingly' contaminated by our biases. We're not as objective as we think we are! A salutary message when we relate this to relationships. It's easy to appreciate this concept. Think how readily we make predictions about people based on appearance. We continuously judge each other and can create a complete profile of their family background, education, what type of car they're likely to have and where they'll go on holiday!

Mainstream neuroscience is now suggesting that the unconscious constantly communicates with the conscious mind via the subconscious to provide meaning to our interactions with the world, filtered through our beliefs and habits. The unconscious communicates through feelings, emotions, imagination, sensations and dreams. This is sounding remarkably similar to Freud's findings! Again, from neuroscience we have the unconscious described as a storage place for repressed memories or memories we don't wish to recall. We can't extract memories at will; however, they can be activated. An example of a trigger is smell; it is easy to evoke memories of a first partner when we later smell the same perfume worn back then and to remember grandma's fruit cake when similar baking transports us back to childhood!

What is the wisdom of the unconscious that we can work with; assuming we can? We're realising we can't rely solely on rational thinking. When we gather data (read evidence) for the performance appraisal which – despite the flaws – is still a preferred process, we have to make some assumptions about the credibility of the information. However, let's challenge this acceptance by focusing on 360-degree feedback. This widely used diagnostic tool is inherently biased. People will complete the feedback forms from their subjective lens of how they view the person. A disgruntled direct report will see the anonymity of response collation as an opportunity to express their true feelings about their manager. The sycophantic career climber will include an easily recognisable statement of praise in the 'other comments' box. Extreme examples excepted, they nevertheless demonstrate that any 'objective' approach chosen will produce flawed responses. My thinking is that this is not an either/or situation but an opportunity to take the best from both intuition and rational thought.

In commending intuition as a valuable resource and key theme in relationship management, let me quote the work of Claxton. In his YouTube video he talks of how 'we signal our emotions and our cognitive state through our body which shows up in our posture and most particularly through facial expressions and as normal functioning intuitive humans we are deeply connected with body and mind.'

When we gain access to intuition, we gain a new equilibrium of connecting with emotional intelligence.

Theme 10 of The Relational Leadership WAY©: Metaphysical informing a 'relational way of being'

We may believe there's just the two of us 'in this relationship.' We may also be missing an energy beyond what's immediately available to us 'in this relationship!'

198

I remember the first time I had a deep sense of connection with a client; an almost hypnotic state when the silence between us brought a deep sense of presence. I didn't know how to 'name' this; I just know on reflection that the state created in the intensity of the moment must have been generated through an accessible energy source from the wider system.

When you've read this far into Theme 10 and are already seeking a tangible connection with relational leadership you may be wondering where we are going with this!

Read on and hopefully you'll gain a sense of new possibilities emerging from reaching into what may be the unknown for you right now.

Metaphysics is a branch of philosophy with many definitions depending on the focus of study. Metaphysics can be rooted in reality, and at the same time can ask the questions about what reality actually is. Everything beyond what our theories and statistical data show to be true becomes metaphysics.

The definition that I believe is relevant for this chapter is simply 'going beyond what we know.'

Noticing levels of energy *in* ourselves *and* others was introduced at the beginning of this chapter. Now we look at energy *between* us. You must have felt the vibrations or lack of them when meeting someone for the first time. Using the analogy of sound, when the 'volume's turned up' these vibrations can feel like an electrical charge; when the sound is 'turned down' or possibly muted, the 'feeling' doesn't exist – nothing – you don't experience any sensation between yourself and another.

Others relate similar instances where having an apparently innate ability to create relationships may lead us to assume that we are 'one part of a larger network, we are all interconnected and interdependent' and through 'realizing we are all a part of the interconnected whole, it's not that we lose *the self*, but we actually expand *the self* to include a much larger sense of interconnection' (Siegel, 2010).

This interconnection to the 'quantum consciousness' concept is further explained by Laszlo (2012) describing 'consciousness.' Our brain receives information not only from our eyes and ears, but directly from the wider world with which we are 'entangled.' Laszlo describes this as a 'consciousness of directly intuited, felt connection to the world. It inspires empathy with people and with nature and brings an experience of oneness and belonging.'

An article featuring quantum intelligence in an Association for Coaching bulletin (Coyne & Mallinson, 2010) describes a new understanding of how our universe works, and again suggests that 'everything is inter-connected and that everything is made of energy and brought into reality when we engage with it.' The claim associated with quantum intelligence is that by connecting with our energy field we develop greater awareness, realise our own potential and establish a connection to the potential of others. 'Working energetically involves… a journey into the quantum world and experiencing [in the relationship] a field of potential or energy available for realisation' (Coyne & Mallinson, 2010).

Subsequently, moving from 'what is' and letting go of your thoughts and becoming open to 'what can be' in a wider vision will help us see possibilities for change and growth. On being open to the 'energy and information flow' Siegel (2010) references the work of Christakis and Fowler (2009) about the 'social networks and the invisible forces' that connect us 'within fields of influence we actually can't see.' We may not see this energy; however, we can feel it, sense it, notice it.

A work or social group open to being connected will always appear motivated, energetic and engaged. They are sharing personal energy and sourcing energy from the wider system. Recall the meetings you resist attending because you know boredom awaits, where the dialogue is flat, monotonous or non-existent, and when you come away feeling negative and world weary. People are not sharing or exploiting their own or others' energy, or the energy in the system. Be unswervingly intent on changing the dynamic and ask the solutions-focused question, 'What needs to happen to make this meeting more exciting?' When people 'become present,' having recovered from the shock of this 'intrusion' into 'thoughts of elsewhere,' you may just raise the energy levels as people's interest is aroused; you've just demonstrated relational leadership.

This reference is likely to appeal to those with heightened spiritual intelligence (Levin, 2001). Barber (2008) talks of a 'fertile void,' 'spaciousness' and 'a willingness to be informed by something beyond ourselves' and 'a spiritual discipline… a quality akin to Buddhism and Taoism which encourages a freeing of the mind and a loosening of the intellect… to be guided by a higher intelligence' (Barber, 2008).

I notice that reference to the 'human heart' or 'speaking from the heart' is dropping into the language commonly used within the coaching community and in some organisations. You'll hear references to 'heart' linked to being 'authentic' and 'speaking your truth,' giving suggestion to a move towards transparency and openness in communications. This 'use of self' or 'way of being' is resonant of relational leadership, where you are the conduit for encouraging quality dialogue and reciprocity.

Referencing the website 'Metaphysics for Life' (2013), the 'human heart' field is reported as 'interacting with and is affected by the electromagnetic field of the Earth, as well as other people, plants, animals – anything that has electromagnetic qualities.'

Exactly how and to what degree our individual heart fields become affected by the environment is still under investigation. However, it is claimed 'that this field connects all of us to each other, the Earth, and space in ways we don't yet fully understand.' Evidently 'the electromagnetic human heart field is a powerful source of energy and information, which can be accessed by the human mind under the right circumstances; it transcends the information we gain through the five physical senses' (Metaphysics for Life, 2013).

The organisation HeartMath (www.heartmath.org) talks of heart intelligence with the belief that 'adding heart increases the love flowing through our system, which can play a large part in solving the collective challenges of these transitional times' (2019). If you want to know more, the HeartMath website has research articles. One of these is 'The Science of Interconnectivity,' which focuses on studying different types of interconnectivity between people and the earth's magnetic fields; involving 1,600 Global Coherence Initiative members that found a number of significant effects of solar and geomagnetic activity on people's mental functions and emotional states.

Metaphysical studies are wide-ranging and not expected to be comprehensively covered here, although the intention is to pursue further research of this field. The purpose of Theme 10 is to alert you to what exists beyond the obvious, beyond the 'you and me' in a relationship. If you are willing to still the busyness of your mind that continuously strives to dominate thoughts and conversation and be open to trusting that silence brings presence, you will access the power that emerges from the energy field that surrounds us. Be patient – it took time to lose the ability to spontaneously access this resource and it will take time to reconnect with it again!

Read on to learn what the future may hold for 'working with the relationship.'

How artificial intelligence (AI) may impact on the future of feedback

8

Why do you stay in prison when the door is so wide open?

Rumi, 'A Community of the Spirit'

Humans will be replaced by artificial intelligence! This is the claim made by scientists in the field of AI. Scary thought or relief? When asked what we would do if we won the lottery, our first thoughts may well go to 'giving up work,' moving to our dream location and spending the rest of our days at leisure. Well, this may become a reality. If it does, then this of course begs the question of who will pay for the lavish lifestyle we want to enjoy? Well, if we're to be replaced by AI, the obvious choice is that the robots will naturally have to be taxed! If they're doing all the work and have taken all the jobs it makes perfect sense that they are taxed just as we are. Presumably this dilemma will sit with the 'owners' of the robots.

Leaving this fantasy to percolate in your imagination, let's return to the purpose of this text in improving the experience of feedback. This chapter offers a glimpse into how feedback may evolve in a future with an integrated workforce of humans and robotics – based on existing knowledge, what is AI likely to contribute to feedback?

How might AI shape the future of work?

This text began with an introduction to the digital age, how AI is already reshaping the world of work and how children today may not yet know about future careers because these jobs haven't been created. We know that digital disruption is already with us and AI is replacing the routine tasks in the workplace – robotics redistributes warehouse stock, bots are more proficient at statistical analysis than humans in the world of finance and chatbots are regularly used for the first sift in the recruitment of new hires. There are many similar scenarios where the influence of AI is easily observable and which is gaining recognition as creating the 'fifth industrial revolution.'

The benefits of programming algorithms to perform anything that is repetitive are obvious. The extent to which AI totally replaces the human workforce remains unknown. What seems to be happening is humans being complacent about the penetration of AI. Perhaps we're enjoying the benefits without thinking too much about the repercussions: '22 per cent of UK households now own a voice-controlled digital home assistant device, such as an Amazon Echo or Google Home, doubling the 11 per cent figure recorded in 2017. Furthermore, according to EY's latest digital home report, 41 per cent of households plan to own one in the next five years' (Stewart, 2019).

'What will happen if robots take over the world and run everything?' was the alarm bell ringing in a broadcast on UK Radio 4 (Ian McEwan and Andrew Marr, BBC R4 15.4.19). 'Our brains don't need a battery, but robots do!' the conversation continued, giving hope that the human race has some advantage over AI. However, the sobering question, 'What happens when the system crashes?' is a cautionary reminder of the wisdom to stay aware of developments and perhaps seriously think about what to expect if AI takes control.

The big question here is how will AI serve us as humans in the workplace and, for the topic of this text – how might people react to feedback from humanoid robots?

Buckingham and Goodall (2019) make realistic interpretations about what we commonly accept as truths about feedback. One of the three is that 'others are more aware than you are of your weaknesses… and the best way to help… is to show you what you cannot see for yourself.' The claim is clear in the assumption that 'my way is necessarily your way.' Presumably the opposite also applies in that people have the option to accept or reject others' opinions. This HBR article reinforces what has emerged from research that 'humans are unreliable raters of other humans.' This brings us back to asking what is reality? We know we see the world through our own lens. Our conditioning through life forms our opinions of others and we unconsciously attribute to others behaviours and assessment of competence. We can see why it's so important that the quality of the relationship enables open-mindedness, a willingness to accept subjective assessment and to seek together a realistic solution to helping each other learn. Perhaps the uncertainty of capturing reality is why we also rely on the anticipated security of societal and organisational cultural norms to add context, a reference point and a sense of stability to our interactions with others? These unanswered questions are shared to make us curious rather than accepting of feedback specifically, unless we're totally trusting of the source.

Let's continue with the AI projections and imagine what the integrated workforce of humans and robotics will offer the feedback dialogue. Singling out the limitations of the human condition as unreliable is an easy target for the argument that the objectivity of robotics can replace us. Knowing that robotics is already in the workplace and forecast to mushroom, what can we predict with our current level of knowledge?

AI appears to be on the 'cusp of Artificial General Intelligence (AGI) that can perform power of reasoning, problem solving and abstract thinking. in which the intelligence of machines can equal humans' (Stiehler & Gantori, 2018).

If we reflect first on the skill of machine learning that, by pattern recognition, can complete routine tasks involving sequential steps, we can see how easily an algorithm can replace and possibly be more accurate than one human's feedback to another. Where a human overrides AI capability is where common sense and reasonableness of judgements are critical or at least desirable. The safety industry is an obvious example of AI currently not having the capability for making common sense decisions about activities that occur outside of a prescribed routine. This is a risk not worth imagining, let alone taking! We can see that AI can instigate feedback with some limitations.

A weakness of AI, and one which is subject of much current debate, is ethics and regulation. One concern is who programmes the algorithms, humans or sophisticated AI, and what bias may be introduced consciously or unconsciously?

If we scrutinise the consistency of programming the activity of feedback based on rater comments:

1. Feedback initially has to be retrieved by the programmer: this can be the first level of bias
2. The feedback usually comes from a number of sources: second, third, perhaps up to five levels of bias

3. AI is programmed with feedback: possibly a sixth level of bias
4. Result is data in = result out.

Although AI may be objective in the delivery of feedback, the data input is likely to be generated by subjective raters. If voice recognition and simple sentence construction is a feature of AI, then responses from the receiver of feedback can only be interpreted by AI to the level of programmed competence. The current capability of AI seems to demonstrate that the conversation deteriorates when communication surpasses the limits of AI comprehension.

How relational is AI compared with humans?

What can we expect if we compare the effectiveness of connectivity that AI will likely have with humans with that of what *humans* predominantly have with humans? How effective is AI at generating a feeling of inclusion in the same way as a nurturing relationship between humans? Can we really feel the warmth from a machine that another human offers? As humans we feel inspired and are motivated when we know important others trust our intention, respect us, accept our limitations and value our contribution. All this complexity is at the same time making us feel safe in the relationship!

An article appearing in Fast Company reported on Microsoft introducing an algorithm that ensures people's talks are 'politically correct and profanity-free.' The software is designed to give live feedback on presentations. In the moment feedback advises people about their delivery including 'spotting language that is culturally insensitive.' Can you imagine similar software adapted for a performance discussion between line manager and direct report? Think of the impact of unsolicited interjections from a software microphone commenting on language. Some may claim such software avoids the potential for using harassing language; others may feel the intrusion of a third voice shatters attempts for creating a safe space for feedback. This is possibly an exaggerated example of technology influencing conversation, although it is offered as an indicator of future possibilities. Some may say this is George Orwell's book *1984* revisited, or at least an update – I heard recently that Alexa will join a conversation uninvited!

Algorithms are predicted to have the ability to read emotions and moods; there's a thought! Who knows, we may prefer the anonymity of AI to that of another human potentially holding up the mirror of judgement to confront us with our shortcomings. The giver of feedback may also welcome relinquishing to AI the task of potentially distressing feedback. AI is unlikely to have a vested interest in connecting with our feelings, despite the ability for recognising emotion. Feedback in this scenario is a transaction and preparation for the feedback conversation is the role of the programmer who decides what will be initiated by AI. This also removes the need for AI to have awareness of verbal communication at a semantic level when the richness of language currently makes it beyond even human understanding. This just seems to be duplicating rather than improving the many misunderstandings when we assume we know what the other person is thinking! We can only presume at this stage of AI development that a fully programmed algorithm or a desire for engaging in understanding the reaction of the other to feedback is not available.

Removing this potential for emotional reaction from the feedback equation may be desirable for some. There is no need to relate with another at a deeper level; the comfort zone for those who prefer a less complicated and more sterile conversation. There's no concern about managing the reaction of the other who receives unexpected feedback. Displays of empathy and compassion, both human attributes, are unlikely to feature. Feedback delivered – job done! If this holds traction, then we are replaceable, and feedback becomes logistical instead of dialogic.

We now know that without transformational feedback we cannot grow, and AI is without agency unless it can deliver.

The digital age also gives us entry to a global platform; a favourable expansion removing office walls, country borders and reducing our carbon footprint. Cognitive load management will be faster and easier as we share information and sense making can be data crunched in seconds. As always, there are consequences to every advantage. Bringing the village mentality to worldwide access means we also attract unprecedented cultural diversity in our universal workplace. Just consider our basic tribal mentality and need for relating with others similar to ourselves and the primal instinct for bonding within secure relationships. We already struggle at times with the relational complexity of our immediate micro world of business. We both relish and tentatively probe the macro opportunities bursting from the anteroom of globalisation by inviting modernism punctuated with the wisdom of caution. The complexion of feedback is likely to change in appearance, content and delivery, with relational leadership and expertise dominating, whatever the future shape of work. I offer a microcosm of the anticipated bigger picture awaiting us:

One of our international coaching skills training programmes included delegates from three continents. In one session, the dialogue ventured into how different cultures react to feedback. The case study involved working with 'ego' and how to overcome the 'blind spot' of someone with the mindset that 'their way was the only way.' They were always right and the idea that they may be contributing to the problem had never entered their thoughts. A snapshot of the dialogue relating to feedback went something like this:

'Well – it's just a case of saying to the person, if an observer was looking into your conversation, what would they be seeing?' The aim of this suggestion was to invite reflection and open a discussion about accepting some responsibility for the breakdown in a relationship.

Response: 'I value this opinion and agree that what you're saying can be effective. However, any hint of someone potentially feeling humiliated – even for someone with a modest self-image – will damage our working relationship and bring the conversation to a close.'

The dialogue continuing within the group recognised that what works in one culture is directly opposed in another. This is how we can so easily make wrong assumptions and unintentionally appear disrespectful.

Many similar scenarios and some yet to emerge face us as a global community and the importance of valuing relationships becomes increasingly evident in oiling the wheels of everyday business transactions. A monumental feat of programming must be confronting scientists if AI is to remotely match human capability – imperfections acknowledged! An integrated workforce means functioning effectively in a multi-cultural context between humans and AI, and presumably between AI and AI!

What do we need to change and how will we get there?

Technological change makes it clear that we need to accept that AI will transform the workplace, probably beyond much of what we recognise right now. We will have to adapt just as we have before to keep pace with technological progress. This may include accepting that feedback is not totally reliant on human intervention. If anything, feedback is likely to become even more important as the human race adjusts. What is more effectively accomplished by AI, what continues to be the domain of humans and what can be co-created by AI and humans working together are fundamental questions. Feedback is central to acknowledging activities best performed by AI, which is no longer seen for its convenience or entertainment value but as a major contributor to industry. This will mean job losses and also job creation. We will stagnate if we assume our roles will be the same; they won't. The presence of another human being showing empathy and compassion for those affected by technological enhancements will likely be the preferred option when the cold detachment of AI is the alternative choice. Honing relational expertise is vital.

AI is rapidly infiltrating a business world fuelled by both human complacency and AI specialists. The rate of advancement is ignored by some and others have no desire to get involved. This is compounded by the eagerness of scientists to be first to the marketplace with potentially lucrative inventions. It's definitely time to get involved. We can use technology to our advantage. We don't have to be victims if we accept responsibility for the drivers of change and play a role in shaping the workplace that best serves the needs of society.

We're building robots that are more intelligent than we are. We don't need to build the architecture anymore – robots can build other robots. It's not obvious how we control something that's more intelligent than we are. When AI is effectively self-reprogrammable, I guess the next level of conversation complexity is possible. Spontaneous creative communication is likely to remain a human skill for the foreseeable future, which is reassuring if AI makes us feel insecure! With another human being we have dialogue; we see each other 'thinking and reflecting'; we feel engagement. AI does not have the same range of expressions or emit the same energy as humans. We have mirror neuron connectivity and build relationships by reacting and responding to signals from each other. We rely on intuition to alert us to situations that need attention and those we can trust – robots don't function at this level. Robots may be programmed to objectively evaluate the validity of data supporting a thought based on intuition. However, AI has no experience of having an intuitive thought! This snapshot of human capability is just scratching the surface of the complexity of cognitive and emotional connections that humans engage in systemically for 'seeing the whole' from interrelationships and patterns of change. This complexity of thinking is outside the range of AI, at the moment.

Generation Z are reported as high performers with the expectation of development being part of the recruitment package on joining a new organisation. Anticipating development seems to have high correlation with the acceptance of feedback; advancement doesn't happen in isolation of feedback. This generation of digital natives will likely respond well to AI feedback in preference to human engagement. However, let's not assume. The awakening of youth to the problems of the world shows an expectation of wanting to be involved in decisions affecting the lifestyle inherited from previous generations. This includes the voice of the young in determining their place in the workplace. Gone are the days of staying with the same organisation; younger generations will seek new opportunities if they fail to realise aspirations with an existing employer.

These turbulent times demand agile leadership; never before have relationships been so problematic and we need to change to survive. Whether or not we agree with the integration of AI into our working lives, perhaps our focus can be redirected to what it can do for us rather than what it takes away. Undoubtedly AI outstrips human capability in many ways already. Our focus for feedback in the future needs to identify what human attributes are important to nurture, retain and distinguish us from AI – our social and relational intelligence. We need feedback to help us grow into what we need to become to regain a habitable world integrated with AI.

My vision of a relational future!

I make no apology for repeatedly extolling the virtues of relational leadership. Caring for others with sensitivity and compassion has never been as important as it is now.

Perhaps more than ever before, we have to react early – now – to make the world of work a better place to be and ensure that humans are well equipped to work with and not against the stealthy presence of AI.

Take a moment to think about the quality of your relationships or those of your clients. Imagine what changes there would be in the working environment and what you and they would be seeing, hearing, thinking and feeling if:

- The workplace was free of interpersonal and intrapersonal struggles
- Everyone was delivering to expectations and possibly beyond
- Everyone was responsible for their personal development
- Company speak was energetic and about possibilities
- Work was fun!

What is this telling you right now that you and others can fix by adopting the ethos of being relational?

A final reminder of practical steps you can take with others in your sphere of influence to act/lead more relationally:

Table 8.1 Personal and interpersonal competences of relational leadership

Personal attributes

Competence	Achieved by	What can you add that you will do
Authenticity	Always speak the truth	
Trust	Be responsive and do what you say you will	
Respect	Be mindful and attentive of others' feelings, thoughts, wishes, and rights	
Connection	Be approachable and available when meeting others	
Passion	Show enthusiasm	
Self-disclosure	Be prepared to be vulnerable	

Interpersonal attributes

Competence	Achieved by	What can you add that you will do
Security	Making people feel safe with you	
Transparency	No hidden agendas	
Interest	Get to know colleagues likes and dislikes	
Creative	Make a habit of looking for new possibilities	
Equality	Be fair in your treatment of others	

Lewis, 2019

Bibliography

Allport, G. (1979). *The Nature of Prejudice*. Cambridge MA: Perseus Books Publishing.

Askew, S., & Carnell, E. (2011). *Transformative Coaching: A Learning Theory for Practice*. London: Institute of Education, University of London.

Bachkirova, T., & Smith, C. (2015). From competencies to capabilities in the assessment and accreditation of coaches. *International Journal of Evidence Based Coaching and Mentoring*, Vol. 13, No. 2, August 2015, pp. 123–140.

Banaji, M. R., Bazerman, M. H., & Chugh, D. (2003). How (Un)ethical Are You? *Harvard Business Review*. December 2003 Issue.

Banaji, M. R., & Greenwald, A. G. (2013). *Blindspot: Hidden Biases of Good People*. New York: Delacorte Press.

Barber, P. (2008). A Brief Review of Gestalt Facilitation (2008) Accessed website 280311 www.gestaltinaction.com/index3.asp?pID=3&ID=3.

Barber, P. (2009). *Becoming a Practitioner-Researcher: A Gestalt Approach to Holistic Enquiry*. London: Middlesex University Press.

Barrett-Lennard, G. T. (2005). *Relationship at the Centre: Healing in a Troubled World*. London/Philadelphia: Whurr.

Barsade, S.G. (2002). The Ripple Effect: Emotional Contagion and its Influence on Group Behavior. *Administrative Science Quarterly*, Johnson Graduate School of Management, Cornell University, Vol. 47, pp. 644–675.

Batson, G. (2007). Revisiting overuse injuries in dance in view of motor learning and somatic models of distributed practice. *Journal of Dance Medicine & Science*, 2007, Vol. 11, No. 3, pp. 70–76.

Baxter, L. A., & Montgomery, B. M. (1996). *Relating: Dialogues and Dialectics*. New York: Guilford Press.

BCC World Service, (1999). Radio 4. Brain Power. 'Emotions' episode: Learning to learn in our everyday lives (BBC World Service First Broadcast 6 October 1999).

Beisser, A. R. (1970). The Paradoxical Theory of Change. In J. Fagan & I. L. Shepherd (Eds.), *Gestalt Therapy Now*. New York: Harper & Row.

Berger, J. G. (2004). Dancing on the Threshold of Meaning: Recognizing and Understanding the Growing Edge. George Mason University. *Journal of Transformative Education*, Vol. 2, No. 4, October 2004, pp. 336–351.

Berne, E. (1964). *Games People Play*. New York: Grove Press, Inc.

Blanchard, K. (2013). *Situational Leadership II: Learn the SLII Model*. USA: The Ken Blanchard Companies publication.

Bloom, P. (2017). *Against Empathy: The Case for Rational Compassion*. Harper Collins.

Bluckert, P. (2006). *Psychological Dimensions of Executive Coaching*. Berkshire: Open University Press McGraw-Hill Education. p. 38, 82, 144.

Bock, L. (2015). *Work Rules! Insights from Inside Google That Will Transform How You Live and Lead*. London: John Murray.

Bohart, A. C., & Tallman, K. (1999). *How Clients Make Therapy Work: The Process of Active Self-Healing*. Washington, DC: American Psychological Association.

Börjeson, L. (2009). Management Consultant CMC and author, Metoda. Metoda™ Coaching skills – Newsletter No. 23, 2009. Editor: Lena Börjeson, Management Consultant CMC, Metoda, lb@metoda.se ISSN nr 1652-7712.

Bourne, A. (2008). Using psychometrics in coaching. In S. Palmer & A. Whybrow (Eds.), *Handbook of Coaching Psychology: A Guide for Practitioners* (pp. 385–403). New York: Routledge/Taylor & Francis Group.

Bowlby, J. (1973). *Attachment and Loss. Vol. 2 Separation Anxiety and Anger*. New York: NY Basic Books.

Boyce, L. A., Jackson, R. J., & Neal, L. J. (2010). Building successful leadership coaching relationships: Examining impact of matching criteria in a leadership coaching program. *Journal of Management Development*, Vol. 29, No. 10, pp. 914–931.

Brann, A. (2017). *Neuroscience for Coaches: How to Use the Latest Insights for the Benefit of Your Clients*. London: Kogan Page.

Brockbank, A., & McGill, I. (2006). *Facilitating Reflective Learning Through Mentoring and Coaching*. London: Kogan Page.

Brown, B. (2007). *I Thought It Was Just Me: Women Reclaiming Power in a Culture of Shame*. New York: Penguin/Gotham.

Brown, B. (2016). Brené Brown collection YouTube https://youtu.be/gBck-4lS7Oo (accessed 19.2.17).

Brown, B. (2019). *Brené Brown: The Call to Courage*. Netflix production.

Brown, P. (2018). A leading neuroscientist speaking at an EMCC EQA holders meeting in November 2018.

Buckingham, M., & Goodall, A. (2019). The feedback fallacy. *Harvard Business Review*, March–April edition, 2019.

Cappelli, P., & Tavis, A. (2016). Assessing performance the performance management revolution. *Harvard Business Review*. October 2016 issue.

Cavanagh, M. J. (2006). Coaching from a systemic perspective: A complex adaptive conversation. In D. R. Stober & A. M. Grant (Eds.), *Evidence Based Coaching Handbook: Putting Best Practice to Work for Your Clients* (pp. 313–354). New York: John Wiley and Sons.

Charon, R. (2006). *Narrative Medicine: Honoring the Stories of Illness*. New York: Oxford.

Charvet, S. R. (2008). The feedback sandwich is out to lunch. *The OCM Coach-Mentor Journal*, No. 8, Spring.

Christakis, N. A., & Fowler, J. H. (2009). *Connected: The Amazing Power of Social Networks and How They Shape Our Lives*. New York: Brown and Company.

CIPD (2017). Chartered Institute of Personnel and Development, 2017 Factsheet on performance appraisal understand the basics of performance appraisals and how to ensure the process adds value to the organisation. Update 27 July 2017: www.cipd.co.uk.

CIPD (2018). The people profession in 2018. *A Survey Exploring the Current State of People Profession, Including Career Journeys and Professional Development*. www.cipd.co.uk accessed 9 May 2019.

CIPD (2019). Fact sheet coaching and mentoring identify ways to apply coaching and mentoring principles as part of an overall learning and development strategy. 20 March 2019.

Claxton, G. (2018). Intelligence in the flesh: The bodily basis of thinking. YouTube video published 2.1.18.

Clutterbuck, D. (2007). *Coaching the Team at Work*. London: Nicholas Brealey.

Clutterbuck, D. (2008). David Clutterbuck Partnership www.davidclutterbuckpartnership.com/wp-content/.

Clutterbuck, D., & Megginson, D. (2009). *Further Techniques for Coaching and Mentoring*. Oxford: Butterworth-Heinemann. p. 37.

Clutterbuck, D., & Megginson, D. (2013). *Beyond Goals: Effective Strategies in Coaching and Mentoring*. Farnham: Gower Pubilshing. pp. 33–34. Surrey 33/34.

Clutterbuck, D., Megginson, D., & Bajer, A. (2016). *Building and Sustaining a Coaching Culture*. London: CIPD.

Clutterbuck, D. et al. (2017). *The SAGE Handbook of Mentoring*. London: Sage.

Cornell, A. W., & McGavin, B. (2008). Inner relationship focusing. *Focusing Folio*, Vol. 21, No. 1, 2008, pp. 21–33.

Cox, E. (2013). *Coaching Understood: A Pragmatic Inquiry into the Coaching Process*. London: Sage Publications.

Coyne, S., & Mallinson, P. (2010). Connective coaching – using the power of quantum intelligence. *Bulletin of the Association for Coaching*, June 2010, Issue 1, www.associationforcoaching.com.

Csikszentmihalyi, M. (2013). TED Talk: 'Flow, the secret to happiness' viewed on YouTube 11.5.13.

Csikszentmihályi, M. (1997). *Finding Flow: The Psychology of Engagement with Everyday Life*. New York: Harper-Collins.

David, S., Clutterbuck, D., & Megginson, D. (2013). Beyond Goals: Effective strategies for coaching and mentoring. In S. David, D. Clutterbuck & D. Megginson. Eds. (p. 14). Farnham, Surrey: Gower Publishing Limited.

de Haan, E. (2008). *Relational Coaching*. Chichester: John Wiley and Sons Ltd.

de Haan, E., & Blass, E. (2007). Using critical moments to learn about coaching. *Training Journal*, April, pp. 54–58 accessed on web 19 March 2010.

de Haan, E., Culpin, V., & Curd, J. (2011). Executive coaching practice: What determines Helpfulness for Coaching Clients. *Personnel Review*, Vol. 40, No. 1, pp. 24–44.

de Haan, E., & Niess, C. (2012). Critical moments in a coaching case study. *Consulting Psychology Journal: Practice and Research*, Vol. 64, No. 3, September 2012, pp. 198–224.

DeFranzo, S. E. (2015). 5 reasons why feedback is important. *SnapSurveys, July 1, 2015.*

Dilthey, W. (1976). The development of hermeneutics. *Dilthey, Selected Writings,* Ed. and trans H. P. Rickman. Cambridge: Cambridge University Press. p. 249.

Dirkx, J. M., & Mezirow, J. (2006). Musings and reflections on the meaning, context, and process of transformative learning. *Journal of Transformative Education,* Vol. 4, No. 2, pp. 123–139.

Drake, D. B. (2011). What do coaches need to know? Using the Mastery. *Window to Assess and Develop Expertise, Coaching: An International Journal of Theory, Research and Practice,* Vol. 4, No. 2, pp. 138–155.

Du Plessis, T., & van Niekerk, A. (2017). Factors influencing managers' attitudes towards performance appraisal. *SA Journal of Human Resource Management/SA Tydskrif Vir Menlikehulpbrønbestuur,* Vol. 15, No. 0, pp. a880 DOI: 104102 sajhrmv15i0880.

Duckworth, A., & de Haan, E. (2009). What clients say about our coaching. *The Training Journal,* pp. 64–67, August.

Duhigg, C. (2012). *The Power of Habit: Why We Do What We Do and How to Change.* New York: Random House.

Duncan, B. L., Miller, S. D., & Sparks, J. A. (2004). *The Heroic Client: A Revolutionary Way to Improve Effectiveness through Client-Directed, Outcome-Informed Therapy.* San Francisco, CA: Jossey-Bass. p. 51.

Dweck, C. S. (2006). *Mindset: How You Can Fulfil Your Potential.* London: Robinson.

Dweck, C. S. (2012). *Mindset: Updated Edition: Changing the Way You Think to Fulfil Your Potential.* London: Robinson.

Dweck, C. S. (2007). *Mindset: The New Psychology of Success.* New York: Ballantine Books an imprint of and division of Penguin Random House LLC.

Dyer, W. W. (2007). *Change Your Thoughts Change Your Llife: Living the Wisdom of the Tao.* New York: Hay House.

Ehrlich, J. (2011). Mindshifting to Mindful Coaching: Managing Your Attention So You Can Think, Focus, and Lead. Available: www.wabccoaches.com [06/06, 2011].

Ellinger, A., Beattie, R., & Hamlin, R. (2014). The 'Manager as Coach'. In E. Cox, T. Bachkirova & D. Clutterbuck (Eds.), *The Complete Handbook of Coaching* (pp. 256–270). London: Sage Publications.

Encyclopaedia Britannica (2012). Intuition. Available at: www.britannica.com/topic/intuition. Accessed 1/11/19.

European Mentoring and Coaching Council (EMCC) (2015). Competence framework for coaches and mentors downloadable at www.emccouncil.org: Quality tab.

Falconier, M. K., et al (2014). Stress from daily hassles in couples: Its effects on intradyadic stress, relationship satisfaction, and physical and psychological well-being. *NCBI,* May 2014.

Fillery-Travis, A., & Lane, D. (2006). Does coaching work or are we asking the wrong question? *International Coaching Psychology Review,* Vol. 1, pp. 23–26.

Freud, S. (1915). *The Unconscious.* XIV (2nd ed.). London: Hogarth Press. 1955.

Gallo, A. (2010). How to give your boss feedback. *Harvard Business Review.* March 24, 2010 edition.

Gallup (2016). Q12® Meta-Analysis report.

Gallwey, T. (2001). *The Inner Game of Work: Focus, Learning, Pleasure, and Mobility in the Workplace.* New York: Random House.

Garvey Berger, J. (2004). Dancing on the Threshold of Meaning: Recognizing and Understanding the Growing Edge. *Journal of Transformative Education*, Vol. 2, No. 4, October 2004, pp. 336–351.

Gendlin, E. T. (2003). *Focusing: How to Gain Direct Access to Your Body's Knowledge*. New York: Random House.

Gilbert, P. (2009a). Introducing compassion-focused therapy advances in psychiatric treatment journal of continuing professional development pp. 199–208, *Royal College of Psychiatrists*. Accessed 17 July 2013: http://apt.rcpsych.org/content/15/3/199.full.pdf+html.

Gilbert, P. (2009b). *The Compassionate Mind*. London: Robinson.

Gilbert, P. et al. (2010a). *Training Our Minds in, with and for Compassion: An Introduction to Concepts and Compassion-Focused Exercises*. Available at: www.getselfhelp.co.uk/docs/GILBERT-COMPASSION-HANDOUT.pdf.

Gilbert, P. (2010b). *The Compassionate Mind*. London: Constable.

Goleman, D. (1995). *Emotional Intelligence: Why It Can Matter More Than IQ*. New York: Bantam Books.

Goleman, D. (2003). Finding happiness: Cajole your brain to lean to the left. *New York Times* 4 Feb. 2003, New York edition, sec. F: p. 5.

Goleman, D. (2007). *Social Intelligence: The New Science of Human Relationships*. London: Arrow Books.

Gordon, J. (2003). BMJ ABC of learning and teaching in medicine: One to one teaching and feedback. www.faculty.londondeanery.ac.uk/e-learnng/feedback, Ed. *British Medical Journal*, p. 544.

Grant, A. (2013). Goodbye to MBTI, the fad that won't die. MBTI, I'm breaking up with you. *It's not me*. It's you. Posted Sep 18, 2013 Psychology Today www.psychologytoday.com/blog/give-and-take/201309/goodbye-mbti-the-fad-won-t-die.

Grant, A. M. (2006). An integrative goal-focused approach to executive coaching. In D. R. Stober & A. M. Grant (2006), (Eds.), *Evidence Based Coaching Handbook Putting Best Practices to Work for Your Clients*, (pp. 153–192). New Jersey: John Wiley & Sons, Inc.

Green, S. (2014). Everything you need to know about giving negative feedback www.hbrascend.in/topics/giving-negative-feedback/. Accessed 15.6.18.

Gregory, K. (2012). Integrative international conference in Romania: *The Psychotherapy of the 21st century*.

Gregory, K. (2016). The emotional regulation system in the brain and body adapted from Paul Gilbert, 2010.

Grossman, R. (1984). *Phenomenology and Existentialism: An Introduction*. London: Routledge and Kegan Paul.

Guynn, J. (2015). Google's "bias busting" workshops target hidden prejudices. *USA Today*. Retrieved from www.usatoday.com/story/tech/2015/05/12/google-unconscious-bias-diversity/27055485/.

Gyllensten, K., & Palmer, S. (2007). The coaching relationship: An interpretative phenomenological analysis. *International Coaching Psychology Review*, Vol. 2, No. 2, pp. 168–177.

Habermas, J. (1970). Technology and science as "ideology". In J. J. Shapiro (trans.), *Toward a Rational Society: Student Protest, Science, and Politics*. Boston: Beacon Press.

Hackman, J. R. (2002). *Leading Teams: Setting the Stage for Great Performances*. USA: Harvard Business Review Press.

Hackney, H. (1978a). The evolution of empathy. *Journal of Counseling & Development*, Accessed Wiley Online Library DOI: 10.1002/j.2164-4918.1978.tb05091.x.

Hackney, H. L. (1978b). The evolution of empathy. *Personnel and Guidance Journal*, 1978, Vol. 57, pp. 35–38.

Harari, Y. N. (2015). *Sapiens: A Brief History of Humankind*. New York: Vintage.

HeartMath (2019). Website www.heartmath.org.

Henneman, T. (2014). You, Biased? No, It's Your Brain. *Workforce Edition* Feburary 9, 2014.

Hernez-Broome (2002). Research & reviews using multisource feedback coaching effectively in executive education. *Academy of Management Learning & Education* 8 (4). Robert Hooijberg and Nancy Lane. Published online: 30 Nov 2017. https://doi.org/10.5465/amle.8.4.zqr483.

Heron, J. (1975). *Helping the Client*. London: Sage Publications.

Heron, J. (1989). *Six Category Intervention. Helping The Client*. 5th edition. UK: Human Potential Resource Project, University of Surrey.

Heron, J. (2009). *Helping the Client: A Creative Practical Guide* – abridged, 4 Sep 2009.

Hersey, P., & Blanchard, K. H. (1977). *Management of Organizational Behavior (3rd edition): Utilizing Human Resources*. New Jersey: Prentice Hall.

Hesketh, E. A., & Laidlaw, J. M. (2002). Developing the teaching instinct: Feedback. *Medical Teacher*, Vol. 24, pp. 245–248.

Hinsliff, G. (2017). We are overdosing on empathy. *Guardian* 18.2.17.

Iacoboni, M. (2008). Interview with Scientific American entitled 'the mirror neuron revolution: explaining what makes humans social' accessed 25.8.13 on www.scientificamerican.com/article.cfm?id=the-mirror-neuron-revolut.

Iacoboni, M. (2009). *Mirroring People: The Science of Empathy and How We Connect with Others*. New York: Picador.

Jarvis, J., Lane, D., & Fillery-Travis, A. (2006). *The Case for Coaching Making Evidence-based Decisions on Coaching*. London: CIPD.

Jeffers, S. (1991). *Feel the Fear and Do It Anyway*. New York: Arrow Books.

John, L. K., Blunden, H., & Liu, H. (2019). Shooting the messenger. *Journal of Experimental Psychology: General*, Vol. 148, No. 4, pp. 644–666.

Jordan, J. V. (1991a). Empathy and self-boundaries. In J. V. Jordan, A. G. Kaplan, J. B. Miller, I. P. Stiver & J. L. Surrey (Eds.), *Women's Growth in Connection: Writings from the Stone Center* (pp. 67–80). New York: Guilford.

Jung, C. G. (1953). *Collected Works: Vol. 12: Psychology and Alchemy*. New York: Pantheon Books.

Kabat-Zinn, J. (2003). Mindfulness-based interventions in context: Past, present, and future. *Clinical Psychology: Science and Practice*, Vol. 10, pp. 144–156.

Kabat-Zinn, J. (2009). *The Science of Mindfulness*. New York: Speaking of Faith, NPR. 18 April 2009.

Kahnemann, D. (2011). *Thinking, Fast and Slow*. Great Britain: Allen Lane.

Kaufmann, W. (1970). *Martin Buber's 'I and Thou': A Translation with a Prologue*. New York: Charles Scribner's Sons.

Kaufmann, W. (1980a). *Discovering the Mind*. Volume One Goethe, Kant and Hegel. New Brunswick: Transaction Publishers.

Kegan, R. (1998). *In Over Our Heads: The Mental Demands of Modern Life*. Boston: Harvard University Press.

Keltner, D. (2004). The compassionate instinct. March 1, 2004 http://greatergood.berkeley. edu/article/item/the_compassionate_instinct/.

Khuna, K. (2017). Compassionate leadership is the future. Published on February 15, 2017.

Kline, N. (2017). *Extract from Time to Think Coach Training Course Syllabus*. England: Oxford.

Kosfeld, M., Heinrichs, M., Zak, P. J., Zak, Fischbacher, U., & Ernst Fehr, E. (2005). Oxytocin increases trust in humans. *Nature 2005 Jun 2*, Vol. 435, No. 7042, pp. 673–676.

Kubler-Ross, E., & Kessler, D. (2005). *On Grief and Grieving: Finding the Meaning of Grief Through the Five Stages of Loss*. London: Simon and Schuster Inc.

Ladyshewsky, R., & Taplin, R. (2018). The interplay between organisational learning culture, the manager as coach, self-efficacy and workload on employee work engagement. *International Journal of Evidence Based Coaching and Mentoring*, Vol. 16, No. 2, pp. 3–19.

Lane, D. A., & Corrie, S. (2006). *The Modern Scientist Practitioner: A Guide to Practice in Psychology*. London: Routledge.

Laszlo, E. (2012). *Quantum Consciousness: Our Evolution, Our Salvation*. Available at: www. ervinlazlo/notebook/2012.

Lawley, J., & Tompkins, P. (2011). Calibrating when what you are doing is working – And when it's not, the developing group, 9 July 2011, James Lawley & Penny Tompkins.

Levin, M. (2001). *Spiritual Intelligence: Awakening the Power of Your Spirituality and Intuition*. London: Hodder and Stoughton.

Lewis, L. (2014a). Cultural Intelligence Matrix Created for APAC conference session on Cultural Diversity.

Lewis, L. (2014b). *Doctoral Research in Executive Coaching: Creating the Conditions for Feedback*. London: Middlesex University.

Lewis, T., Amini, F., & Lannon, R. (2001). *A General Theory of Love*. New York: Vintage.

Locke, C. C. (2015). When it's safe to rely on intuition (and when it's not) HBR April 30, 2015.

Locke, E. A., & Latham, G. P. (1990). *A Theory of Goal Setting and Task Performance*. Englewood Cliffs, NJ: Prentice Hall.

Marreli, A. F. (2011). Problems and remedies in performance management. *Industrial and Organisational Psychology*, Vol. 4, No. 2, pp. 169–172.

McCraty, R., Deyhle, A., & Childre, D. (2012). The global coherence initiative: Creating a coherent planetary standing wave. *Global Advances in Health and Medicine*, Vol. 1, No. 1, pp. 64–77.

McDowall, A., Harris, M., & McGrath, M. (2009). Feedback: Evidence from psychology for best practice. British Psychological Society. *Assessment and Development Matters*, Vol. 2, No. 3, pp. 20–26.

McGoldrick, M., Giordano, J., & Pearce, J. K. (Eds.). (1996). *Ethnicity in Family Therapy* (2nd ed.). New York: Guildford.

McMillan, M., & McLeod, J. (2006). Letting go: The client's experience of relational depth. *Person-Centered and Experiential Psychotherapies*, Vol. 5, No. 4, pp. 277–292.

Mearns, D. (2004c). Person-centred therapy: The leading edge. Paper presented at the North West Counselling Association, Manchester.

Mearns, D., & Cooper, M. (2005). *Working at Relational Depth in Counselling*. London: SAGE Publishers Ltd. pp. ix and xi.

Metaphysics for Life (2013). www.metaphysics-for-life.com.

Mezirow, J. (1981). A critical theory of adult learning and education. *Adult Education*, Vol. 32, No. 1, pp. 3–24.

Mezirow, J. (2000). *Learning as Transformation*. San Francisco, CA: John Wiley & Sons, Inc.

Milliken, K. (2017). *Posner Fellowship: The Seeds of Scholarship. Student and Professor Forge a Lasting Bond by Unpacking a Famous Film March 07, 2017*. NorthWestern Now. North Western University. Evanston IL 60208.

Milner, M. (1987). Suppressed madness of sane men, forty-four years of exploring psychoanalysis, location 3707-3712 of 7122. Taylor & Francis e-library 2005.

Morgan, H. (2013). WBECS e-conference session: Critical aspects of coaching – especially for more knowledgeable or smarter people. Accessed online May 2013 www.wbecs.com.

Muzio, E., Fisher, D. J., Erv, T., & Peters, R. (2007). Soft Skills Quantification (SSQ) foi project manager competencies. *Project Management Journal*, Vol. 38, No. 2, pp. 30–38. June 2007. DOI: 10.1177/875697280703800204.

Nakamura, J., & Csikszentmihalyi, M. (2009). Flow theory and research. In C. R. Snyder & S. J. Lopez (Eds.), *Handbook of Positive Psychology* (pp. 195–206). Oxford: Oxford University Press.

Neff, K. (2009). Self Compassion. In M. R. Leary & R. H. Hoyle (Eds.), *Handbook of Individual Differences in Social Behavior* (pp. 561–573). New York: Guilford.

Neff, K. (2013). The space between self-esteem and self compassion. Sourced from TED TALKS.

Nichols, T. W., & Erakovich, R. (2013). Authentic leadership and implicit theory: A normative form of leadership?. *Leadership & Organization Development Journal*, Vol. 34, No. 2, pp. 182–195.

O'Brien, B. (2019). Right speech from the Buddhist Eightfold Path. *Learn Religions*, Apr. 17, 2019, learnreligions.com/right-speech-450072.

O'Broin, A., & Palmer, S. (2008). Reappraising the coach-client relationship: The unassuming change agent in coaching. In S. Palmer & A. Whybrow (Eds.), *Handbook of Coaching Psychology: A Guide for Practitioners* (pp 295–324). New York: Routledge.

O'Neill, M. B. (2000). *Executive Coaching with Backbone and Heart: A Systems Approach to Engaging Leaders with Their Challenges*. San Francisco: Jossey-Bass Publishers. p. 35.

Oetting, E. R. (1999). Primary socialization theory: developmental stages, spirituality, government institutions, sensation seeking, and theoretical implications. *Substance Use Misuse V 1999*, Vol. 34, No. 7, pp. 947–982. Informa Allied Health.

P'Pool, K. (2012). Using Dweck's Theory of motivation to determine how a student's view of intelligence affects their overall academic achievement. *Masters Theses & Specialist Projects*. Paper 1214. http://digitalcommons.wku.edu/theses/1214.

Palmer, W. (1994). *The Intuitive Body: Discovering the Wisdom of Conscious Embodiment and Aikido*. Berkeley, CA: Blue Snake Books. pp. 79–80.

Parsloe, E., & Leedham, M. (2009). *Coaching and Mentoring: Practical Conversations to Improve Learning* (2nd ed.). London and Philadelphia: Kogan and Page, p. 132.

Passmore, J., & Whybrow, A. (2008). Motivational interviewing: A specific approach for coaching psychologists. In S. Palmer & A. Whybrow (Eds.), *Handbook of Coaching Psychology: A Guide for Practitioners* (pp. 160–173). New York: Routledge.

Pelham, G. (2016). *The Coaching Relationship in Practice*. London: Sage.

Plimmer (2013). *FT.com* web page.

Prochaska, J., DiClemente, C., & Norcross, J. (1992). In search of how people change: Application to addictive behaviours. *American Psychologist*, Vol. 47, pp. 1102–1114.

Pulakos, E. D., & O'Leary, R. S. (2011). Why is performance management broken?. *Industrial and Organisational Psychology*, Vol. 4, No. 2, pp. 146–164.

Rancourt, K. L. (1995). Real-time coaching boosts performance. *Training & Development: April 95*, Vol. 49, No. 4, p. 53.

Ricard, M. (2015). *Altruism: The Power of Compassion to Change Yourself and the World*. London: Atlantic Books.

Rock, D. (2008). SCARF: A brain based model for collaborating with and influencing others. *NeuroLeadership JOURNAL*, Issue 1, 2008, pp. 1–9.

Rock, D. (2009). *Your Brain at Work: Strategies for Overcoming Distraction, Regaining Focus, and Working Smarter All Day Long*. New York: HarperCollins.

Rock, D., & Schwartz, J. (2006). The Neuroscience of Leadership: Breakthroughs in brain research explain how to make organizational transformation succeed. *Leadership*, Vol. 43, 30 May 2006/Summer 2006.

Rock, D., & Schwartz, J. (2006). The Neuroscience of Leadership. *Strategy Business Magazine*.

Rodenburg, P. (2007). *Presence: How to Use Positive Energy for Success in Every Situation*. London: Penguin Books Ltd.

Rogers, C. R. (1957). The necessary and sufficient conditions of therapeutic personality change. *Journal of Consulting Psychology*, Vol. 21, No. 2, pp. 95–103.

Rogers, C. R. (1959). A theory of therapy, personality and interpersonal relationships as developed in the client-centered framework. In S. Koch (Ed.), *Psychology: A study of a science. Vol. 3: Formulations of the Person and the Social Context* (pp. 184–256). New York: McGraw Hill.

Rogers, C. R. (1986). A client-centered person-centered approach to therapy. In I. L. Kutash & A. Wolf (Eds.), *Psychotherapists Casebook* (p. 197). San Francisco: Jossey.

Rosinski, P. (2003). *Coaching Across Cultures: New Tools for Leveraging National, Corporate and Professional Differences*. London: Nicholas Brealey Publishing.

Ross, A. (2008). *Exploring Unconscious Bias*. Washington: Cook Ross Inc. Diversity Best Practices.

Rothmann, S., & Coetzer, E. P. (24 October 2003). The big five personality dimensions and job performance. *SA Journal of Industrial Psychology*, Vol. 29. DOI: 10.4102/sajip. v29i1.88.

Salzman, M. (2017). 5 generations in the workplace (and why we need them all). *Entrepreneur*, February 10, 2017.

Sartre, J. P. (1943). *Being and Nothingness: An Essay on Phenomenological Ontology* (French: *L'Être et le néant: Essai d'ontologie phénoménologique*), sometimes published with the subtitle *A Phenomenological Essay on Ontology*.

Schpancer, N. (2017). Fear Is Nothing to Be Feared. A phenomenon known as 'fear of fear' is at the core of most anxiety disorders. Posted Dec 26, 2017. *Psychology Today*.

Schultz, S. E., & Schultz, D. (2010). *Psychology and Work Today*. New York: Prentice Hall.

Scott, C. (1984). Empathy – Examination of a crucial concept. *Journal of the British Association for Counselling*, Vol. 49, pp. 3–6, British Association for Counselling and Psychotherapy.

Scoular, A. (2011). *FT Guide to Business Coaching*. New Jersey: Prentice Hall.

Seligman, M. E. P. (2011). *Flourish: A New Understanding of Happiness and Wellbeing: The Practical Guide to Using Positive Psychology to Make you Happier and Healthier*. Sydney: Random House Australia.

Seppala, E. (2015). Why compassion is a better managerial tactic than toughness. May 07, 2015.

Seto, L., & Geithner, T. (2018). Metaphor magic in coaching and coaching supervision. *International Journal of Evidence Based Coaching and Mentoring*, Vol. 16, No. 2, pp. 99–111.

Shah, R. (2015). Working beyond five generations in the workplace. *Forbes Magazine Feb 23, 2015*.

Siegel, D. (2009). The brain and the developing mind. http://fora.tv/2009/06/30/Dan_Siegel_The_Brain_and_the_Developing_Mind.

Siegel, D. (2010). The mindful therapist: a teleseminar session with Daniel Siegel, and Ruth Buczynski. The National Institute for the Clinical Application of Behavioral Medicine. Accessed 23. 8.13at: www.gobookee.net/mindful-therapist-siegel/.

Sinek, S. (2011). *Start with Why: How Great Leaders Inspire Everyone to Take Action*. London: Penguin.

Smither, J. W., London, M., & Reilly, R. R. (2005). Does performance improve following multisource feedback?: A theoretical model, meta-analysis, and review of empirical findings. *Personnel Psychology*, Vol. 58, pp. 33–66.

Spinelli, E. (2005). *The Interpreted World: An Introduction to Phenomenological Psychology* (2nd ed.). London: SAGE Publications Ltd, pp. 20–21.

Starr, J. (2012). *Brilliant Coaching: How to Be a Brilliant Coach in Your Workplace*. Harlow: Pearson Education Limited.

Stern, D. N. (2004). *The Present Moment in Psychotherapy and Everyday Life*. London: W.W. Norton and Company Ltd..

Stern, S., & Cooper, C. (2017). *Myths of Management: What People Get Wrong About Being the Boss*. London: Kogan Page Publishers.

Stewart, T. (2019). Almost a quarter of UK households are home to a smart assistant device. *Mobile Marketing*. Thursday 04-04-2019.

Stiehler, A., & Gantori, S. (2018). Longer term investments. Automation and robotics. Chief Investment Office WM | 2 March 2018. Sourced from UBS.com.

Stober, D. R., & Grant, A. M. (2006). Toward a contextual approach to coaching models. In D. R. Stober & A. M. Grant (Eds.), *Evidence Based Coaching Handbook Putting Best Practices to Work for Your Clients* (pp. 77–102). New Jersey: John Wiley & Sons, Inc.

Stone, D., & Heen, S. (2014). *Thanks for the Feedback: The Science and Art of Receiving Feedback Well*. London: Portfolio Penguin.

Strozzi-Heckler, R. (2009). *Embodied Trust Learning Day*. Roffey Park London: Embodied Leadership. April 2009.

Sveen, L. (2015). Welcoming millennials to the workforce? Prepare. *They're Change Agents*. The Denver Post Published: May 1, 2015 at 2:30 pm | Updated: June 6, 2016 at 1:58 pm.

Taylor, F. W. (1911). *The Principles of Scientific Management*. New York and London: Harper & Brothers, LCCN 11010339, OCLC 233134.

Thach, E. C. (2002). The impact of executive coaching and 360 feedback on leadership effectiveness, *Leadership & Organization Development Journal*, Vol. 23, No. 4, pp. 205–214.

Tolle, E. (2004). *The Power of Now: A Guide to Spiritual Enlightenment*. Vancouver BC Canada: New World Library CA | Namaste Publishing.

Tolle, E. (2013). Dialogue between Dr. James Doty and Eckhart Tolle about his life's work and what role compassion may have played. YouTube CCARE, published on Feb 21, 2013.

Tolle, E. (2017). *Becoming a Teach of Presence: Bringing Awareness to the Service of Others.* British Columbia, Canada and California: Eckhart Teachings, Inc.. Unabridged edition (July 1, 2017).

Torrington, D., Hall, L., Taylor, S., & Atkinson, C. (2009). *Fundamentals of Human Resource Management.* London: Pearson.

Trompenaars and Hampden-Turner's Seven Dimensions of Culture, in *Organizational Management and Administration: A Guide for Managers and Professionals.* Available online at http://alangutterman.typepad.com/files/cms---trompenaars-seven-dimensions.pdf.

VandeWalle, D., Ganesan, S., Challagalla, G. N., & Brown, S. P. (2000). An integrated model of feedback seeking behaviour: Disposition, context and cognition. *Journal of Applied Psychology,* Vol. 85, No. 6, pp. 996–1003.

Vardaki, Z. (2018). Graduate of Bluesky International Diploma for Professional Coaches/Mentors. Cyprus 2017/8.

Venosa, A. (2015). Prejudice in the Brain. How evolutionary valuable brain processes have turned problematic. *Medical Daily* 23 July 2015.

Waitzkin, J. (2007). *The Art of Learning: An Inner Journey to Optimal Performance.* New York: Simon & Schuster.

Wallace, B. A., & Shapiro, S. L. (2006). Mental balance and well-being: building bridges between Buddhism and Western psychology October 2006. *American Psychologist,* Vol. 61, No. 7, pp. 690–701.

Warner, J. (2012). Coaching and mentoring, giving and receiving feedback. December 14, 2012.

Warner, J. (2013). Dealing positively with criticism in giving and receiving feedback. April 19, 2013.

Wasylyshyn, K. M. (2003). Executive coaching: An outcome study. *Leadership Development. Consulting Psychology Journal: Practice and Research,* Vol. 55, No. 2, pp. 94–106.

Whitworth, L., Kimsey-House, K., Kimsey-House, H., & Sandahl, P. (2007). *Co-active Coaching: New Skills for Coaching People Toward Success in Work and Life* (2nd ed.). Mountain View, CA: Davies-Black Publishing.

Wikipedia (2018). Big five personality traits.

Yalom, I. D. (1980). *Existential Psychotherapy, Yalom Family Trust.* New York: Basic Books.

Zak, P. J. (2017). The neuroscience of trust. *Harvard Business Review.* January-February 2017 issue.

Zenger, J. (2016). What is your fear of feedback costing you? Forbes.com/leadership. July 11, 2016.

Zinker, J. (1994). *In Search of Good Form.* Massachussetts: GIC Press. Cambridge Massachussetts Gestalt Institute of Cleveland. Distributed by The Analytic Press Inc Hillsdale New Jersey.

Index

ability tests 73
accountability 51, 66, 121
active listening 92
agreeableness 73
algorithms 43, 52, 61, 203, 204, 205–206
Allport, G. 151
Amazon 85
anger 189, 191, 192
anxiety 17, 24, 33–34; compassion 127–128; continuum of transformational change 38; cortisol 190, 191; limbic system 189; managing emotions 184; stress 115; unsolicited feedback 93
appraisals 20, 22–23, 62–70, 74, 198
Armstrong, Andrew 45
artificial intelligence (AI) 16, 43, 52, 54, 186, 202–209
Askew, S. 174
attachment styles 136
authenticity 102, 200; authentic leadership 2, 183, 210; authentic relationships 19, 162; confidence 109; objectivity 155

Baden-Powell, Robert 143
balance 142
Banaji, Mahzarin 151, 155
Barber, P. 25, 101, 195, 200
Barrett-Lennard, G. T. 100
Batson, G. 180
Baxter, L. A. 59
Beisser, A. R. 162

belonging, sense of 59
Berger, Garvey 172–173
Berger, J. G. 37, 38
Berne, Eric 153–154
biases 11, 21, 67, 110, 197; artificial intelligence 204–205; Clean Language framework 117; conscious 151–152; objectivity 142, 146; presence 159; psychometric tests 76; self-management 107; setting aside 111; unconscious 74, 97, 152–156, 178
Big 5 Personality Traits 73
blame 1, 122, 156, 185
Blanchard, K. H. 65
Blass, E. 174
Bloom, P. 131
Bluckert, P. 7, 54, 67, 72, 85, 111, 117, 145, 175
Bock, Laszlo 69
body language 43, 58, 92, 137, 182; see also non-verbal communication
Bohart, A. C. 145
Börjeson, L. 112
Bourne, A. 84
Boyce, L. A. 83–84
brain 26–28, 118; adrenaline levels 183; compassion 128–129; desire for novelty 159; emotions 85–86, 188–191; neural pathways 27, 28, 164, 167; neuroplasticity 28, 29, 30–32, 155; space for reflection 158; unconscious biases 153; see also neuroscience

breaking flow 144, 168–169
Brockbank, A. 174
Brown, Brené 100, 122, 182
Brown, P. 183–184, 188
Buber, Martin 86
Buckingham, M. 17, 203
bullying 5–6, 23, 185–186

capability 4, 5, 21–22, 92–93
career progression 3, 4
Carnell, E. 174
Cavanagh, M. J. 17, 82–83
centred presence 120
challenge stress 98–99
challenge/support continuum 93, 156
change 27–28, 29, 39, 40, 162; coaching
    54; compassion 130; continuum
    of transformational 38; Kubler-
    Ross change curve 140; readiness
    for 135, 147; relational objectivity
    156; resistance to 84–85; space for
    reflection 158; technological 207–208;
    Transtheoretical Stages of Change
    model 147–148
Charon, R. 12
Charvet, S. R. 78
Christakis, N. A. 200
CIPD 20, 35, 36, 43–44, 49, 54
Claxton, G. 198
Clean Language framework 117
client-centred approach 87, 100, 101
Clutterbuck, D. 24, 96, 135, 148, 161, 168,
    172, 187
coaching 5, 7, 13, 24, 39, 41, 57–58; case
    example 55–57; coach as critical friend
    48; competency frameworks 71,
    171–172, 187; contracting 133; external
    68; feed-forward 78–79; feedback
    techniques 76; growing popularity
    of 66; impact on performance 66;
    practitioner perspective 52–55;
    preparation 135; presence 145–146;
    purpose of feedback 44; rapport 83–84;
    relationships 12, 20, 82–83, 85–86;
    research 9; timing of feedback 170–171,
    174
communication: cultural awareness and
    intelligence 97; information sharing 99;
    misunderstandings 179–180; non-verbal
    20, 43, 129, 189; 'Right Speech' 36–37
compassion 55, 183, 209; artificial
    intelligence 206; client-centred

approach 87; emotional intelligence
    113; human capacity for 208; kindness
    193; physicality 182; self-management
    10, 107, 108–109, 121–132
competency frameworks 63–64, 70–71,
    110, 171–172, 187
concentration 25, 103, 144, 156, 159, 165
conditioning 119–120
confidence: coaching 53, 56–57; loss of
    32; self-management 10, 107, 108–109,
    116–120
confirmation bias 151–152
connection 59, 88, 148–149; intuition 84,
    195; mindfulness 142, 157; mirror
    neurons 208; physicality 181; presence
    160, 161, 199; productive relationships
    102; quantum intelligence 199–200;
    relational depth 42, 84, 165; relational
    leadership 210
conscientiousness 73
consciousness 199
constructive feedback 7, 46
continuous improvement 2, 19, 44, 133
Cooper, M. 86, 87, 99–100, 165
cooperation 51, 183
Cornell, A. W. 160
Corrie, S. 12
cortisol 190, 191
countertransference 149–150, 189
Cox, E. 157, 171, 174
Coyne, S. 200
creativity 101, 102, 210
credibility 24, 46, 135, 198
'critical moments' 174
critical:positive ratio 61, 77
criticism 5, 18, 77–78
Csikszentmihályi, M. 149, 165
culture 40, 44, 96–98; biases 152;
    compassion 127; emotional climate
    185–188; evaluation of cultural climate
    50; generative 43; improvement 17–18;
    multi-cultural context 207; societal 71
curiosity 121, 160; continuum of
    transformational change 38; learning
    goal orientation 135; objectivity 146,
    150, 156; rapport 83; relationships 103;
    timing of feedback 175

Dalai Lama 123
data sources 21, 106
David, S. 135
de Haan, E. 43, 71, 81, 83, 102, 174

DEB/DESC Feedback Framework 45–47
decision-making 151
DeFranzo, S. E. 22
demographics 1, 96, 124, 186
'developmental' feedback 18, 22, 24
DiClemente, C. 147–148
digital natives 96, 208–209
digital technology 1, 2, 3, 52, 81, 96; see also
    artificial intelligence
Dilthey, W. 146
Dirkx, J. M. 12
disciplinary procedures 24
discretion 99
disenchantment 5
disengagement 5, 48, 94
disharmony 85, 144–145
diversity 96–97, 130, 185, 206
documentation 62, 63, 69
dopamine 189, 190, 191
Drake, D. B. 12, 66, 102
Du Plessis, T. 63
Duckworth, A. 83
Duhigg, C. 30–31
Duncan, B. L. 101
Dweck, C. S. 9, 30, 61
Dyer, Wayne 155

'edge of knowing' 37, 38, 172–173
Ehrlich, J. 157
Einstein, Albert 195
electromagnetic human heart field 187,
    200–201
EMCC see European Mentoring and
    Coaching Council
emotional climate 185–188
emotional contagion 189–190
emotional intelligence 1, 67, 109, 112–115,
    124
emotional skills 24
emotions 33–34; artificial intelligence 205–
    206; brain processes 85–86, 129, 155;
    compassion 130; emotional states 11,
    15, 16, 178–179, 184–193; mindfulness
    157; relationship building 82; self-
    management 10, 107, 108; unconscious
    processes 194–195, 198
empathy 12, 88, 100, 101, 103, 131; artificial
    intelligence 206; brain processes 129;
    client-centred approach 87; compassion
    122, 123; consciousness 199; human
    capacity for 208; mindfulness 157;
    somatic 181–182

employees 41, 44, 55–59, 62–70
endorphins 190, 191
energy 11, 33, 83, 161; emotional states
    179; metaphysics 199–200, 201;
    physicality 182, 183–184; sense of
    presence 199
engagement 1, 67, 188
equality 102, 210
Erakovich, R. 2
European Mentoring and Coaching
    Council (EMCC) 82, 110, 171–172, 187
expectations 145–146, 165, 186
extraversion 73

Falconier, M. K. 114–115
fear 25–27, 44, 137, 192; cortisol 190,
    191; of giving feedback 18–19; limbic
    system 189; neuroscience of 27–28;
    protection of self 29; reducing 24
feed-forward 53, 61, 78–79
feedback: business case for 43–44; definitions
    of 19–22; feedback formula 77; feedback
    'sandwich' 61, 77–78; impact of artificial
    intelligence 202–209; importance of
    2; perception of 7, 13, 17–40; practices
    13, 60–79; purpose of 34–39, 41–42, 44;
    reactions to 18, 22, 25, 107, 139–140;
    readiness for 11, 15, 106–107, 132–141;
    relationships 13–14, 80–104; research
    3–5, 9–10; resentment towards
    6–7; stakeholders 13, 40–41, 44–59;
    360-degree 25, 71–72, 74, 82, 198; timing
    of 8, 11, 15, 136, 143, 145, 169–179
Feedback Wheel 46, 47–48
feminine energy 184
Fillery-Travis, A. 86
FIRO-B 75
first impressions 91
fixed mindset 30, 61
'flight or fight' syndrome 26–27, 130, 190,
    191
flow 11, 144, 149, 165–169, 170
Fowler, J. H. 200
Freud, Sigmund 196, 197

Gallo, A. 79
Gallwey, Tim 51, 167
Gantori, S. 204
gender differences 184
Gendlin, E. T. 160
Gestalt perspective 101, 117, 118, 161–162,
    175, 187

Gilbert, P. 11, 33, 100, 123, 130, 190
goals 22, 24, 51, 62, 165
Goleman, Daniel 103, 114, 193
Goodall, A. 17, 203
Google 68–69, 99
Gordon, J. 66, 76
Grant, A. M. 83, 135
Green, S. 61, 123
Greenwald, A. G. 155
Gregory, K. 118, 122
Grossman, R. 110
GROW model 79
growth mindset 9, 30, 46, 61, 99
Gyllensten, K. 83

Habermas, J. 171
habits 27, 30–31, 164
Hackman, J. R. 51
Hackney, H. L. 100
happiness 187, 188, 192
harassment 5–6, 23, 94
heart 187, 200–201
HeartMath 201
Heen, S. 61
Hernez-Broome, G. 74
Heron, John 19, 36, 42, 93, 193
Hersey, P. 65
Hesketh, E. A. 76, 175
HEXACO model of personality 73
hierarchy 90
Hinsliff, G. 131
honesty 46, 155
human capital 186
'human factor' 5, 25
human heart 187, 200–201
human resource professionals 41, 49–50

Iacoboni, M. 101, 189
ICF see International Coach Federation
identity 59
impactfulness 107, 132, 137–141
individual differences 24, 135
information sharing 99
Inner Game approach 167–168
interest 102, 210
International Coach Federation (ICF) 110
interpersonal dynamics 91–92
interpersonal skills 1, 67
intimidator power 94
intuition 11, 15, 16, 178–179, 193–198;
    artificial intelligence 208; bodily 173;
    brain processes 129; connecting 84

Jarvis, J. 54, 135
Jeffers, S. 26
job crafting 99
Johari window model 34
John, L. K. 47
Jordan, J. V. 86
Jung, Carl 197

Kabat-Zinn, J. 157
Kahnemann, D. 197
Kant, Immanuel 111
Katzenbach, J. 51
Kaufmann, W. 86
Kegan, R. 81
Keltner, D. 129
Kessler, D. 139
Kline, N. 137–138
Kosfeld, M. 118
Kubler-Ross, E. 139, 140

Laidlaw, J. M. 76, 175
Lane, D. A. 12, 43, 86
Laszlo, E. 199
Latham, G. P. 135
Lawley, J. 175
leaders 13, 41, 44–49, 60–61; authentic
    2, 183; presence 162–163, 164;
    relational 186–187, 209–210; Situational
    Theory of Leadership 65–66; teams
    50–51
learning: goals 24; Inner Game approach
    168; learning goal orientation 135;
    reciprocal 19; relationships 48–49;
    responsibility for one's own 122;
    transformative 10; unconscious biases
    153
Leedham, M. 78, 172
Lewis, L. 125
Lewis, T. 189
likeability 67, 74
'limbic resonance' 189–190
listening 92, 177
Locke, C. C. 196
Locke, E. A. 135
Losada ratio 77
love 192

Mallinson, P. 200
managers 5, 13, 44–49; effective
    conversations 43; emotional
    intelligence 67; fear of giving feedback
    18–19, 23–24; perception of feedback 7;

performance appraisals 63, 64; self-talk 126; transactional style 90
Marra, Brad 45–46
matrix style 90
MBTI 75
McCraty, R. 190
McDowall, A. 25
McGavin, B. 160
McGill, I. 174
McLeod, J. 86–87
McMillan, M. 86–87
meaning making 111, 175
Mearns, D. 86, 87, 99–100, 165
Megginson, D. 24, 161, 172, 187
mentoring 7, 13, 17, 41; attachment styles 136; competency frameworks 71, 171–172, 187; contracting 133; external 68; practitioner perspective 52–55
metaphysics 11, 15, 16, 178–179, 198–201
Mezirow, J. 10, 12, 55, 171
Microsoft 205
millennials 61, 124
Milner, M. 6
mindfulness 11, 15, 142, 144, 156–159; compassion 130; emotions 192–193; neural pathways 164; presence 88
mirror neurons 29–30, 101, 189, 208
mistakes 156
Montgomery, B. M. 59
Morgan, H. 145
motivation 44, 61, 69, 121, 176
motivator power 95
multi-source feedback 46, 47

Nakamura, J. 165
Neff, K. 123–124
negative brain plasticity 31
negative feedback 46, 76, 77–78, 88–90, 175
Netflix 25
neurons 29–30, 101, 189, 208
neuroplasticity 28, 29, 30–32, 155
neuroscience 27–28, 119, 178; biases 197; compassion 122, 128–129; emotional intelligence 114; emotions 85–86, 188–191; energy 183–184; neuroplasticity 155; relationships 98, 99, 101, 103; unconscious processes 198; see also brain
neuroticism 73
neurotransmitters 167
Nichols, T. W. 2

Niess, C. 43
non-judgmentality 11, 22, 110, 142, 160, 168
non-verbal communication 20, 43, 129, 189; see also body language
not-for-profit organisations 176

objectivity 11, 15, 142, 143–144, 146–156; appraisals 67; artificial intelligence 205; breaking flow 169; importance of 84; relational leadership 59
O'Brien, B. 36–37
O'Broin, A. 82
Oetting, E. R. 20
O'Neill, M. B. 101
openness 17, 24, 46, 73; culture of 43; learning goal orientation 135; managing bias 152; relationship of 172, 188
OPQ32 and OPQ32r Personality Questionnaires 75
Orwell, George 205
oxytocin 98, 118–119, 127–128, 129, 190

Palmer, S. 82, 83
Palmer, W. 173–174
Parsloe, E. 78, 172
passion 101, 102, 210
pay 69
peer-assessment 69
peer feedback 68
Pelham, G. 109
performance 21–22, 36, 69, 167, 168
performance appraisals 20, 22–23, 62–70, 74, 198
performance management 2, 5, 18, 35–36, 49
personality 73, 75, 88
phenomenological approach 110–111, 175
physicality 11, 15, 16, 178, 179–184
physiology 101, 178–179
Picasso, Pablo 165
positive feedback 47, 76, 77–78
positive psychology 42, 188
positivity 187, 189
power dynamics 84–85, 93–95, 144
P'Pool, K. 61
praise 61, 67, 77–78
prefrontal cortex 129
preparation 105–106, 108, 134, 135, 141, 143
presence 11, 15, 142, 144, 145–146, 159–169; calming your feelings 193; centred

120; mindfulness 157, 158–159; rapport
84; silence 199
presenteeism 72
Prochaska, J. 147–148
psychometrics 21, 61, 72–76

quantum intelligence 199–200
quantum physics 190
questioning 93

Rancourt, K. L. 66
rapport 83–84, 103
ratios 61, 77
readiness for change 135, 147
readiness for feedback 11, 14, 106–107,
132–141
receptivity 11, 24, 44, 139, 170, 174;
encouraging 126; gauging 134–135;
learning goal orientation 135; relational
leadership 59; relationships 83, 85, 86
reciprocity 9, 58, 84, 103, 125, 172, 200
recruitment 3–4, 72
reflection 10, 57, 158, 168, 171; see also
self-reflection
regular feedback conversations 23
relational depth 42, 87, 99, 165
Relational Feedback WAY 2, 10–12, 13–16,
42, 65, 92, 104; Part 1 105–141; Part 2
142–176; Part 3 177–201; relationships
43, 81, 82, 83
relationships 3, 12, 13–14, 20, 80–104, 198,
209; authentic 19, 162; compassion
121, 132; emotional climate 187;
harmonious 42; human capital 186;
intuition 195–196; learning 48–49; need
for 206; presence 160, 162; quality of
6; Relational Feedback WAY 10; signals
43, 208; systemic forces 8–9; timing
of feedback 174–175; transference
and countertransference 149–150;
trusting 36
resilience 3, 88, 114, 131, 179
respect 109, 210
responsibility 17–18, 57, 87; for action 172;
for change 39; coaches/mentors 52;
emotional intelligence 113; employees
44; joint 72, 103; self-feedback 35; self-
responsibility 156; shared 166
Ricard, M. 123
'Right Speech' 36–37
Rock, D. 175

Rodenburg, Patsy 163–164
Rogers, C. R. 87
role modelling 50, 78, 172

Sartre, Jean Paul 197
Schpancer, N. 33
Schultz, D. 66
Schultz, S. E. 66
Scott, C. 100
Scoular, A. 20, 47, 172, 178
security 102, 210
selection 3–4, 72
Self 1 and Self 2 concept 167–168
self-assessment 69, 71–72
self-awareness 6, 21, 24, 25; authentic
leadership 2; brain processes 129;
coaching feedback 53; compassion
127, 131; confidence 117; cultural
diversity 97; cultural values 71;
emotional intelligence 113, 114; impact
of feedback 137; presence 159, 160;
raising 37, 66, 85; reflective practice
171; Relational Feedback WAY 42;
self-assessment 69; self-feedback
35; self-management 108–109, 112;
self-monitoring 145; transformational
change 11
self-compassion 123–124, 130
self-criticism 100, 123
self-disclosure 87, 102, 187, 210
self-esteem 3, 25, 35, 44, 88, 107, 116
self-feedback 35
self-management 10, 14, 71, 106–107,
108–132, 146
self-reflection 21, 39, 41, 97, 171; see also
reflection
self-talk 31, 32–33, 34, 57, 126
self, use of 3, 4, 9, 87, 200; coaching 53;
confidence 117; motivator power 95;
Relational Feedback WAY 11; self-
learning 115
Seligman, M. E. P. 188
Seppala, E. 121
shame 122, 185, 191, 192
Shapiro, S. L. 174
Siegel, D. 88, 101–102, 128–129, 157, 199,
200
silence 158, 182, 199, 201
Sinek, Simon 59
Situational Theory of Leadership 65–66
16pf tool 75

Smither, J. W. 74
social intelligence 103, 109, 131, 209
social media 52, 62, 187
socialization 20
soft skills 1, 42, 193
Solutions Focus 79
somatic empathy 181–182
somatic indicators 180–181
Spinelli, E. 110, 175
stakeholders 13, 40–41, 44–59
standards 70, 71
Starr, J. 20, 172
stereotypes 21, 91, 97, 138, 146, 153, 155
Stewart, T. 203
Stiehler, A. 204
Stone, D. 61
strengths 53
Strengths Deployment Inventory (SDI)
    74
stress 98–99, 114–116, 118, 190
Strozzi-Heckler, R. 119
Strozzi Institute 119–120
succession planning 72
summarising 93
'supportive' feedback 18
System 1 and System 2 theory 197

talent management 72
Tallman, K. 145
targets 23–24, 49
Taylor, F. W. 122
teams 41, 50–52, 189
technology 43, 85; see also artificial
    intelligence; digital technology
Thach, E. C. 60, 106
Thai proverb 3
thinking enhancers 137–138
thinking inhibitors 138
360-degree feedback 25, 71–72, 74, 82,
    198
timing of feedback 8, 11, 15, 136, 143, 145,
    169–179
Tolle, E. 127, 160
Tompkins, P. 175
training 48, 49, 63
Transactional Analysis 78, 153–155
transactional style 90
transference 149, 189, 190

transparency 40, 43, 102, 103, 134;
    compassion 130; confidence 108, 109;
    culture of 17; managing bias 152;
    relational leadership 210; relational
    objectivity 155
Transtheoretical Stages of Change model
    147–148
trends 46
trust 83, 98, 102, 171; building 13, 118–120;
    culture of 43; mutual 117; relational
    leadership 210; relationship of 103, 172,
    188; sense of connection 88

unconditional positive regard 87, 149
unconscious biases 74, 97, 152–156, 178
unconscious processes 29–30, 178, 179,
    194–195, 196–198
upward feedback 7, 79

values 40, 91, 101; competency
    frameworks 70; cultural awareness and
    intelligence 97; misunderstandings 179;
    objectivity 146, 150; setting aside 111;
    unconscious biases 153
van Niekerk, A. 63
VandeWalle, D. 24
Vardaki, Zena 88–90
verbal communication 19
voice 101, 163–164
volunteers 176
vulnerability 99, 122, 162, 173, 183

Waitzkin, J. 165
Wallace, B. A. 174
Warner, J. 18, 78
Wasylyshyn, K. M. 72, 82
ways of being 3, 4, 9, 104, 200; presence
    163; relational 105, 106, 143, 144,
    157; Relational Feedback WAY 11, 13;
    style for giving feedback 171; trusting
    relationships 36
wellbeing 3, 88, 109, 181, 186
withdrawal through abdication 5–6

Yalom, I. D. 101

Zak, P. J. 98–99
Zinker, J. 118